THE GAY SCIENCE

THE
GAY SCIENCE

*with a prelude in rhymes
and an appendix of songs*

Friedrich Nietzsche

Translated, with Commentary, by

WALTER KAUFMANN

VINTAGE BOOKS
A Division of Random House
NEW YORK

VINTAGE BOOKS EDITION, March 1974
Copyright © 1974 by Random House, Inc.
All rights reserved under International and Pan-American Copyright
Conventions. Published in the United States by Random House, Inc.,
New York, and simultaneously in Canada by Random House of Canda
Limited, Toronto. Originally published by Random House, Inc., in 1974.

Library of Congress Cataloging in Publication Data
Nietzsche, Friedrich Wilhelm, 1844–1900.
The gay science.
"This translation is based on the second edition of
Die fröhliche Wissenschaft, published in 1887."
1. Philosophy. 2. Man. 3. Religion—Philosophy.
4. Power (Philosophy) 5. Ethics. I. Kaufmann,
Walter Arnold, tr. II. Title.
[B3313.F72E5   1974b]   193   73–10479
ISBN 0–394–71985–9

Manufactured in the United States of America
E98765432

For

MY JOYFUL SOPHIA

A Note on the Text

This translation is based on the second edition of *Die Fröhliche Wissenschaft*, published in 1887, which agrees with the first edition of 1882, but contains three substantial additions: an important ten-page Preface, Book V (sections 343–384), and an Appendix of Songs. Nietzsche also changed the title page and replaced the motto from Emerson with a four-liner of his own.

When citing the original German in the notes, I have modernized the spelling (changing *th* to *t*).

The text of the book that appears in various collected German editions is also that of the second edition—except for some small, unacknowledged changes, noted in the commentary. One of these changes is rather serious (in section 370).

One collected edition that I refer to occasionally is *Gesammelte Werke, Musarionausgabe*, 23 volumes, Musarion Verlag, Munich, 1920–29. Two other German works are quoted a number of times: *Friedrich Nietzsches Briefe an Peter Gast*, ed. Peter Gast, Insel Verlag, Leipzig, 1908, and *Friedrich Nietzsches Briefwechsel mit Franz Overbeck*, ed. Richard Oehler and Carl Albrecht Bernoulli, Insel Verlag, Leipzig, 1916.

Abbreviations

BWN: *Basic Writings of Nietzsche,* Translated and Edited, with Commentaries, by Walter Kaufmann. The Modern Library, Random House, New York, 1968. This volume contains *The Birth of Tragedy, Beyond Good and Evil, On the Genealogy of Morals, The Case of Wagner,* and *Ecce Homo,* as well as additional selections.

VPN: *The Portable Nietzsche,* Selected and Translated, with an Introduction, Prefaces, and Notes by Walter Kaufmann. The Viking Press, New York, 1954. This volume contains *Thus Spoke Zarathustra, Twilight of the Idols, The Antichrist,* and *Nietzsche contra Wagner,* as well as additional selections.

Kaufmann: Walter Kaufmann, *Nietzsche: Philosopher, Psychologist, Antichrist.* Third Edition. Princeton University Press, Princeton, 1968, and Vintage Books, Random House, New York, 1968. Nietzsche Bibliography on pp. 477–502.

NOTE: Arabic figures after these three abbreviations refer to *pages* in these editions.

The Will to Power, Edited, with Commentary, by Walter Kaufmann, Vintage Books, Random House, New York, 1968, is cited by referring to the numbers of the 1067 notes.

CONTENTS

BOOK ONE 71

BOOK TWO   119

BOOK THREE 165

BOOK FOUR: *Sanctus Januarius* 221

BOOK FIVE: *We Fearless Ones*   277

Appendix: Songs of Prince Vogelfrei   349

Acknowledgments   376

Index   377

THE GAY SCIENCE

Translator's Introduction

The Gay Science is one of Nietzsche's most beautiful and important books. Why then, it may be asked, has it not been made available in English before this, except for a single inadequate translation published before World War I that even had the title of the book wrong?

The "Prelude in German Rhymes" and the Appendix of "Songs" must have led many a would-be translator to wonder whether they could be done in English, and a look at the old version suggested that they might well be untranslatable. If you give up Nietzsche's meters and rhymes in order to produce a literal version, the whole spirit and tone of this book are betrayed; if you give up Nietzsche's meaning, if only now and then, the reader is led astray; and if you simply omit the Prelude and Appendix, a substantial part of the book is left out.

This may help to explain the fate of the book in English, and why the first translator left it to two others to furnish the "poetry versions." Now that interest in Nietzsche has become widespread, this book can no longer be ignored. Here, then, is a new translation; and in fairness to Nietzsche, the original German rhymes and songs are furnished on facing pages.

2
The Title

The first English translation was entitled *The Joyful Wisdom,* which quite misses Nietzsche's meaning. *Wissenschaft* means science and never wisdom. He himself had called his book:

Die
fröhliche Wissenschaft.
("la gaya scienza")

In my *Nietzsche* (1950) I therefore referred to the book as *The Gay Science.* I continued to use this title in subsequent publications; many other Nietzsche scholars followed suit; and by now this is the way the book is generally cited.

Meanwhile, the word "gay" has acquired a new meaning, and people are beginning to assume that it has always suggested homosexuality. But even in the early 1960s that connotation was still quite unusual. Standard dictionaries did not list it at all, while Eric Partridge, in the Supplement of *A Dictionary of Slang and Unconventional English* (1961), listed "gay boy. A homosexual: Australian: since ca. 1925," with no literary occurrence before 1951—and "gay girl; gay woman. A prostitute . . ."[1] If homosexuality is what now comes to mind first when the word "gay" is heard or read, the decisive change was brought about only in 1969 by the establishment of the "Gay Liberation Front."[2]

Under the circumstances, one might give up the title *The Gay Science* and resort to "The Cheerful Science." But in the first place *fröhlich* means *gay,* while *heiter* means *cheerful*—a word that also has a prominent place in the book, but not in its title. Secondly, Nietzsche's subtitle suggests forcibly that *The Gay Science* is what is wanted. Finally, it is no accident that the

[1] Partridge has several entries under "gay," including, noun: "A dupe: Australian . . ."

[2] In *A Supplement to the Oxford English Dictionary,* vol I, *A-G* (1972), the article on "gay" went to press in 1970 and includes five new listings of which only one deals with what is now widely taken for the only meaning, and that is still designated as "slang."

homosexuals as well as Nietzsche opted for "gay" rather than "cheerful." "Gay science," unlike "cheerful science," has overtones of a light-hearted defiance of convention; it suggests Nietzsche's "immoralism" and his "revaluation of values."

Superficially, the parallel extends even further: Nietzsche says some very unkind things about women, and he extols friendship and the Greeks. But it is to be hoped that the title of this book will not be misconstrued as implying that Nietzsche was homosexual or that the book deals with homosexuality.[3]

What Nietzsche himself wanted the title to convey was that serious thinking does not have to be stodgy, heavy, dusty, or, in one word, Teutonic. The German *Wissenschaft* does not bring to mind only—perhaps not even primarily—the natural sciences but any serious, disciplined, rigorous quest for knowledge; and this need not be of the traditional German type or, as Nietzsche is fond of saying in this book, "northern"; it can also be "southern," by which he means Mediterranean—and he refers again and again to Genoa and the Provence. Those who cannot readily understand Nietzsche's feelings for "the south" should think of another Northerner who discovered the Provence at the same time: Van Gogh.

It was in the Provence that modern European poetry was born. William IX, Count of Poitiers around 1100 A.D., is said to be the poet whose verses are the oldest surviving lyrics in a modern European language. He was followed by other, greater troubadours of which the most famous are probably Bertran de Born (1140–1215) and Arnaut Daniel, his contemporary. Both are encountered in Dante's *Inferno* (Cantos 28f.); Bertran de Born is also the hero of two remarkable German poems, one by Ludwig Uhland, the other by Heinrich Heine.[4] The Albigensian Crusade (1209–1229) all but destroyed the culture of the troubadours; but in the fourteenth century the *gai saber* or *gaia sciensa* was still cultivated in the Provence by lesser poets; and under "gay" *The Shorter Oxford English Dictionary* (1955)

---

[3] On the question whether Nietzsche was homosexual, see Kaufmann, 34n.

[4] Both poems are included in *Twenty German Poets: A Bilingual collection.* Edited, translated and introduced by Walter Kaufmann. Random House, New York, 1962.

duly lists "The gay science (= Pr [ovençal] *gai saber*) : the art of poetry."

Nietzsche, of course, meant not only the art of poetry; but he definitely meant this, too, and therefore began his book with the "Prelude in German Rhymes"[5] and later, in the second edition, added the Appendix of songs. In the last poem we even encounter the troubadours. It is also of some interest that in *Beyond Good and Evil* Nietzsche says that "love *as passion*—which is our European specialty—" was invented by "the Provençal knight-poets, those magnificent and inventive human beings of the *'gai saber'* to whom Europe owes so many things and almost owes itself" (section 260, BWN, 398).

In the section on *The Gay Science* in *Ecce Homo,* Nietzsche says specifically that the songs in the Appendix, "written for the most part in Sicily,[6] are quite emphatically reminiscent of the Provençal concept of *gaya scienza*—that unity of *singer, knight,* and *free spirit* which distinguishes the wonderful early culture of the Provençals from all equivocal cultures. The very last poem above all, 'To the Mistral,' an exuberant dancing song in which, if I may say so, one dances right over morality, is a perfect Provençalism" (BWN, 750).

The second section of the second chapter of *Ecce Homo* is also relevant. After deriding the Germans, Nietzsche says: "List the places where men with *esprit* are living or have lived, where wit, subtlety, and malice belonged to happiness, where genius found its home almost of necessity: all of them have excellent dry air. Paris, Provence, Florence, Jerusalem, Athens—these names prove something . . ." (BWN, 696).

---

[5] "As for the title *'Gay Science,'* I thought *only* of the *gaya scienza* of the troubadours—hence also the little verses," Nietzsche wrote in a letter to his friend Erwin Rohde, in the winter 1882–83.

[6] Nietzsche's *Idyllen aus Messina* were published in 1882, but never reprinted. When Nietzsche used these poems in the Appendix, he made many changes. Cf. Musarion edition, vol. XII, p. 356ff., and above all Erich Podach, *Ein Blick in Notizbücher Nietzsches,* Wolfgang Rothe Verlag, Heidelberg, 1963; pp. 174–83. Regarding Podach's limitations, see Kaufmann, 424–52. In the *Kritische Gesamtausgabe* of Nietzsche's *Werke,* Berlin 1967ff., the *Idyllen* are to appear in the same volume with *Die Fröhliche Wissenschaft.*

Thus the title of the book has polemical overtones: it is meant to be anti-German,[7] anti-professorial, anti-academic and goes well with the idea of "the good European" that is encountered in these pages. It is also meant to suggest "light feet," "dancing," "laughter"—and ridicule of "the spirit of gravity."

3
Emerson

What should be gay is *science*—not wisdom. "Science," as I have said, suggests seriousness, discipline, and rigor; and these matter to Nietzsche. Consider what he said about Ralph Waldo Emerson in a letter to Franz Overbeck, December 22, 1884: "I do not know how much I would give if only I could bring it about, *ex post facto*, that such a glorious, great nature, rich in soul and spirit, might have gone through some *strict* discipline, a really *scientific education*. As it is, in Emerson we have *lost a philosopher*" (VPN, 441).

Emerson was one of Nietzsche's great loves ever since he read him as a schoolboy. But while Nietzsche was at home in Latin and Greek, French and Italian, he read Emerson in German translations. He not only *read* him but also copied dozens of passages into notebooks and wrote extensively on the margins and flyleaves of his copy of the *Essays*. In 1874 he lost a bag with a volume of Emerson in it, but soon bought another copy.[8] In 1881, when he wrote *The Gay Science*, he was re-reading Emerson, and the first edition of *The Gay Science* actually carried as an epigraph a quotation from Emerson: *Dem*

---

[7] Cf. the letter in which Nietzsche informed his friend Franz Overbeck that *The Gay Science* was on its way to him: "This book is in every way *against* German taste *and the present*; and I myself even more so" (August 22, 1882).

[8] Cf. Eduard Baumgarten, *Der Pragmatismus: R. W. Emerson, W. James, J. Dewey*, Frankfurt, 1938, pp. 81–88 and 396–407, and "Mitteilungen und Bemerkungen über den Einfluss Emersons auf Nietzsche" in *Jahrbuch für Amerikastudien*, ed. Walther Fischer, vol I, Heidelberg, 1956, pp. 93–152. See also Stanley Hubbard, *Nietzsche und Emerson*, Basel, 1958.

Much of what follows in the text above is not to be found in any previous study of Nietzsche's relation to Emerson.

*Dichter und Weisen sind alle Dinge befreundet und geweiht,
alle Erlebnisse nützlich, alle Tage heilig, alle Menschen göttlich.*
Literally: To the poet and sage, all things are friendly and hallowed, all experiences profitable, all days holy, all men divine.
Oddly, no edition of Nietzsche nor any of the articles or books
on Nietzsche and Emerson that I have seen gives a reference
for this quotation and Emerson's original wording. Emerson's
own words are found in the thirteenth paragraph of "History,"
an essay that had had some influence on Nietzsche's own "untimely meditation" on history: "To the poet, to the philosopher,
to the saint, all things are friendly and sacred, all events profitable, all days holy, all men divine."[9]

Emerson had even called himself "a professor of the Joyous
Science." An entry in his *Journals* made July 6, 1841, poses a
puzzle. It reads: "Ah ye old ghosts! ye builders of dungeons in
the air! why do I ever allow you to encroach on me a moment;
a moment to win me to your hapless company? In every week
there is some hour when I read my commission in every cipher
of nature, and know that I was made for another office, a professor of the Joyous Science [!], a detector & delineator of
occult harmonies & unpublished beauties, a herald of civility,
nobility, learning, & wisdom; an affirmer of the One Law, yet
as one who should affirm it in music or dancing, a priest of
the Soul, yet one who would better love to celebrate it through
the beauty of health & harmonious power."[10]

Nietzsche could not have known the *Journals*. But on January
20, 1842, Emerson gave a lecture entitled "Prospects" in Bos-
ton, and subsequently repeated it elsewhere. In the opening

---

[9] On Christmas day, 1882, Nietzsche wrote Overbeck: ". . . If I do not
discover the alchemists' trick of turning even this—filth into *gold*, I am
lost. —Thus I have the *most beautiful* opportunity to prove that for me
'all experiences are profitable, all days holy, and all human beings
divine'!!!!" For the biographical context, see Kaufmann, 59, where
almost the whole letter is quoted—with the comment: "All experiences
were useful for Nietzsche, and he turned his torments into his later
books . . ."

[10] *The Journals and Miscellaneous Notebooks*, vol. VIII: 1841–1843, ed.
William H. Gilman and J. E. Parsons, Cambridge, Mass., 1970, p. 8.
A footnote in this edition refers to the other passages I cite.

paragraph he made use of his journal entry, changing it slightly:[11] ". . . I am sorry to read the observation of M. De Tocqueville that a cloud always hangs on an American brow.[12] Least of all is it to be pardoned in the literary and speculative class. I hate the builders of dungeons in the air. 'Ascending souls sing Paean,' said the Magian. Ascending souls congratulate each other on the admirable harmonies of the world. We read another commission in the cipher of nature: we were made for another office, professors of the Joyous Science . . ."

From that point on the text follows the journal entry through "music or dancing" with only minor variations. (It continues in the plural: "detectors and delineators . . .") Even if Nietzsche had read a translation of this lecture—and I have no evidence that he did—he could scarcely have known that in his manuscript Emerson had ascribed the two sentences on ascending souls to Zoroaster, and that Emerson thus associated his Joyous Science with Zarathustra! (Zoroaster is the Greek name of the Persian prophet whom the Persians called Zarathushtra.)

Emerson's editors refer us to an article on "The Oracles of Zoroaster," from which, though they do not mention it at this point, Emerson quoted on many other occasions. Zoroaster is also mentioned in the *Essays*, which Nietzsche read so many times; for example, two-thirds of the way through "Experience." The immediately preceding paragraph begins with three lines of verse and ends: "the question ever is, not, what you have done or forborne, but, at whose command you have done or forborne it." Whatever the precise meaning of that may be, the imagery of commanding and obeying recurs in Nietzsche's *Zarathustra*. In the fifth paragraph from the end of "Experience," the dictum "The life of truth is cold" sounds like Nietzsche; and a sentence a few lines later goes a long way toward explaining Nietzsche's love of Emerson: "A sympathetic person is placed in the dilemma of a swimmer among drowning men, who all catch at him, and if he give so much as a leg or

---

[11] *The Early Lectures*, vol. III: 1838–1842, ed. Robert E. Spiller and Wallace E. Williams, Cambridge, Mass., 1972, p. 367f.

[12] In his manuscript Emerson referred to de Tocqueville's *Democracy in America*, Pt. II, transl. Henry Reeve, New York, 1840, p. 144.

a finger, they will drown him." As usual, the similarity becomes much less striking as one reads on, and one would never mistake a whole page of Emerson for a page of Nietzsche.

In the last chapter ("Prospects") of Emerson's early book. *Nature,* he introduces four paragraphs in quotes that, he says, "a certain poet sang to me." Again, a couple of sentences sound rather like Nietzsche's *Zarathustra:* "A man is a god in ruins" and "Man is the dwarf of himself." But what is even more striking is the conclusion: "Thus my Orphic poet sang." Was this perhaps the seed of "Thus Spoke Zarathustra"? It would be utterly improbable if we did not know that Nietzsche, long steeped in Emerson, reread him and annotated him again during the period of *The Gay Science* and just before he wrote *Zarathustra.*[13]

To return to Emerson's "Joyous Science," he used the passage from his *Journals* once more in the second paragraph of his lecture on "The Scholar," at the University of Virginia, June 28, 1876. This time he referred twice to the "intellectual conscience" (six years later Nietzsche called the second section of his *Gay Science* "The intellectual conscience"!) before he said: "I think the peculiar office of scholars in a careful and gloomy generation is to be (as the poets were called in the Middle Ages) Professors of the Joyous Science, detectors and delineators of occult symmetries"—and so forth, down through "music and dancing."[14]

Again, I have no evidence that Nietzsche ever read this lecture, or any passage whatever in which Emerson referred to Joyous Science. As it happens, one E. S. Dallas published a work entitled *The Gay Science* in London in 1866, in two volumes. The work deals with literary criticism, and Nietzsche was surely unaware of it. But in view of what has been said here about *gai saber,* it is hardly surprising that several writers should have tried to revive this notion.

To investigate in detail Nietzsche's relation to Emerson would lead us too far afield. Previous writers have covered the

---

[13] See Baumgarten, 1956.
[14] *Complete Works,* Riverside Edition, vol. X, Cambridge, Mass., 1883, p. 250.

same ground again and again, but unfortunately without comparing Nietzsche's German excerpts with the original English text—and context! Hubbard confined himself almost entirely to Nietzsche's German copy of the *Essays*, telling us what Nietzsche marked, while Baumgarten reports at length about the excerpts Nietzsche copied. Both call our attention to passages in Nietzsche's books that they consider similar to passages in Emerson; but a critical reader will often wonder whether there really is any great similarity. To be sure, I have just called attention to some parallels that do not seem to have been noticed before; and in section 142 I have found a quotation from Emerson that seems to have been overlooked. Hence it might seem that, even if one denied some similarities, a great many others would be left. On balance, however, it seems to me that most of those who have written on this subject have exaggerated the kinship of these men, and that the differences are far more striking.

Still, it is of considerable interest—and rather at odds with many popular notions about Nietzsche—that he loved Emerson from first to last. A section in *Twilight of the Idols*, written in 1888, during Nietzsche's last great creative spurt, bears the title "Emerson,"[15] and here Nietzsche's affection contrasts strongly with the tone of his comments on a number of other writers in the preceding sections. Emerson's coinage "The Over-soul" (the title of one of the essays) surely influenced Nietzsche's choice of the term *Übermensch*—and this makes my translation, "overman," doubly appropriate. I take it that Nietzsche knew that the original had "over-soul," although this was translated in his copy as *Die höhere Seele*, the higher soul, which undoubtedly influenced his phrase, "the higher men."

Volume XI of the Musarion edition of Nietzsche's works in the original German contains almost 200 pages of his notes from the period during which he worked on *The Gay Science*, including these two notes:

---

[15] VPN, 522. The gentle but by no means hostile irony of the final two sentences in that section was surely prompted by a passage in "Experience," in the same paragraph where Zoroaster is mentioned: "Why should I fret myself ?"

"*Emerson.*—Never have I felt so much at home in a book, and in *my* home, as—I may not praise it, it is too close to me."

"The author who has been richest in ideas in this century so far has been an American (unfortunately made obscure by German philosophy—frosted glass)" (p. 283f.).

Nietzsche also speaks of Emerson in *The Gay Science* (section 92). But to place Emerson in Nietzsche's world one would have to go beyond the references to Emerson; one would have to consider his love of Claude Lorrain, the seventeenth-century landscape painter, and Adalbert Stifter, the nineteenth-century Austrian novelist—as well as the place of Epicurus in his thought. For I take it that Emerson was basically as unlike Nietzsche as these three men were, although Nietzsche cannot be understood apart from the attraction that their serene cheerfulness and calm, harmonious humanity always held for him. Always? If some widely credited legends were true, no evidence of any such taste could be found in Nietzsche's later works, beginning with *Zarathustra.* In fact, not only his love of Emerson still finds expression in *Twilight,* which was written in 1888, but Claude Lorrain is still apotheosized in Nietzsche's last creative weeks, in *Nietzsche contra Wagner,* in *Ecce Homo,* and in some letters in the fall of 1888,[16] and Adalbert Stifter and Gottfried Keller still appear together in *The Will to Power* (note 1021) as they did earlier in *The Wanderer and His Shadow* (section 109).

Nietzsche's taste remained the same—which is to say, utterly different from what most writers about him take for granted—and in *Zarathustra,* for example, this taste finds expression again and again, and occasionally veers into sentimentality. It is Nietzsche's philosophical views that change to some extent as he keeps thinking; and *The Gay Science,* written partly before and partly after *Zarathustra,* reflects both his abiding taste and the development of his thought. It is instructive in this connection to pursue his discussions of Epicurus through this volume

---

[16] *Nietzsche contra Wagner,* A Music Without a Future, VPN, 608; *Ecce Homo,* the last sentence of the section on *Twilight,* BWN, 772; letters to Gast, October 30, to Overbeck, November 13, and to Meta von Salis, November 14.

—a much maligned philosopher for whom Nietzsche had a deep feeling and to whom he returns again and again in these pages; in the end, critically.

To return to science, Nietzsche certainly rejected the simplistic alternative of being either "for" science, like some positivists, or "against" science, like some neoromantics. In his first book, *The Birth of Tragedy,* he had tried *"to look at science in the perspective of the artist"* (Preface; BWN, 19); but this did not mean that he was "for" art and "against" science. The position to which his intricate dialectic finally led was, in his own words, an "artistic Socrates"—a philosopher with an intellectual conscience *and* with the feeling for art that the historical Socrates had lacked. Indeed, not only a *feeling* for art. Nietzsche also spoke of "a Socrates who makes music"—a philosopher who also *is* an artist. But for Nietzsche that never meant being a philosopher six days and a poet on the sabbath, or writing a conventional philosophical book with some poetry at the beginning and the end; it meant—gay science, philosophy that sings and sizzles.[17]

4
The Structure of The Gay Science

The first edition lacked the preface, began directly with the rhymes of the Prelude, and ended with section 342 which, except for minute changes indicated in my commentary, consisted literally of the beginning of Nietzsche's next book *Thus Spoke Zarathustra.* That is to say, the ending was poetic, though not rhymed. It was preceded by two other very remarkable sections. The first of these (340) is called *The dying Socrates* and was clearly placed so close to the end because Nietzsche considered it a particularly fitting coda and testament. It begins: "I admire the courage and wisdom of Socrates in everything he did, said—and did not say." A striking statement, utterly at odds with much of the literature on Nietzsche. This section is

---

[17] For a discussion of Nietzsche's conception of the way in which he was scientific and a contrast with Hegel, who thought *he* was scientific, see Kaufmann, Chapter 2.

discussed in the commentary. Nietzsche found reasons to believe that Socrates considered life a disease and death a cure, and the section ends: "We must overcome even the Greeks!"

What follows is section 341: *The greatest weight*." It is here that Nietzsche first announces his famous doctrine of the eternal recurrence of the same events at immense intervals— a literal recurrence even of "this spider and this moonlight between the trees." Actually, the doctrine, which has been alluded to in three earlier sections (109, 233, and 285), is not proclaimed even here. Rather the question is raised how you would react to it if a demon spelled it out to you, and Nietzsche suggests that most people would consider this recurrence a curse and that it would require the most impassioned love of life *"to crave nothing more fervently than this ultimate eternal confirmation and seal."* With this doctrine, then, Nietzsche overcomes even Socrates—and Epicurus, and Emerson. What is suggested at this point transcends all gaiety and serenity and involves *passion*.

Then comes the last section, entitled *Incipit tragoedia*, the tragedy begins. Zarathustra gives up the serenity of his ten years of solitude and decides to go down among men. The last words of this section and thus of the first edition of this book are ambiguous: *untergehen* means go down, but also drown or perish. This ambiguity is discussed in the commentary; but the final sentence would strike almost any reader as meaning first of all: "Thus began Zarathustra's destruction."

The end of Hermann Hesse's last hero, Josef Knecht, the *magister ludi* of the *Glasperlenspiel* or bead game, echoes this passage. Nietzsche's immense influence on Hesse has long been recognized, and Hesse often acknowledged it. In 1919, right after the end of World War I, he published a pamphlet with the title *Zarathustras Wiederkehr* ("Zarathustra's Return"; but *Wiederkehr* is also the word Nietzsche had used often for his conception of the recurrence). Some writers have supposed, following a remark by Hesse, that in his later work the influence of Nietzsche became less significant for him; but this is surely false. Nietzsche's impact on Hesse had been so formative and so deep that it is quite as evident in Hesse's last novel as in his earlier work. In the Epilogue of my *Nietzsche* I have quoted two notes—one early Nietzsche, the other late—that suggest the basic conception of Hesse's last and greatest novel, the need for secular monasteries and "education free from politics, nationality, and newspapers." But it should also be noted that in the end Knecht leaves his serene retreat to go down among men —and drowns.

To return to the problem of structure, the final section about Zarathustra is not merely tacked on but rather carefully led up to by the sections that precede it. And Book V, written after *Zarathustra* and *Beyond Good and Evil*, and added only in the second edition, picks up themes introduced earlier.

What may at first seem to be a haphazard sequence of aphorisms turns out to be a carefully crafted composition in which almost every section means much more in context than will ever be noted by readers who assume, in flat defiance of Nietzsche's own repeated pleas to the contrary, that each section is a self-sufficient aphorism. The structure is extremely important, and it is one of the functions of my commentary to show this.

To anticipate a single example: there would have been less doubt about what Nietzsche might have meant in the parable of the madman when he says "God is dead" if section 125 had not generally been treated as if it stood by itself instead of being part of a long train of thought. The idea of the eternal recurrence has to be understood against this background.

5
The Eternal Recurrence

Nietzsche had encountered the idea of the eternal recurrence in his reading and did not suppose that it was his own brain-child. But its significance for him was new and different. This point is readily illustrated by quoting a passage from a posthumously published book by Heinrich Heine that Nietzsche, who greatly admired Heine, had in his library.[18] This passage con-

---

[18] *Letzte Gedichte und Gedanken von H. Heine,* ed. Adolf Strodtmann, Hamburg 1869. In 1899 H. Lichtenberger cited this passage but said expressly that Nietzsche did not know it. In 1908, C. A. Bernoulli pointed out that it was to be found in Strodtmann's book and that Nietzsche

tains a clearer and more succinct formulation of Nietzsche's "doctrine" than is to be found in *The Gay Science* and in Nietzsche's later works. In *Zarathustra* there are many allusions to this conception before it is finally stated very poetically near the end, in "The Drunken Song." In his next books, *Beyond Good and Evil, On the Genealogy of Morals,* and *The Case of Wagner,* the idea is not discussed at all, while in *Twilight of the Idols* and *Ecce Homo* we are told what immense importance Nietzsche attaches to the doctrine, but he does not bother to formulate it. For more information about it, one has to turn to his notebooks.[19] Here, then, is Heine's formulation:

> And she answered with a tender voice: "Let us be good friends."—But what I have told you here, dear reader, that is not an event of yesterday or the day before. . . . For time is infinite, but the things in time, the concrete bodies, are finite. They may indeed disperse into the smallest particles; but these particles, the atoms, have their determinate number, and the number of configurations that, all of themselves, are formed out of them is also determinate. Now, however long a time may pass, according to the eternal laws governing the combinations of this eternal play of repetition, all configurations that have previously existed on this earth must yet meet, attract, repulse, kiss, and corrupt each other again. . . . And thus it will happen one day that a man will be born again, just like me, and a woman will be born, just like Mary—only that it is to be hoped that the head of this man may contain a

---

therefore *could* have read it. In 1950, I added "that Nietzsche actually possessed the book." For the details, see Kaufmann, 318; for a comprehensive exposition and discussion of the conception, *ibid.*, 316–33; for some other recent analyses see Joan Stambaugh, *Nietzsche's Thought of Eternal Return,* Baltimore and London, 1972, and *Nietzsche: A Collection of Critical Essays,* ed. Robert C. Solomon, Garden City, N.Y., 1973, essays 16–18.

[19] Especially, *The Will to Power,* notes 55, 417, 462, 617, 1041, 1050, and 1053–67, and the notes of the period of *The Gay Science* and *Zarathustra* that are collected in vols. XI and XIV of the *Musarionausgabe.*

little less foolishness—and in a better land they will meet and contemplate each other a long time; and finally the woman will give her hand to the man and say with a tender voice: "Let us be good friends."

The playful spirit of this passage is as different from Nietzsche's tone when he speaks of this conception as the details of the theory are similar. Only two differences need to be noted: Nietzsche prefers to speak of power quanta instead of atoms, and the ironic conceit "that it is to be hoped that the head of this man may contain a little less foolishness" is ruled out by Nietzsche's theory, which precludes any variation, however small.

Nietzsche's associations with this doctrine are complex, but they cannot be understood unless one realizes that (1) his primary reaction is that no idea could be more gruesome. Nevertheless, (2) he takes it for "the most *scientific* of all possible hypotheses"[20] and feels that any refusal to accept it because it is such a terrifying notion would be a sign of weakness. Then (3) he discovers that there are moments and perhaps even ways of life that make this idea not only bearable but beautiful, and (4) he asks whether it might not serve a positive function. Naturally, different interpreters have fastened on different dimensions of the eternal recurrence, but all accounts that omit even one of these four points are bound to be partial at best and serious distortions of Nietzsche's philosophy at worst.

This is not the place for a detailed analysis of the eternal recurrence. The title of the section in *The Gay Science* in which Nietzsche presents his idea (*"The greatest weight"*) has to be understood in terms of the fourth point: the search for a positive function. A modern poet has asked: "What still has weight?" In his parable of the madman (section 125) Nietzsche suggests that during the Victorian era this question was not yet asked widely, but that before long the sense that whatever we do is of hardly any consequence will spread like a disease. This terrifying sense of weightlessness might be called *nihilism*—to use a term that looms large in Nietzsche's notes, especially in

20 *The Will to Power*, note 55.

The Will to Power. Now it occurs to Nietzsche that the belief that whatever I do now I shall do again and again, eternally, may cure this weightlessness by becoming "the greatest weight."

In a way, the notion that everything recurs eternally in identical fashion reduces life to "a tale told by an idiot, full of sound and fury, signifying nothing." It might be considered "the most extreme form of nihilism." But it is also, as Nietzsche sees it, the self-overcoming of nihilism, a self-conquest that requires no recourse beyond science. For Nietzsche considered this doctrine more scientific than other hypotheses because he thought that it followed from the denial of any absolute beginning, any creation, any infinite energy—any god. Science, scientific thinking, and scientific hypotheses are for Nietzsche not necessarily stodgy and academic or desiccated.

In the second section of the "untimely meditation" on history, Nietzsche refers to the ancient Pythagorean notion "that when the heavenly bodies are in the same constellation, the same events must also be repeated on earth, down to every small particular—so that every time the stars stand in a certain relation to each other, a Stoic will form an alliance with an Epicurean and murder Caesar, and when they reach another position Columbus will again discover America." When Nietzsche had come to take seriously this ancient doctrine, which he had earlier dismissed, and was wondering how to present it in *The Gay Science,* the same images were in his mind again. Nietzsche devotes a memorable section (98) to Brutus's murder of Caesar, which is not discussed by him in any other book; and the Columbus theme is one of the leitmotifs of *The Gay Science* that turns up again and again. Thus works the unconscious.

As late as January 25, 1882, Nietzsche still referred to *The Gay Science* as "Book VI, VII, and VIII of *The Dawn* [his last book, published in 1881]" and was planning to work on Books IX and X "next winter—I am not yet *mature* enough for the elemental ideas that I want to present in these final books. Among them is one idea that really requires 'millennia' to *become* something. From where am I to take the courage to pronounce it!" (Letter to Gast).

The feeling that it requires enormous courage to present the conception of the eternal recurrence finds expression over and over again in *Zarathustra*, till it becomes rather tiresome. But to understand Nietzsche it is important to realize how frightful he himself found the doctrine and how difficult it was for him to accept it. Evidently, he could endure it only by accepting it joyously, almost ecstatically. That is what he said more indirectly when he finally presented the idea in *"The greatest weight."*

After the "tremendous moment" of which Nietzsche speaks in that section and the exuberant affirmation of the eternal recurrence of the same events, intolerable physical and spiritual agonies and depressions had not been exorcised once and for all. Apparently while working on *Zarathustra*, Nietzsche, in a moment of despair, said in one of his notes: "I do not want life *again*. How did I endure it? Creating. What makes me stand the sight of it? The vision of the overman who *affirms* life. I have tried to affirm it *myself*—alas!"[21]

One can read an exclamation like that merely as a poignant personal document; but it can also be read as a reflection on the ideas of the overman and the recurrence; and it seems reasonable to read it both ways. Supposing that the eternal recurrence of the same events *were* the most scientific hypothesis, we might still find it impossible to live creative lives while actually joyously affirming this idea. If so, we might live with the idea of the overman and think of him as a type that *would* be able to accept the eternal recurrence gladly.[22]

In January 1882 Nietzsche did not yet think of his forthcoming book as *The Gay Science*. On June 19 he wrote Gast to ask "whether you will be *able* to help me with the proofs of *The Gay Science*—my last work, as I suppose— (whether you 'want to,' I do not ask, my faithful old friend). Honesty unto death! Right?" And August 20: *"The Gay Science* has come; I immediately send you the first copy. A number of things will be new to you: even when reading the final proofs I still

---

[21] Musarion ed., vol. XIV, p. 121. Cf. also *ibid.* p. 110, quoted in Kaufmann, 327.
[22] See Kaufmann, Chapter 11, "Overman and Eternal Recurrence" for the compatibility of these two ideas.

changed this and that and hope that I *improved* a few things.
Read, for example, the conclusions of Books II and III; about
Schopenhauer, too, I have spoken more explicitly (perhaps I
shall *never* again comment on him and on Wagner; I *had* to
clarify my relationship now, in view of my *former* opinions—
for ultimately I am a *teacher* and have the duty to say in what
respects I remain the *same* and how I have become *different*).
. . . Above all: is *Sanctus Januarius* [Book IV] at all *compre-
hensible?* After everything I have experienced since I am among
men again, my *doubt* about that is *tremendous!*"

A few days later, Nietzsche wrote his friend Paul Rée:
'. . . Is *The Gay Science* in your hands—the *most personal* of
all my books? Considering that everything very personal is
essentially *comical,* I really anticipate a 'gay' effect.—Do read
Sanctus Januarius in context! There my private morality will be
found together, as the sum of the conditions of *my* existence
which prescribe an *ought* only if I *want myself.*"[23]

Indeed, not only Book IV but the entire work needs to be
read in context; but of the first four books which comprised
the original edition, *Sanctus Januarius* is the most impressive.
There is a steady crescendo. Book I is inferior to what follows;
Book II gradually picks up strength; Book III is far better still;
and Book V is late Nietzsche and belongs with the major works
of his maturity. But upon closer scrutiny one continues to discover connections that escape cursory readers. Thus the first
section of the work, "The teachers of the purpose of existence,"
introduces the theme that culminates in the doctrine of the
recurrence, and the second section, "The Intellectual Conscience," is one of the most important in the book. *The Gay*

---

[23] *Friedrich Nietzsche, Paul Rée, Lou von Salomé: Die Dokumente
ihrer Begegnung,* ed. Ernst Pfeiffer, Frankfurt am Main, 1970, p. 224.
The last words are: *"falls ich* mich *selber* will." If Pfeiffer's text is correct, then Rudolph Binion's rendering ("they prescribe only an *ought,*
in case I do not *want* to *myself*") is mistaken. Certainly, the Pfeiffer
reading makes more sense. See Binion's *Frau Lou: Nietzsche's Wayward
Disciple,* with a Foreword by Walter Kaufmann, Princeton, 1968, p. 87.
A much briefer treatment, based on the documents, is to be found in
Kaufmann, 48–64.

Science does represent a crescendo; it is also a storehouse of treasures that contains some of Nietzsche's most sustained treatments of important epistemological questions as well as some of his most profound observations about art and ethics, usually in large consecutive units; it also contains his famous celebration of living dangerously, some splendid prose poems, and ever so much else.

6
Germans, Jews, and Women

Among the many subjects taken up by Nietzsche in a series of consecutive sections are the Germans and the Jews. Both subjects come up again and again in his books. Looked at superficially, Nietzsche's comments may appear to be the sort of generalizations that it was then fashionable to toss off with a dogmatic air, of a piece with Nietzsche's dicta about women. On closer inspection, his comments on Germans and Jews at least have the virtue of being untimely, of going against the grain of the age.

It is arguable that generalizations of this sort are unworthy of a great thinker and that, however a close reading may lead us to interpret them, Nietzsche's book might be better if he had left them out. But Nietzsche was clearly not timeless in *that* sense. He lived on the edge of disaster and knew it; he saw himself as a kind of prophet and compared himself in this respect to monkeys (in a letter cited in the commentary); and the Germans and the Jews did turn out to be central in the events that came to pass in the twentieth century. What, then, can we make of what Nietzsche had to say about them?

First of all, it is important to see his comments on the Jews and the Germans together. Not only does this yield more interesting readings, but as soon as one adopts this perspective one discovers an intricate and clearly deliberate counterpoint. Secondly, one must attend to Nietzsche's conception of the relationship of Christianity to Judaism. And finally, one has to keep in mind the historical context of Nietzsche's comments.

To begin with the last point, some of Nietzsche's comments

on the Jews in sections 135 ff., and especially in 140, are bound
to strike many of today's readers very differently from the way
they struck—and were meant to strike—Victorian readers. The
modern reader is apt to find evidence of anti-Semitism where
Victorian readers were shocked by the suggestion that Jesus
was considered a Jew not only in name. This is a central motif
not only in these sections but also, much later, in *The Antichrist:* Jesus and Christianity were "Jewish" precisely in the
sense in which nineteenth-century Christians used to look down
on what was "Jewish."[24]

There is thus an *ad hominem* quality to Nietzsche's argument: he confronts anti-Semitic readers with a *tu quoque*—you
are doing it, too, and are actually worse. But he himself realizes that in scoring against one type of reader he may well be
taken to agree with anti-Semites who have little or no sympathy
for Christianity. He may be read as a racist. Hence he goes out
of his way in *The Gay Science* no less than in *Beyond Good
and Evil* and *The Antichrist* to dissociate himself from every
kind of proto-Nazism; and he does this scathingly, usually in
sections that deal with the Germans; for example, sections 134,
149, and 377 of this book.

The problem of interpretation is not illuminated by asking
whether a reading is "gentle" or "tough." Crane Brinton, who
introduced the distinction between "gentle Nietzscheans" and
"tough Nietzscheans" in his *Nietzsche* (1941) said in a review
of my *Nietzsche* (1950): "To my mind Mr. Kaufmann is—
marginally, of course—a 'tough' Nietzschean."[25] He knew that
I had treated Nietzsche's views concerning race in general and
the Jews and anti-Semitism in particular at length, and that I had
disparaged the gentle/tough dichotomy because it distracts attention from the question whether an interpretation is sound and
instead of this puts a premium on "toughness."

To gain some historical perspective on Nietzsche's comments
on the Jews, it is obviously best to see what other writers of

---

[24] Cf. the much fuller treatment of these problems in Kaufmann, Chapter
10; also the Editor's Preface to *The Antichrist* (VPN, 565–67), and the
notes on sections 248, 250, and 251 in *Beyond Good and Evil* (BWN,
374–79).

[25] *Saturday Review,* January 13, 1951.

his time said about Jews. But with one exception, this dreary literature is not easily accessible, and dredging up some little known tracts would be pointless. The exception is Karl Marx's essay "On the Jewish Question" (1843), and especially Part Two of that, which comprises about eight pages. These pages are reprinted in many Marx anthologies.[26] Seeing how Marx's tone here approximates that of Nazi literature on the Jews, it is ironical that in the Soviet Union, twenty-five years after World War II, Nietzsche's alleged anti-Semitism was still considered proof of his proto-Nazism

What other German literature on the Jews during the Victorian era could one profitably compare with Nietzsche's remarks? Heine, a Jew whose attitude toward Jews was too complex to be discussed here, also made some comments about Jews that are offensive to the hypersensitive—and Richard Wagner, the most influential anti-Semite of his time, unquestionably influenced Hitler, as Nietzsche did not. In response to Wagner's many minions, who were "Christian" anti-Semites, Nietzsche delighted in picturing Christianity more and more as the abortion of Judaism and as more "Jewish" in the anti-Semitic sense of that word than the Old Testament had been. In his view, the Old Testament at its best was superior even to ancient Greek literature, while the New Testament represents a low point in human history. Whatever may be wrong with this view, its motivation is clearly anti-anti-Semitic.

Although some of Nietzsche's remarks about the Germans in *The Gay Science* are vitriolic, his attitude is not yet as totally hostile as in *Twilight of the Idols, The Antichrist*, and *Ecce Homo*, which were written in the summer and fall of 1888. In 1886, when Nietzsche wrote Book V of *The Gay Science*, he still placed some hope in the humanity of Crown Prince Friedrich, whose father, Wilhelm I, was then 89 years old. But in June 1888 Friedrich III died of cancer after a reign of a mere hundred days and was succeeded by Wilhelm II. It was then that Nietz-

---

[26] See, e.g., *Writings of the Young Marx on Philosophy and Society*, transl. L. D. Easton and G. H. Guddat, Garden City, N.Y., 1967, and *The Marx-Engels Reader*, ed. R. C. Tucker, New York, 1972. For some pertinent quotations and discussion see Kaufmann, *Without Guilt and Justice* (1973), section 58.

sche despaired utterly of Germany. These matters do not seem to have been noted before, but I have tried to give supporting evidence in notes 84 and 87 on sections 357 and 358.

What Nietzsche says about Germans and Jews tends to be unconventional and leads us to see things in a new light. It is often thought-provoking even if after due reflection we do not agree with him. He broke the tyranny of stereotyped views that were false and made it possible for us to take a fresh look. His reflections on women, on the other hand, generally have little merit and originality. They show the influence of La Rochefoucauld, Chamfort, and Schopenhauer, without equaling in either venom or absurdity Schopenhauer's famous diatribe "On Women." In sum, they are on the whole strikingly inferior to the rest of his work.

One theme that Nietzsche introduces in his discussion of women is of considerable interest but has so far received little or no attention: roles. This concept has become very fashionable, and the *International Encyclopedia of the Social Sciences* devotes separate articles to "Psychological Aspects" and "Sociological Aspects" (vol. 13, 1968); but both articles find the beginnings of role theory in the 1920s. In *The Gay Science* the concept is discussed at length in section 356 (*role* and *role faith* are emphasized by Nietzsche) along with the faith of men in certain types of societies, including American society, that one *can manage almost any role*. In section 361 this concept is taken up again, but it is actually used first in the sections on women, especially 68 and 71.

There is a good deal of material in Nietzsche on what he calls "the problem of the actor," on histrionics, on play-acting, and on the mask. Not all of these passages are equally relevant to the concept of roles in the contemporary sense.[27] Many sec-

---

[27] A glance at the indices of the Kaufmann editions of *Beyond Good and Evil* and *The Will to Power* will quickly yield over two dozen references.

Notes 68, 78, 289, and 434 in *The Will to Power* are especially relevant to the problems discussed in *The Gay Science*, and so are at the very least two formulations in *Beyond Good and Evil*: "untruth as a condition of life" (section 4), and "every word also a mask" (section 289).

tions deal specifically with the need for masks by those who are especially profound.

Translation and Commentary
7

My translation of *The Gay Science* follows the same principles as my previous versions of nine of Nietzsche's books and of *The Will to Power*. The aim is, in one word, faithfulness— to Nietzsche's meaning, tone, nuances, style, and manner. Important terms are generally rendered consistently—*Wissenschaft* as science, *Geist* as spirit—and when it seemed helpful, the original German words are furnished in notes. If one rendered *Geist* now as spirit, now as mind, now as intellect, this would impede serious discussions of Nietzsche's views.

In the original German every numbered section, no matter how long, comprises a single paragraph. I have again broken up long paragraphs to make the structure of Nietzsche's arguments clearer.

I had translated a few passages before and published them here and there. Instead of simply reprinting them, I have gone back to the original text and have done my best to improve them. This also applies to some of the poems in the Prelude and Appendix and to the verses on the title page of Book IV, which are quoted in *Ecce Homo*.

Once again it has been made easy for any reader who is so minded to read straight through Nietzsche without ever being interrupted by the commentary which, except for this Introduction, is offered entirely in the form of footnotes. But in the past too many readers have browsed in Nietzsche's aphoristic works instead of actually reading them, and the aim of the commentary is to facilitate a more thoughtful approach—to open up a world that it is a joy to discover.

This book is a microcosm in which we find almost all of Nietzsche: epigrams and songs, aphorisms and sustained discussions of philosophical problems, ethics and theory of knowledge, reflections on art and on the death of God, the eternal recurrence and even Zarathustra. The abundant material Nietzsche added to the second edition, translated here, makes plain that he did not consider this book dated by *Zarathustra* and *Beyond Good and Evil*. It is not merely one corner of a large edifice or one fraction of a system. It mirrors all of Nietzsche's thought and could be related in hundreds of ways to his other books, his notes, and his letters. And yet it is complete in itself. For it is a work of art.

Die

fröhliche Wissenschaft.

Von

Friedrich Nietzsche.

> „Dem Dichter und Weisen sind alle Dinge be-
> freundet und geweiht, alle Erlebnisse nützlich,
> alle Tage heilig, alle Menschen göttlich."
>
> *Emerson.*

———•◦◦◦•———

Chemnitz 1882.

Verlag von Ernst Schmeitzner.

Paris	St. Petersburg	Rom
C. Klincksieck	H. Schmitzdorff	(Turin, Florenz)
11 Rue de Lille.	(C. Roettger)	Loescher & Co.
	Kais. Hof-Buchhandlung.	307 Via del Corso.
	5 Newsky Prospekt.	

New-York	London
E. Steiger	Williams & Norgate
22 u. 24 Frankfort Street.	14 Henrietta Street,
	Covent Garden.

Mit diesem Buche kommt eine Reihe von Schriften FRIEDRICH NIETZSCHE's zum Abschluss, deren gemeinsames Ziel ist, ein neues Bild und Ideal des Freigeistes aufzustellen. In diese Reihe gehören:

Menschliches, Allzumenschliches. Mit Anhang: Vermischte Meinungen und Sprüche.

Der Wanderer und sein Schatten.

Morgenröthe. Gedanken über die moralischen Vorurtheile.

Die fröhliche Wissenschaft.

Frühere Schriften desselben Verfassers:

Die Geburt der Tragödie aus dem Geiste der Musik.

Unzeitgemässe Betrachtungen. 1. David Strauss der Bekenner und der Schriftsteller. 2. Vom Nutzen und Nachtheil der Historie für das Leben. 3. Schopenhauer als Erzieher. 4. Richard Wagner in Bayreuth.

Druck von B. G. Teubner in Leipzig.

Die
fröhliche Wissenschaft.

(„la gaya scienza")

Von

FRIEDRICH NIETZSCHE.

Ich wohne in meinem eignen Haus,
Hab Niemandem nie nichts nachgemacht
Und — lachte noch jeden Meister aus,
Der nicht sich selber ausgelacht.

Ueber meiner Hausthür.

Neue Ausgabe

mit einem Anhange:

Lieder des Prinzen Vogelfrei.

—>+ǁ+<—

LEIPZIG.
Verlag von E. W. Fritzsch.
1887.

The illustrations on the preceding three pages show (1) the title page of the original edition of 1882 (the Emerson quotation is discussed in the Translator's Introduction), (2) the back cover of the same edition (a translation follows below), and (3) the title page of the second edition of 1887 (translated on the next page).

Here is what Nietzsche said on the back of the original edition:

> This book marks the conclusion of a series of writings by FRIEDRICH NIETZSCHE whose common goal it is to erect *a new image and ideal of the free spirit*. To this series belong:
>
> *Human, all too human*. With Appendix: Mixed Opinions and Aphorisms.
> *The Wanderer and his Shadow.*
> *Dawn: Thoughts about the prejudices of morality.*
> *The Gay Science.*
>
> ———
>
> Earlier writings by the same author:
> *The Birth of Tragedy out of the Spirit of Music.*
> *Untimely Meditations.* 1. David Strauss, the Confessor and Writer. 2. Of the Use and Disadvantage of History for Life. 3. Schopenhauer as Educator. 4. Richard Wagner in Bayreuth.
>
> ———

THE
GAY SCIENCE

("la gaya scienza")

BY

Friedrich Nietzsche

I live in my own place,
have never copied nobody even half,
and at any master who lacks the grace
to laugh at himself—I laugh.

OVER THE DOOR TO MY HOUSE

NEW EDITION
WITH AN APPENDIX:
Songs of Prince Vogelfrei

—

LEIPZIG
E. W. Fritzsch
1887

Preface for the Second Edition

This book may need more than one preface, and in the end there would still remain room for doubt whether anyone who had never lived through similar experiences could be brought closer to the *experience* of this book by means of prefaces. It seems to be written in the language of the wind that thaws ice and snow: high spirits, unrest, contradiction, and April weather are present in it, and one is instantly reminded no less of the proximity of winter than of the triumph over the winter that is coming, must come, and perhaps has already come.

Gratitude pours forth continually, as if the unexpected had just happened—the gratitude of a convalescent—for *convalescence* was unexpected. "Gay Science": that signifies the saturnalia of a spirit who has patiently resisted a terrible, long pressure—patiently, severely, coldly, without submitting, but also without hope—and who is now all at once attacked by hope, the hope for health, and the *intoxication* of convalescence. Is it any wonder that in the process much that is unreasonable and foolish comes to light, much playful tenderness that is lavished even on problems that have a prickly hide and are not made to be caressed and enticed? This whole book is nothing but a bit of merry-making after long privation and powerlessness, the rejoicing of strength that is returning, of a reawakened faith in a tomorrow and the day after tomorrow, of a sudden sense and anticipation of a future, of impending adventures, of seas that are open again, of goals that are permitted again, believed again. And what did not lie behind me then! This stretch of desert, exhaustion, disbelief, icing up in the midst of youth, this interlude of old age at the wrong time, this tyranny of pain even excelled by the tyranny of pride that refused the *conclusions* of pain—and conclusions are consolations—this radical retreat into solitude as a self-defense against a contempt for men that had become pathologically clairvoyant—this determined self-limitation to what was bitter, harsh, and hurtful to know, prescribed by the *nausea* that had gradually developed out of an incautious and pampering spiritual diet, called romanticism —oh, who could reexperience all of this? But if anyone could, he would surely pardon more than a little foolishness, exuberance, and "gay science"—for example, the handful of songs that have now been added to this book—songs in which a poet makes fun of all poets in a way that may be hard to forgive. Alas, it is not only the poets and their beautiful "lyrical sentiments" on whom the resurrected author has to vent his sarcasm: who knows what victim he is looking for, what monster of material for parody will soon attract him? *"Incipit tragoedia"* we read at the end of this awesomely aweless book. Beware! Something downright wicked and malicious is announced here: *incipit parodia*, no doubt.[1]

2

But let us leave Herr Nietzsche: what is it to us that Herr Nietzsche has become well again?

For a psychologist there are few questions that are as attractive as that concerning the relation of health and philosophy, and if he should himself become ill, he will bring all of his scientific curiosity into his illness. For assuming that one is a person, one necessarily also has the philosophy that belongs to that person; but there is a big difference. In some it is their deprivations that philosophize; in others, their riches and strengths.[2] The former *need* their philosophy, whether it be as a prop, a sedative, medicine, redemption, elevation, or self-alienation. For the latter it is merely a beautiful luxury—in the

---

[1] "The tragedy begins": This is the title of section 342 which concluded the first edition—and the text of that section is the beginning of Nietzsche's next book, *Thus Spoke Zarathustra*. What Nietzsche is saying, then, is that *Zarathustra* is something of a parody—which it surely is—although most readers during the first half of the twentieth century failed to see this.

[2] Cf. the last three paragraphs of section 370.

best cases, the voluptuousness of a triumphant gratitude that eventually still has to inscribe itself in cosmic letters on the heaven of concepts. But in the former case, which is more common, when it is distress that philosophizes, as is the case with all sick thinkers—and perhaps sick thinkers are more numerous in the history of philosophy—what will become of the thought itself when it is subjected to the *pressure* of sickness? This is the question that concerns the psychologist, and here an experiment is possible. Just as a traveler may resolve, before he calmly abandons himself to sleep, to wake up at a certain time, we philosophers, if we should become sick, surrender for a while to sickness, body and soul—and, as it were, shut our eyes to ourselves. And as the traveler knows that something is *not* asleep, that something counts the hours and will wake him up, we, too, know that the decisive moment will find us awake, and that something will leap forward then and catch the spirit *in the act:* I mean, in its weakness or repentance or resignation or hardening or gloom, and whatever other names there are for the pathological states of the spirit that on healthy days are opposed by the *pride* of the spirit (for the old saying is still valid: "the proud spirit, peacock, and horse are the three proudest beasts on earth").

After such self-questioning, self-temptation, one acquires a subtler eye for all philosophizing to date; one can infer better than before the involuntary detours, side lanes, resting places, and *sunny* places of thought to which suffering thinkers are led and misled on account of their suffering; for now one knows whether the sick *body* and its needs unconsciously urge, push, and lure the spirit—toward the sun, stillness, mildness, patience, medicine, balm in some sense. Every philosophy that ranks peace above war, every ethic with a negative definition of happiness, every metaphysics and physics that knows some *finale*, some final state of some sort, every predominantly aesthetic or religious craving for some Apart, Beyond, Outside, Above, permits the question whether it was not sickness that inspired the philosopher. The unconscious disguise of physiological needs under the cloaks of the objective, ideal, purely spiritual goes to frightening lengths—and often I have asked myself whether, taking a large view, philosophy has not been merely an interpretation of the body and a *misunderstanding of the body*.

Behind the highest value judgments that have hitherto guided the history of thought, there are concealed misunderstandings of the physical constitution—of individuals or classes or even whole races. All those bold insanities of metaphysics, especially answers to the question about the *value* of existence, may always be considered first of all as the symptoms of certain bodies. And if such world affirmations or world negations *tout court* lack any grain of significance when measured scientifically, they are the more valuable for the historian and psychologist as hints or symptoms of the body, of its success or failure, its plenitude, power, and autocracy in history, or of its frustrations, weariness, impoverishment, its premonitions of the end, its will to the end.

I am still waiting for a philosophical *physician* in the exceptional sense of that word—one who has to pursue the problem of the total health of a people, time, race or of humanity—to muster the courage to push my suspicion to its limits and to risk the proposition: what was at stake in all philosophizing hitherto was not at all "truth" but something else—let us say, health, future, growth, power, life.

3

You see that I do not want to take leave ungratefully from that time of severe sickness whose profits I have not yet exhausted even today. I am very conscious of the advantages that my fickle health gives me over all robust squares.[3] A philosopher who has traversed many kinds of health, and keeps traversing them, has passed through an equal number of philosophies; he simply *cannot* keep from transposing his states every time into the most spiritual form and distance: this art of transfiguration *is* philosophy. We philosophers are not free to divide body from soul as the people do; we are even less free to divide soul from spirit. We are not thinking frogs, nor objectifying and registering mechanisms with their innards removed: constantly, we have to give birth to our thoughts out of our pain and, like

---

[3] *Vierschrötigen des Geistes.*

mothers, endow them with all we have of blood, heart, fire, pleasure, passion, agony, conscience, fate, and catastrophe. Life —that means for us constantly transforming all that we are into light and flame[4]—also everything that wounds us; we simply can do no other. And as for sickness: are we not almost tempted to ask whether we could get along without it?[5] Only great pain is the ultimate liberator of the spirit, being the teacher of *the great suspicion* that turns every U into an X, a real, genuine X, that is the letter before the penultimate one.[6]

Only great pain, the long, slow pain that takes its time—on which we are burned, as it were, with green wood—compels us philosophers to descend into our ultimate depths and to put aside all trust, everything good-natured, everything that would interpose a veil, that is mild, that is medium—things in which formerly we may have found our humanity. I doubt that such pain makes us "better"; but I know that it makes us more *profound.*

Whether we learn to pit our pride, our scorn, our will power against it, equaling the American Indian who, however tortured, repays his torturer with the malice of his tongue; or whether we withdraw from pain into that Oriental Nothing—called Nirvana—into mute, rigid, deaf resignation, self-forgetting, self-extinction: out of such long and dangerous exercises of self-mastery one emerges as a different person, with a few more question marks—above all with the *will* henceforth to question further, more deeply, severely, harshly, evilly and quietly than one had questioned heretofore. The trust in life is gone: life itself has become a *problem.* Yet one should not jump to the

---

[4] Cf. poem #62 in the Prelude.

[5] Nietzsche later reprinted the last two sections of this Preface, with some revisions, as the "Epilogue" of *Nietzsche contra Wagner* (VPN, 680–83). Up to this point the text was changed extensively while most of what follows was retained with only minor changes.

[6] There is a German expression for deceiving someone that means literally: passing off a *u* as an *x*. Originally it referred to the Roman numerals, V and X, and meant passing off a five for a ten. The suspicion of which Nietzsche speaks does not inflate conventional values; it insists that they are not really known but rather unknown quantities—the *x* of the mathematicians.

conclusion that this necessarily makes one gloomy. Even love of life is still possible, only one loves differently. It is the love for a woman that causes doubts in us.

The attraction of everything problematic, the delight in an *x*, however, is so great in such more spiritual, more spiritualized men that this delight flares up again and again like a bright blaze over all the distress of what is problematic, over all the danger of uncertainty, and even over the jealousy of the lover. We know a new happiness.

4

In the end, lest what is most important remain unsaid: from such abysses, from such severe sickness, also from the sickness of severe suspicion, one returns *newborn*, having shed one's skin, more ticklish and malicious, with a more delicate taste for joy, with a tenderer tongue for all good things, with merrier senses, with a second dangerous innocence in joy, more child-like and yet a hundred times subtler than one has ever been before.

How repulsive pleasure is now, that crude, musty, brown pleasure as it is understood by those who like pleasure, our "educated" people, our rich people, and our rulers! How maliciously we listen now to the big county-fair boom-boom with which the "educated" person and city dweller today permits art, books, and music to rape him and provide "spiritual pleasures"—with the aid of spirituous liquors! How the theatrical scream of passion now hurts our ears, how strange to our taste the whole romantic uproar and tumult of the senses have become, which the educated mob loves, and all its aspirations after the elevated, inflated, and exaggerated! No, if we convalescents still need art, it is another kind of art—a mocking, light, fleeting, divinely untroubled, divinely artificial art that, like a pure flame, licks into unclouded skies. Above all, an art for artists, for artists only! We know better afterward what above all is needed for this: cheerfulness, any cheerfulness, my friends—also as artists: let me prove it. There are a few things we now know too well, we knowing ones: oh, how we now learn to forget well, and to be good at *not* knowing, as artists!

And as for our future, one will hardly find us again on the paths of those Egyptian youths who endanger temples by night, embrace statues, and want by all means to unveil, uncover, and put into a bright light whatever is kept concealed for good reasons.[7] No, this bad taste, this will to truth, to "truth at any price," this youthful madness in the love of truth, have lost their charm for us: for that we are too experienced, too serious, too merry, too burned, too *profound.* We no longer believe that truth remains truth when the veils are withdrawn; we have lived too much to believe this. Today we consider it a matter of decency not to wish to see everything naked, or to be present at everything, or to understand and "know" everything.

"Is it true that God is present everywhere?" a little girl asked her mother; "I think that's indecent"—a hint for philosophers! One should have more respect for the bashfulness with which nature has hidden behind riddles and iridescent uncertainties. Perhaps truth is a woman who has reasons for not letting us see her reasons? Perhaps her name is—to speak Greek—*Baubo?*[8]

Oh, those Greeks! They knew how to live. What is required for that is to stop courageously at the surface, the fold, the skin, to adore appearance, to believe in forms, tones, words, in the whole Olympus of appearance. Those Greeks were superficial—*out of profundity.* And is not this precisely what we are again coming back to, we daredevils of the spirit who have climbed the highest and most dangerous peak of present thought and looked around from up there—we who have looked *down* from there? Are we not, precisely in this respect, Greeks? Adorers of forms, of tones, of words? And therefore—*artists?*

Ruta, near Genoa,
in the fall of 1886

---

[7] An allusion to Friedrich Schiller's great ballad "The Veiled Image at Sais."

[8] *Baubo:* A primitive and obscene female demon; according to the *Oxford Classical Dictionary,* originally a personification of the female genitals.

"JOKE, CUNNING, AND REVENGE"*

PRELUDE IN GERMAN RHYMES

---

* *"Scherz, List und Rache"*: This had been the title of a *Singspiel* (a libretto) by Goethe. Nietzsche's friend Peter Gast (1854–1918; his real name was Heinrich Köselitz) had set it to music and was seeking a publisher for it. Nietzsche's correspondence with Gast in 1882 is full of references to it; and Gast helped Nietzsche with the printer's proof.

1
Einladung

Wagt's mit meiner Kost, ihr Esser!
Morgen schmeckt sie euch schon besser
Und schon übermorgen gut!
Wollt ihr dann noch mehr,—so machen
Meine alten sieben Sachen
Mir zu sieben neuen Mut.

2
Mein Glück

Seit ich des Suchens müde ward,
Erlernte ich das Finden.
Seit mir ein Wind hielt Widerpart,
Segl' ich mit allen Winden.

3
Unverzagt

Wo du stehst grab tief hinein!
Drunten ist die Quelle!
Lass die dunklen Männer schrein:
„Stets ist drunten—Hölle!"

4
Zwiegespräch

A. War ich krank? Bin ich genesen?
   Und wer ist mein Arzt gewesen?
   Wie vergass ich alles das!

B. Jetzt erst glaub' ich dich genesen:
   Denn gesund ist, wer vergass.

1
Invitation

Take a chance and try my fare:
It will grow on you, I swear;
Soon it will taste good to you.
If by then you should want more,
All the things I've done before
Will inspire things quite new.[1]

2
My Happiness

Since I grew tired of the chase
And search, I learned to find;
And since the wind blows in my face,
I sail with every wind.

3
Undaunted

Where you stand, dig deep and pry!
Down there is the well.
Let the obscurantists cry:
"Down there's only—hell!"

4
Dialogue

A. Was I ill? Have I got well?
   Who was my doctor? Can you tell?
   Oh, my memory is rotten!
B. Only now you're truly well.
   Those are well who have forgotten.

---

[1] The modesty of the first three lines is striking. Literally, the fare will taste better tomorrow, and good only the day after tomorrow.

5
An die Tugendsamen

Unseren Tugenden auch soll'n leicht die Füsse sich heben,
Gleich den Versen Homers müssen sie kommen
und gehn!

6
Welt-Klugheit

Bleib nicht auf ebnem Feld!
Steig nicht zu hoch hinaus!
Am schönsten sieht die Welt
Von halber Höhe aus.

7
Vademecum—Vadetecum

Es lockt dich meine Art und Sprach',
Du folgest mir, du gehst mir nach?
Geh nur dir selber treulich nach:—
So folgst du mir—gemach! gemach!

8
Bei der dritten Häutung

Schon krümmt und bricht sich mir die Haut,
Schon giert mit neuem Drange,
So viel sie Erde schon verdaut,
Nach Erd' in mir die Schlange.
Schon kriech' ich zwischen Stein und Gras
Hungrig auf krummer Fährte,
Zu essen das, was stets ich ass,
Dich, Schlangenkost, dich, Erde!

5
To the Virtuous

Why should our virtues be grave? We like ours
    nimble-footed:
Even like Homer's verse, they have to come *and go!*[2]

6
Worldly Wisdom

Do not stay in the field!
Nor climb out of sight.
The best view of the world
Is from a medium height.

7
Vademecum—Vadetecum[3]

Lured by my style and tendency,
you follow and come after me?
Follow your own self faithfully—
take time—and thus you follow me.

8
Shedding the Third Skin

My skin is cracking, as the snake
Inside me lusts, as if it had
Not eaten enough earth, to slake
Its thirst with more earth. Between blade
And stem I crawl, far from the beaten
Track, hungry and yet full of mirth
To eat what I have always eaten:
You, fare of snakes, you, earth!

---

[2] I.e., our virtues should occasionally leave us in peace.
[3] *Vademecum*: a manual or guidebook; literally, "go with me."
Vadetecum: go with yourself.

9
Meine Rosen

Ja! Mein Glück—es will beglücken,—
Alles Glück will ja beglücken!
Wollt ihr meine Rosen pflücken?

Müsst euch bücken und verstecken
Zwischen Fels und Dornenhecken,
Oft die Fingerchen euch lecken!

Denn mein Glück—es liebt das Necken!
Denn mein Glück—es liebt die Tücken!—
Wollt ihr meine Rosen pflücken?

10
Der Verächter

Vieles lass' ich fall'n und rollen,
Und ihr nennt mich drum Verächter.
Wer da trinkt aus allzuvollen
Bechern, lässt viel fall'n und rollen,—
Denkt vom Weine drum nicht schlechter.

11
Das Sprichwort spricht

Scharf und milde, grob und fein,
Vertraut und seltsam, schmutzig und rein,
Der Narren und Weisen Stelldichein:
Dies alles bin ich, will ich sein,
Taube zugleich, Schlange und Schwein!

12
An einen Lichtfreund

Willst du nicht Aug' und Sinn ermatten,
Lauf auch der Sonne nach im Schatten!

9
My Roses

Yes, my joy wants to amuse,
Every joy wants to amuse.
Would you like to pick my roses?

You must stoop and stick your noses
Between thorns and rocky views,
And not be afraid of bruises.

For my joy—enjoys good teases.
For my joy—enjoys good ruses.
Would you like to pick my roses?

10
Scorn

There is much I drop and spill:
I am full of scorn, you think.
If your beaker is too full,
There is much you drop and spill
Without scorning what you drink.

11
The Proverb Speaks

Sharp and mild, rough and fine,
Strange and familiar, impure and clean,
A place where fool and sage convene:
All this I am and wish to mean,
Dove as well as snake and swine.

12
To a Light-Lover

If you don't want your eyes and mind to fade
Pursue the sun while walking in the shade.

13
Für Tänzer

Glattes Eis
Ein Paradeis
Für den, der gut zu tanzen weiss.

14
Der Brave

Lieber aus ganzem Holz eine Feindschaft
Als eine geleimte Freundschaft!

15
Rost

Auch Rost tut not; Scharfsein ist nicht genung!
Sonst sagt man stets von dir: „er ist zu jung!"

16
Aufwärts

„Wie komm' ich am besten den Berg hinan?"—
„Steig nur hinauf und denk nicht dran!"

17
Spruch des Gewaltmenschen

Bitte nie! Lass dies Gewimmer!
Nimm, ich bitte dich, nimm immer!

18
Schmale Seelen

Schmale Seelen sind mir verhasst:
Da steht nichts Gutes, nichts Böses fast.

19
Der unfreiwillige Verführer

Er schoss ein leeres Wort zum Zeitvertreib
Ins Blaue—und doch fiel darob ein Weib.

13
For Dancers

Smooth ice
is paradise
for those who dance with expertise.

14
The Good Man

Better a whole-hearted feud
Than a friendship that is glued.

15
Rust

You need some rust; sharpness does not suffice:
Else you will seem too young and too precise:

16
Up

If you want to get to the peak, you ought
To climb without giving it too much thought.

17
The Maxim of the Brute

Never ask! Why cry and shake?
Please, I ask you, simply take!

18
Narrow Souls

Narrow souls I cannot abide;
There's almost no good or evil inside.

19
The Involuntary Seducer

He shot an empty word, just for a ball,
Into the blue—it made a woman fall.

20
Zur Erwägung

Zwiefacher Schmerz ist leichter zu tragen
Als Ein Schmerz: willst du darauf es wagen?

21
Gegen die Hoffahrt

Blas dich nicht auf: sonst bringet dich
Zum Platzen schon ein kleiner Stich.

22
Mann und Weib

„Raub' dir das Weib, für das dein Herze fühlt!"—
So denkt der Mann; das Weib raubt nicht, es stiehlt.

23
Interpretation

Leg' ich mich aus, so leg' ich mich hinein:
Ich kann nicht selbst mein Interprete sein.
Doch wer nur steigt auf seiner eignen Bahn,
Trägt auch mein Bild zu hellerm Licht hinan.

24
Pessimisten-Arznei

Du klagst, dass nichts dir schmackhaft sei?
Noch immer, Freund, die alten Mucken?
Ich hör' dich lästern, lärmen, spucken—
Geduld und Herz bricht mir dabei.
Folg' mir, mein Freund! Entschliess dich frei,
Ein fettes Krötchen zu verschlucken,
Geschwind und ohne hinzugucken!—
Das hilft dir von der Dyspepsei!

25
Bitte

Iche kenne mancher Menschen Sinn
Und weiss nicht, wer ich selber bin!

20
For your Consideration

Double pain is easier to bear
Than single pain: Do you accept my dare?

21
Against Airs

Those who inflate themselves are cursed
When pricked by a small pin to burst.

22
Man and Woman

Seize forcibly the wench for whom you feel!
Thus thinks a man. Women don't rob, they steal.

23
Interpretation

Interpreting myself, I always read
Myself into my books. I clearly need
Some help. But all who climb on their own way
Carry my image, too, into the breaking day.

24
Medicine for Pessimists

Nothing tastes good to you, my friend?
I'm tired of your belly-aching.
You spit, rage, slander without end;
My patience and my heart are breaking.
I have a remedy; just follow
My good advice and rest assured:
A toad is what you need to swallow,
And your dyspepsia will be cured.

25
Request

The minds of others I know well;
But who *I* am, I cannot tell:

Mein Auge ist mir viel zu nah—
Ich bin nicht, was ich seh' und sah.
Ich wollte mir schon besser nützen,
Könnt' ich mir selber ferner sitzen.
Zwar nicht so ferne wie mein Feind!
Zu fern sitzt schon der nächste Freund—
Doch zwischen dem und mir die Mitte!
Erratet ihr, um was ich bitte?

26
Meine Härte

Ich muss weg über hundert Stufen,
Ich muss empor und hör' euch rufen:
„Hart bist du! Sind wir denn von Stein?"—
Ich muss weg über hundert Stufen,
Und niemand möchte Stufe sein.

27
Der Wanderer

„Kein Pfad mehr! Abgrund rings und Totenstille!"—
So wolltest du's! Vom Pfade wich dein Wille!
Nun, Wandrer, gilt's! Nun blicke kalt und klar!
Verloren bist du, glaubst du—an Gefahr.

28
Trost für Anfänger

Seht das Kind umgrunzt von Schweinen,
Hilflos, mit verkrümmten Zehn!
Weinen kann es, nichts als weinen—
Lernt es jemals stehn und gehn?
Unverzagt! Bald, sollt' ich meinen,
Könnt das Kind ihr tanzen sehn!
Steht es erst auf beiden Beinen,
Wird's auch auf dem Kopfe stehn.

My eye is much too close to me,
I am not what I saw and see.
It would be quite a benefit
If only I could sometimes sit
Farther away; but my foes are
Too distant; close friends, still too far;
Between my friends and me, the middle
Would do. My wish? *You* guess my riddle.

26
My Hardness

A hundred steps I have to climb.
I must ascend, but hear you groan:
"You're cruel! Are we made of stone?"
A hundred steps I have to climb:
Who wants to be a step? Not one.

27
The Wanderer

"No path, abysses, death is not so still!"—
You wished it, left the path by your own will.
Now remain cool and clear, O stranger;
For you are lost if you believe in danger.

28
Consolation for Beginners

See the child lost among swine,
Helpless, he can't even talk.
He is always, always cryin'—
Will he ever learn to walk?
Don't despair! Soon he will treat
You to dances. It is said,
Once he can stand on his feet,
He will soon stand on his head.

29
Sternen-Egoismus

Rollt' ich mich rundes Rollefass
Nicht um mich selbst ohn' Unterlass,
Wie hielt' ich's aus, ohne anzubrennen,
Der heissen Sonne nachzurennen?

30
Der Nächste

Nah hab' den Nächsten ich nicht gerne:
Fort mit ihm in die Höh' und Ferne!
Wie würd' er sonst zu meinem Sterne?—

31
Der verkappte Heilige

Dass dein Glück uns nicht bedrücke,
Legst du um dich Teufelstücke,
Teufelswitz und Teufelskleid.
Doch umsonst! Aus deinem Blicke
Blickt hervor die Heiligkeit!

32
Der Unfreie

A. Er steht und horcht: was konnt ihn irren?
   Was hört er vor den Ohren schwirren?
   Was war's, das ihn darniederschlug?
B. Wie jeder, der einst Ketten trug,
   Hört überall er—Kettenklirren.

33
Der Einsame

Verhasst ist mir das Folgen und das Führen.
Gehorchen? Nein! Und aber nein—Regieren!
Wer sich nicht schrecklich ist, macht niemand Schrecken:

29
The Egoism of the Stars

If I did not, a rolling cask,
Keep turning endlessly, I ask,
How would I keep from burning when
I run after the blazing sun?

30
The Neighbor

I do not love my neighbor near,
but wish he were high up and far.
How else could he become my star?

31
The Disguised Saint

Lest your happiness oppress us
Cloak yourself in devilish tresses
Devilish wit and devilish dress.
All in vain! Your eye expresses
Your angelic saintliness.

32
The Unfree Man

A. He stands and harks: what does he hear?
What sound is ringing in his ear?
What struck him down? What mortal fear?
B. Who once wore chains, will always think
That he is followed by their clink.

33
The Solitary

I hate to follow and I hate to lead.
Obey? Oh no! And govern? No indeed!
Only who dreads himself inspires dread.

Und nur wer Schrecken macht, kann andere führen.
Verhasst ist mir's schon, selber mich zu führen!
Ich liebe es, gleich Wald- und Meerestieren,
Mich für ein gutes Weilchen zu verlieren,
In holder Irrnis grüblerisch zu hocken,
Von ferne her mich endlich heimzulocken,
Mich selber zu mir selber—zu verführen.

34
Seneca et hoc genus omne

Das schreibt und schreibt sein unaussteh-
lich weises Larifari,
Als gält' es primum scribere,
Deinde philosophari.

35
Eis

Ja! Mitunter mach' ich Eis:
Nützlich ist Eis zum Verdauen!
Hättet ihr viel zu verdauen,
O wie liebtet ihr mein Eis!

36
Jugendschriften

Meiner Weisheit A und O
Klang mir hier: was hört' ich doch!
Jetzo klingt mir's nicht mehr so,
Nur das ew'ge Ah! und Oh!
Meiner Jugend hör' ich noch.

37
Vorsicht

In jener Gegend reist man jetzt nicht gut;
Und hast du Geist, sei doppelt auf der Hut!

And only those inspiring dread can lead.
Even to lead myself is not my speed.
I love to lose myself for a good while,
Lik animals in forests and the sea,
To sit and think on some abandoned isle,
And lure myself back home from far away,
Seducing myself to come back to me.

34
Seneca et hoc genus omne[4]

They write and write their insufferably
sagacious larifari,
As if to *primum scribere,
Deinde philosophari.*[5]

35
Ice

Yes, at times I do make ice,
For it helps us to digest.
If you had much to digest,
You would surely love my ice!

36
Juvenilia

My youthful wisdom's A and O
I heard again. What did I hear?
Words not of wisdom but of woe:
Only the endless Ah and Oh
Of youth lies heavy in my ear.[6]

37
Caution

That region is not safe for strangers,
And having wit doubles the dangers.

---

[4] Seneca and his ilk.
[5] First write, afterward philosophize.
[6] "A and O" — alpha and omega, the beginning and the end or the be-all and end-all.

Man lockt und liebt dich, bis man dich zerreisst:
Schwarmgeister sind's—: da fehlt es stets an Geist!

38
Der Fromme spricht

Gott liebt uns, weil er uns erschuf!—
„Der Mensch schuf Gott!"—sagt drauf ihr Feinen.
Und soll nicht lieben, was er schuf?
Soll's gar, weil er es schuf, verneinen?
Das hinkt, das trägt des Teufels Huf.

39
Im Sommer

Im Schweisse unsres Angesichts
Soll'n unser Brot wir essen?
Im Schweisse isst man lieber nichts,
Nach weiser Ärzte Ermessen.
Der Hundsstern winkt: woran gebricht's?
Was will sein feurig Winken?
Im Schweisse unsres Angesichts
Soll'n unsern Wein wir trinken!

40
Ohne Neid

Ja, neidlos blickt er: und ihr ehrt ihn drum?
Er blickt sich nicht nach euren Ehren um;
Er hat des Adlers Auge für die Ferne,
Er sieht euch nicht!—er sieht nur Sterne, Sterne!

41
Heraklitismus

Alles Glück auf Erden,
Freunde, gibt der Kampf!
Ja, um Freund zu werden,

They lure and love you, then tear you to bits:
They are enthusiasts, and that type lacks wits.

38
The Pious Retort

God loves us, *because* we are made *by him*.
"But man made God!" say the refined.
Should he not love what he designed?
Should he, *because* he made him, now *deny him*?
That inference limps; it has a cloven mind.

39
In the Summer

In the sweat of our brow
We should eat our bread?
Good doctors don't allow
Eating when in a sweat.
The Dog Star twinkles now.
Of what is this a sign?
In the sweat of our brow
We should drink our wine!

40
Without Envy

His look is free of envy; hence you laud him;
He does not notice whether you applaud him;
He has the eagle's eye for what is far,
He does not see you, he sees only stars.

41
Heraclitean

Only fighting yields
Happiness on earth,
And on battlefields

Braucht es Pulverdampf!
Eins in Drein sind Freunde:
Brüder vor der Not,
Gleiche vor dem Feinde,
Freie—vor dem Tod!

42
Grundsatz der Allzufeinen

Lieber auf den Zehen noch
Als auf allen Vieren!
Lieber durch ein Schlüsselloch
Als durch offne Türen!

43
Zuspruch

Auf Ruhm hast du den Sinn gericht?
Dann acht' der Lehre:
Beizeiten leiste frei Verzicht
Auf Ehre!

44
Der Gründliche

Ein Forscher ich? O spart dies Wort!—
Ich bin nur schwer—so manche Pfund!
Ich falle, falle immerfort
Und endlich auf den Grund!

45
Für immer

„Heut komm ich, weil mir's heute frommt"—
Denkt jeder, der für immer kommt.
Was ficht ihn an der Welt Gered':
„Du kommst zu früh! Du kommst zu spät!"

Friendship has its birth.
One in three are friends:
Brothers in distress,
Equals, facing foes,
Free—when facing death!

42
Principle of the Overly Refined

Rather on your toes, up high,
Than crawling on all fours!
Rather through a keyhole spy
Than through open doors!

43
Admonition

What you want is fame?
Then note the price:
All claim
To honor you must sacrifice.

44
The Thorough Who Get to the Bottom of Things

A seeker, I? Oh, please be still!
I'm merely *heavy*—weigh many a pound.
I fall, and I keep falling till
At last I reach the ground.

45
Forever

"I come today
Because I feel that way,"
Thinks everyone who comes to stay
Forever. And he gives no weight
To what the world may say:
"You're rather early! You are late!"

46
Urteile der Müden

Der Sonne fluchen alle Matten;
Der Bäume Wert ist ihnen—Schatten!

47
Niedergang

„Er sinkt, er fällt jetzt"—höhnt ihr hin und wieder;
Die Wahrheit ist: er steigt zu euch hernieder!
Sein Überglück ward ihm zum Ungemach,
Sein Überlicht geht eurem Dunkel nach.

48
Gegen die Gesetze

Von heut an hängt an härner Schnur
Um meinen Hals die Stundenuhr;
Von heut an hört der Sterne Lauf,
Sonn', Hahnenschrei und Schatten auf,
Und was mir je die Zeit verkünd't,
Das ist jetzt stumm und taub und blind:—
Es schweigt mir jegliche Natur
Beim Tiktak von Gesetz und Uhr.

49
Der Weise spricht

Dem Volke fremd und nützlich doch dem Volke,
Zieh' ich des Weges, Sonne bald, bald Wolke—
Und immer über diesem Volke!

46
Judgments of the Weary

They hate the sun, find steep the grade,
And love trees only for their shade.

47
Decline

"He sinks, he falls, he's done"—says who?
The truth is: he climbs down to you.
His over-bliss became too stark,
His over-light pursues your dark.[7]

48
Against the Laws

Suspended by a hair, the clock
As of today hangs round *my* neck:
As of today, the stars, the sun,
Cockcrow and shadows are all done;
Whatever used to tell the time
Is mute and deaf and blind, and I
Find nature silent as a rock
At the ticktock of law and clock.

49
The Sage Speaks

A stranger to the crowd, yet useful to the crowd,
I point a way, now sun and now a cloud—
and always far above the crowd.

---

[7] Cf. section 342 and the Prologue to *Zarathustra*, the beginning of Nietzsche's next book.

50
Den Kopf verloren

Sie hat jetzt Geist—wie kam's, dass sie ihn fand?
Ein Mann verlor durch sie jüngst den Verstand.
Sein Kopf war reich vor diesem Zeitvertreibe:
Zum Teufel ging sein Kopf—nein! nein! zum Weibe!

51
Fromme Wünsche

„Mögen alle Schlüssel doch
Flugs verloren gehen,
Und in jedem Schlüsselloch
Sich der Dietrich drehen!"
Also denkt zu jeder Frist
Jeder, der—ein Dietrich ist.

52
Mit dem Fusse schreiben

Ich schreib' nicht mit der Hand allein:
Der Fuss will stets mit Schreiber sein.
Fest, frei und tapfer läuft er mir
Bald durch das Feld, bald durchs Papier.

53
„Menschliches, Allzumenschliches." Ein Buch

Schwermütig scheu, solang du rückwärts schaust,
Der Zukunft trauend, wo du selbst dir traust:
O Vogel, rechn' ich dich den Adlern zu?
Bist du Minervas Liebling U-hu-hu?

54
Meinem Leser

Ein gut Gebiss und einen guten Magen—
Dies wünsch' ich dir!
Und hast du erst mein Buch vertragen,
Verträgst du dich gewiss mit mir!

50
Lost His Head

Why is she clever now and so refined?
On her account a man's out of his mind,
His head was good before he took this whirl:
He lost his wits—to the aforesaid girl.

51
Pious Wishes

"All keys ought to go to hell, anon,
And in every keyhole be replaced
by a skeleton!"
That has always been the taste
Of all who feel they matter
Because they are the latter.

52
Writing with One's Feet

Not with my hand alone I write:
My foot wants to participate.
Firm and free and bold, my feet
Run across the field—and sheet.

53
Human, All Too Human: *A Book*

You're sad and shy when looking at the past,
But trust the future when yourself you trust:
Are you some kind of eagle in pursuit?
Or just Minerva's favorite hootootoot?

54
To My Reader

I am the cook.
Good teeth, strong stomach with you be!
And once you have got down my book,
You should get on with me.

55
Der realistische Maler

„Treu die Natur und ganz!"—Wie fängt er's an:
Wann wäre je Natur im Bilde abgetan?
Unendlich ist das kleinste Stück der Welt!—
Er malt zuletzt davon, was ihm gefällt.
Und was gefällt ihm? Was er malen kann!

56
Dichter-Eitelkeit

Gebt mir Leim nur: denn zum Leime
Find' ich selber mir schon Holz!
Sinn in vier unsinn'ge Reime
Legen—ist kein kleiner Stolz!

57
Wählerischer Geschmack

Wenn man frei mich wählen liesse,
Wählt' ich gern ein Plätzchen mir
Mitten drin im Paradiese:
Gerner noch—vor seiner Tür!

58
Die krumme Nase

Die Nase schauet trutziglich
Ins Land, der Nüster blähet sich—
Drum fällst du, Nashorn ohne Horn,
Mein stolzes Menschlein, stets nach vorn!
Und stets beisammen find't sich das:
Gerader Stolz, gekrümmte Nas'.

59
Die Feder kritzelt

Die Feder kritzelt: Hölle das!
Bin ich verdammt zum Kritzelnmüssen?—

55
Realistic Painters

"True to nature, all the truth: that's art."
This hallowed notion is a threadbare fable.
Infinite is nature's smallest part.
They paint what happens to delight their heart.
And what delights them? What to paint they're able.

56
Poet's Vanity

Give me glue and in good time
I'll find wood myself. To crowd
Sense into four silly rhymes
Is enough to make one proud.

57
Choosy Taste

If it depended on my choice,
I think it might be great
To have a place in Paradise;
Better yet—outside the gate.

58
A Crooked Nose

Its nostrils proud and pliant,
The nose looks out defiant.
That's why, a rhino without horn,
You fall forward, proud little man;
And straight pride generally grows
Together with a crooked nose.

59
The Pen is Stubborn

The pen is stubborn, sputters—hell!
Am I condemned to scrawl?

So greif' ich kühn zum Tintenfass
Und schreib' mit dicken Tintenflüssen.
Wie läuft das hin, so voll, so breit!
Wie glückt mir alles, wie ich's treibe!
Zwar fehlt der Schrift die Deutlichkeit—
Was tut's? Wer liest denn, was ich schreibe?

60
Höhere Menschen

Der steigt empor—ihn soll man loben!
Doch jener kommt allzeit von oben!
Der lebt dem Lobe selbst enthoben,
Der ist von droben!

61
Der Skeptiker spricht

Halb ist dein Leben um,
Der Zeiger rückt, die Seele schaudert dir!
Lang schweift sie schon herum
Und sucht, und fand nicht—und sie zaudert hier?

Halb ist dein Leben um:
Schmerz war's und Irrtum Stund um Stund dahier!
Was suchst du noch? Warum?——
Dies eben such' ich—Grund um Grund dafür!

62
Ecce homo

Ja! Ich weiss, woher ich stamme!
Ungesättigt gleich der Flamme
Glühe und verzehr' ich mich.
Licht wird alles, was ich fasse,
Kohle alles, was ich lasse:
Flamme bin ich sicherlich!

Boldly I dip it in the well,
My writing flows, and all
I try succeeds. Of course, the spatter
Of this tormented night
Is quite illegible. No matter:
Who reads the stuff I write?

60
Higher Men

He should be praised for climbing; yet
The other man comes always from a height
And lives where praise can never get—
Beyond your sight.

61
The Skeptic Speaks

Half of your life is done,
The hand moves on, you feel a sudden chill.
You have roamed long, and run,
And sought, and found not—why this sudden frill?

Half of your life is done,
And it was pain and error through and through:
Why do you still seek on?
Precisely this I seek: The reason why!

62
Ecce Homo

Yes, I know from where I came!
Ever hungry like a flame,
I consume myself and glow.
Light grows all that I conceive,
Ashes everything I leave:
Flame I am assuredly.

63
Sternenmoral

Vorausbestimmt zur Sternenbahn,
Was geht dich, Stern, das Dunkel an?

Roll' selig hin durch diese Zeit!
Ihr Elend sei dir fremd und weit!

Der fernsten Welt gehört dein Schein:
Mitleid soll Sünde für dich sein!

Nur Ein Gebot gilt dir: sei rein!

63
Star Morals

Called a star's orbit to pursue,
What is the darkness, star, to you?

Roll on in bliss, traverse this age—
Its misery far from you and strange.

Let farthest world your light secure.
Pity is sin you must abjure.

But one command is yours: be pure!

BOOK ONE

The teachers of the purpose of existence.— Whether I contemplate men with benevolence or with an evil eye, I always find them concerned with a single task, all of them and every one of them in particular: to do what is good for the preservation of the human race. Not from any feeling of love for the race, but merely because nothing in them is older, stronger, more inexorable and unconquerable than this instinct—because this instinct constitutes *the essence* of our species, our herd. It is easy enough to divide our neighbors quickly, with the usual myopia, from a mere five paces away, into useful and harmful, good and evil men; but in any large-scale accounting, when we reflect on the whole a little longer, we become suspicious of this neat division and finally abandon it. Even the most harmful man may really be the most useful when it comes to the preservation of the species; for he nurtures either in himself or in others, through his effects, instincts without which humanity would long have become feeble or rotten. Hatred, the mischievous delight in the misfortunes of others, the lust to rob and dominate, and whatever else is called evil belongs to the most amazing economy of the preservation of the species. To be sure, this economy is not afraid of high prices, of squandering, and it is on the whole extremely foolish. Still it is *proven* that it has preserved our race so far.

I no longer know whether you, my dear fellow man and neighbor, are at all *capable* of living in a way that would damage the species; in other words, "unreasonably" and "badly." What *might* have harmed the species may have become extinct many thousands of years ago and may by now be one of those things that are not possible even for God. Pursue your best or your worst desires, and above all perish! In both cases you are probably still in some way a promoter and benefactor of humanity and therefore entitled to your eulogists—but also to your detractors. But you will never find anyone who could wholly mock you as an individual, also in your best qualities, bringing home to you to the limits of truth your boundless, flylike, frog-like wretchedness! To laugh at oneself as one would have to laugh in order to laugh *out of the whole truth*—to do that even the best so far lacked sufficient sense for the truth, and the most gifted had too little genius for that. Even laughter may yet have a future. I mean, when the proposition "the species is everything, *one* is always none" has become part of humanity, and this ultimate liberation and irresponsibility has become accessible to all at all times. Perhaps laughter will then have formed an alliance with wisdom, perhaps only "gay science" will then be left.

For the present, things are still quite different. For the present, the comedy of existence has not yet "become conscious" of itself. For the present, we still live in the age of tragedy, the age of moralities and religions. What is the meaning of the ever new appearance of these founders of moralities and religions, these instigators of fights over moral valuations, these teachers of remorse and religious wars? What is the meaning of these heroes on this stage? Thus far these have been the heroes, and everything else, even if at times it was all that could be seen and was much too near to us, has always merely served to set the stage for these heroes, whether it was machinery or coulisse or took the form of confidants and valets. (The poets, for example, were always the valets of some morality.)

It is obvious that these tragedians, too, promote the interests of the *species*, even if they should believe that they promote the interest of God or work as God's emissaries. They, too, promote the life of the species, *by promoting the faith in life.* "Life is worth living," every one of them shouts; "there is something to life, there is something behind life, beneath it; beware!"

From time to time this instinct, which is at work equally in the highest and the basest men—the instinct for the preservation of the species—erupts as reason and as passion of the spirit. Then it is surrounded by a resplendent retinue of reasons and tries with all the force at its command to make us forget that at bottom it is instinct, drive, folly, lack of reasons. Life *shall* be loved, *because*—! Man *shall* advance himself and his neighbor, *because*—! What names all these Shalls and Becauses receive and may yet receive in the future! In order that what happens necessarily and always, spontaneously and without any purpose, may henceforth appear to be done for some purpose and strike man as rational and an ultimate commandment, the ethical teacher comes on stage, as the teacher of the purpose of existence; and to this end he invents a second, different existence and unhinges by means of his new mechanics the old, ordinary existence. Indeed, he wants to make sure that we do not *laugh* at existence, or at ourselves—or at him: for him, *one* is always one, something first and last and tremendous; for him there are no species, sums, or zeroes. His inventions and valuations may be utterly foolish and overenthusiastic; he may badly misjudge the course of nature and deny its conditions—and all ethical systems hitherto have been so foolish and anti-natural that humanity would have perished of every one of them if it had gained power over humanity—and yet, whenever "the hero" appeared on the stage, something new was attained: the gruesome counterpart of laughter, that profound emotional shock felt by many individuals at the thought: "Yes, I am worthy of living!" Life and I and you and all of us became *interesting* to ourselves once again for a little while.

There is no denying that *in the long run* every one of these great teachers of a purpose was vanquished by laughter, reason, and nature: the short tragedy always gave way again and returned into the eternal comedy of existence; and "the waves of uncountable laughter"—to cite Aeschylus—must in the end overwhelm even the greatest of these tragedians. In spite of all this laughter which makes the required corrections, human nature has nevertheless been changed by the ever new appearance of these teachers of the purpose of existence: It now has one additional need—the need for the ever new appearance of such teachers and teachings of a "purpose."

Gradually, man has become a fantastic animal that has to fulfill one more condition of existence than any other animal: man *has to* believe, to know, from time to time *why* he exists; his race cannot flourish without a periodic trust in life—without faith in *reason in life.* And again and again the human race will decree from time to time: "There is something at which it is absolutely forbidden henceforth to laugh." The most cautious friend of man will add: "Not only laughter and gay wisdom but the tragic, too, with all its sublime unreason, belongs among the means and necessities of the preservation of the species."

Consequently—. Consequently. Consequently. O, do you understand me, my brothers? Do you understand this new law of ebb and flood? There is a time for us, too!

2

The intellectual conscience.— I keep having the same experience and keep resisting it every time. I do not want to believe it although it is palpable: *the great majority of people lacks an intellectual conscience.* Indeed, it has often seemed to me as if anyone calling for an intellectual conscience were as lonely in the most densely populated cities as if he were in a desert. Everybody looks at you with strange eyes and goes right on handling his scales, calling this good and that evil. Nobody even blushes when you intimate that their weights are underweight; nor do people feel outraged; they merely laugh at your doubts. I mean: *the great majority of people* does not consider it contemptible to believe this or that and to live accordingly, without first having given themselves an account of the final and most certain reasons pro and con, and without even troubling themselves about such reasons afterward: the most gifted men and the noblest women still belong to this "great majority." But what is goodheartedness, refinement, or genius to me, when the person who has these virtues tolerates slack feelings in his faith and judgments and when he does not account *the desire for certainty* as his inmost craving and deepest distress—as that which separates the higher human beings[1] from the lower.

Among some pious people I found a hatred of reason and was well disposed to them for that; for this at least *betrayed* their bad intellectual conscience. But to stand in the midst of this *rerum concordia discors*[2] and of this whole marvelous uncertainty and rich ambiguity of existence *without questioning*, without trembling with the craving and the rapture of such questioning, without at least hating the person who questions, perhaps even finding him faintly amusing—that is what I feel

---

[1] *die höheren Menschen.* Cf. section 301. Regarding "the desire for certainty," cf. section 347, especially note 25.

[2] Discordant concord of things: Horace, *Epistles,* I.12.19.

to be *contemptible,* and this is the feeling for which I look first in everybody. Some folly keeps persuading me that every human being has this feeling, simply because he is human. This is my type of injustice.[3]

3

Noble and common.— Common natures consider all noble, magnanimous feelings inexpedient and therefore first of all incredible. They blink when they hear of such things and seem to feel like saying: "Surely, there must be some advantage involved; one cannot see through everything." They are suspicious of the noble person, as if he surreptitiously sought his advantage. When they are irresistibly persuaded of the absence of selfish intentions and gains, they see the noble person as a kind of fool; they despise him in his joy and laugh at his shining eyes. "How can one enjoy being at a disadvantage? How could one desire with one's eyes open to be disadvantaged? Some disease of reason must be associated with the noble affection." Thus they think and sneer, as they sneer at the pleasure that a madman derives from his fixed idea. What distinguishes the common type is that it never loses sight of its advantage, and that this thought of purpose and advantage is even stronger than the strongest instincts; not to allow these instincts to lead one astray to perform inexpedient acts—that is their wisdom and pride.

Compared to them, the higher type is more *unreasonable,* for those who are noble, magnanimous, and self-sacrificial do succumb to their instincts, and when they are at their best, their reason *pauses.* An animal that protects its young at the risk of its life, or that during the mating period follows the female even into death, does not think of danger and death; its reason also pauses, because the pleasure in its young or in the female and the fear of being deprived of this pleasure dominate it totally: the animal becomes more stupid than usual—just like those who are noble and magnanimous. They have some feel-

---

[3] Many interpretations of Nietzsche's thought are invalidated by this very important and characteristic section. Nietzsche never renounced it. Cf. sections 319, 335, 344, and *The Antichrist,* sections 50–55.

ings of pleasure and displeasure that are so strong that they reduce the intellect to silence or to servitude: at that point their heart displaces the head, and one speaks of "passion." (Now and then we also encounter the opposite and, as it were, the "reversal of passion"; for example, somebody once laid his hand on Fontenelle's heart, saying to him, "What you have there, dear sir, is another brain."[4])

The unreason or counterreason of passion is what the common type despises in the noble, especially when this passion is directed toward objects whose value seems quite fantastic and arbitrary. One is annoyed with those who succumb to the passion of the belly, but at least one comprehends the attraction that plays the tyrant in such cases. But one cannot comprehend how anyone could risk his health and honor for the sake of a passion for knowledge. The taste of the higher type is for exceptions, for things that leave most people cold and seem to lack sweetness; the higher type has a singular value standard. Moreover, it usually believes that the idiosyncrasy of its taste is *not* a singular value standard; rather, it posits its values and disvalues as generally valid and thus becomes incomprehensible and impractical. Very rarely does a higher nature retain sufficient reason for understanding and treating everyday people as such; for the most part, this type assumes that its own passion is present but kept concealed in all men, and this belief even becomes an ardent and eloquent faith. But when such exceptional people do not see themselves as the exception, how can they ever understand the common type and arrive at a fair evaluation of the rule? Thus they, too, speak of the folly, inexpediency, and fantasies of humanity, stunned that the course of the world should be so insane, and puzzled that it won't own up to what "is needful."—This is the eternal injustice of those who are noble.[5]

---

[4] Bernard le Bovier de Fontenelle (1657–1757; *sic*!). For the anecdote, cf. A. Laborde-Milaà, *Fontenelle*, Paris, 1905, p. 53: "Ce n'est pas un coeur que vous avez là, lui disait un jour Mme de Tencien en lui mettant la main sur la poitrine: c'est de la cervelle, comme dans la tete.' El il souriait, sans dire non." For Fontenelle cf. section 94.

[5] Cf. the conclusion of section 2.

4

What preserves the species.— The strongest and most evil spirits have so far done the most to advance humanity: again and again they relumed the passions that were going to sleep— all ordered society puts the passions to sleep—and they re-awakened again and again the sense of comparison, of contradiction, of the pleasure in what is new, daring, untried; they compelled men to pit opinion against opinion. model against model. Usually by force of arms, by toppling boundary markers, by violating pieties—but also by means of new religions and moralities. In every teacher and preacher of what is *new* we encounter the same "wickedness" that makes conquerors notorious, even if its expression is subtler and it does not immediately set the muscles in motion, and therefore also does not make one that notorious. What is new, however, is always *evil*, being that which wants to conquer and overthrow the old boundary markers and the old pieties; and only what is old is good. The good men are in all ages those who dig the old thoughts, digging deep and getting them to bear fruit—the farmers of the spirit. But eventually all land is exploited, and the ploughshare of evil must come again and again.

Nowadays there is a profoundly erroneous moral doctrine that is celebrated especially in England: this holds that judgments of "good" and "evil" sum up experiences of what is "expedient" and "inexpedient." One holds that what is called good preserves the species, while what is called evil harms the species. In truth, however, the evil instincts are expedient, species-preserving, and indispensable to as high a degree as the good ones; their function is merely different.[6]

---

[6] This section illuminates Nietzsche's "immoralism" as well as his consistent opposition to utilitarianism.

Nietzsche's refusal to accept any simplistic contrast of good and evil is one of the central motifs of his philosophy. All interpretations that overlook this anti-Manichaean subtlety and assume that he simply reverses traditional valuations are untenably crude. A commentary could call attention to this theme again and again, but it may suffice to list here a very few of the following sections that illustrate it especially well: 14, 19, 21, 23, 24, 27, 28, 35–37, 49.

5

Unconditional duties.— All those who feel they need the strongest words and sounds, the most eloquent gestures and postures, in order to be effective *at all*—such as revolutionary politicians, socialists, preachers of repentance with or without Christianity, all of whom cannot tolerate semisuccesses—talk of "duties," and actually always of duties that are supposed to be unconditional. Without that they would lack the justification for their great pathos, and they understand this very well. Thus they reach for moral philosophies that preach some categorical imperative, or they ingest a goodly piece of religion, as Mazzini did,[7] for example. Because they desire the unconditional confidence of others, they need first of all to develop unconditional self-confidence on the basis of some ultimate and indisputable commandment that is inherently sublime, and they want to feel like, and be accepted as, its servants and instruments.

Here we have the most natural and usually very influential opponents of moral enlightenment and skepticism; but they are rare. Yet a very comprehensive class of such opponents is to be found wherever self-interest requires submission while reputation and honor seem to prohibit submission. Whoever feels that his dignity is incompatible with the thought of being the *instrument* of a prince or a party or sect or, even worse, of a financial power—say, because he is after all the descendant of an old and proud family—but who nevertheless wants to or must be such an instrument before himself and before the public, requires pompous principles that can be mouthed at any time; principles of some unconditional obligation to which one may submit

---

[7] There is a large literature on Giuseppe Mazzini (1805–72), the Italian revolutionist. He hoped at one time to write a history of Italy "to enable the working class to apprehend . . . the 'mission' of Italy in God's providential ordering of the world." The work remained unwritten; "no one, however, can read even the briefest and most occasional writing of Mazzini without gaining some impression of the simple grandeur of the man, the lofty elevation of his moral tone, his unwavering faith in the living God, who is ever revealing Himself in the progressive development of humanity." (*Encyclopaedia Britannica*, 11th ed., vol. 17, p. 945).

without shame. Refined servility clings to the categorical imperative and is the mortal enemy of those who wish to deprive duty of its unconditional character; that is what decency demands of them, and not only decency.

6

Loss of dignity.— Reflecting has lost all the dignity of its form: the ceremony and solemn gestures of reflecting have become ridiculous, and an old-style wise man would be considered intolerable. We think too fast, even while walking or on the way, or while engaged in other things, no matter how serious the subject. We require little preparation, not even much silence: it is as if we carried in our heads an unstoppable machine that keeps working even under the most unfavorable circumstances. Formerly, one could tell simply by looking at a person that he wanted to think—it was probably a rare occurrence—that he now wished to become wiser and prepared himself for a thought: he set his face as for prayer and stopped walking; yes, one even stood still for hours in the middle of the road when the thought arrived—on one leg or two legs. That seemed to be required by the dignity of the matter.

7

Something for the industrious.— Anyone who now wishes to make a study of moral matters opens up for himself an immense field for work. All kinds of individual passions have to be thought through and pursued through different ages, peoples, and great and small individuals; all their reason and all their evaluations and perspectives on things have to be brought into the light. So far, all that has given color to existence still lacks a history. Where could you find a history of love, of avarice, of envy, of conscience, of pious respect for tradition, or of cruelty? Even a comparative history of law or at least of punishment is so far lacking completely. Has anyone made a study of different ways of dividing up the day or of the consequences of a regular schedule of work, festivals, and rest? What is known of the moral effects of different foods? Is there any philosophy of nutrition? (The constant revival of noisy agitation for and against vegetarianism proves that there is no such philosophy.) Has anyone collected men's experiences of living together—in monasteries, for example? Has the dialectic of marriage and friendship ever been explicated? Have the manners of scholars, of businessmen, artists, or artisans been studied and thought about? There is so much in them to think about.

Whatever men have so far viewed as the conditions of their existence—and all the reason, passion, and superstition involved in such a view—has this been researched exhaustively? The most industrious people will find that it involves too much work simply to observe how differently men's instincts have grown, and might yet grow, depending on different moral climates. It would require whole generations, and generations of scholars who would collaborate systematically, to exhaust the points of view and the material. The same applies to the demonstration of the reasons for the differences between moral climates ("why is it that the sun of one fundamental moral judgment and main standard of value shines here and another one there?"). And it would be yet another job to determine the erroneousness of all these reasons and the whole nature of moral judgments to date.

If all these jobs were done, the most insidious question of all would emerge into the foreground: whether science can furnish goals of action after it has proved that it can take such goals away and annihilate them; and then experimentation would be in order that would allow every kind of heroism to find satisfaction—centuries of experimentation that might eclipse all the great projects and sacrifices of history to date. So far, science has not yet built its cyclopic buildings; but the time for that, too, will come.

8

Unconscious virtues.— All the human qualities of which we are conscious—and especially those whose visibility and obviousness for others, too, we take for granted—are subject to altogether different laws of development than are those qualities which we know either badly or not at all and which also conceal themselves by means of their subtlety even from very subtle observers, knowing how to hide, as it were, behind nothing at all. It is similar with the subtle sculptures on the scales of reptiles: it would be wrong to take them for ornaments or weapons, for they become visible only under a microscope, under an artificially sharpened eye that similar animals for which these little sculptures might signify ornaments or weapons simply lack.

Our visible moral qualities, and especially those we *believe* to be visible, follow their own course; and the invisible ones that have the same names but are in relation to other men neither ornaments nor weapons, also follow their own course—probably, a wholly different course; and they probably have lines, subtleties, and sculptures that might give pleasure to a god with a divine microscope. Thus we have, for example, our industry, our ambition, our acuteness—all the world knows about that—but in addition to all that we probably also have *our* industry, *our* ambition, *our* acuteness; but for these reptile scales no microscope has been invented as yet.

At this point the friends of instinctive morality will say: "Bravo! At least he considers unconscious virtues possible—and that suffices us." O, you are satisfied with so little!

9

Our eruptions.— Countless things that humanity acquired in earlier stages, but so feebly and embryonically that nobody could perceive this acquisition, suddenly emerge into the light much later—perhaps after centuries; meanwhile they have become strong and ripe. Some ages seem to lack altogether some talent or some virtue, as certain individuals do, too. But just wait for their children and grandchildren, if you have time to wait that long: they bring to light what was hidden in their grandfathers and what their grandfathers themselves did not suspect. Often the son already betrays his father—and the father understands himself better after he has a son.[8]

---

[8] Cf. *Zarathustra*, II, "On the Tarantulas": "What was silent in the father speaks in the son; and often I found the son the unveiled secret of the father" (VPN, 212).

All of us harbor concealed gardens and plantings; and, to use another metaphor, we are, all of us, growing volcanoes that approach the hour of their eruption; but how near or distant that is, nobody knows—not even God.

10

A kind of atavism.— I prefer to understand the rare human beings of an age as suddenly emerging late ghosts of past cultures and their powers—as atavisms of a people and its *mores*: that way one really can *understand* a little about them. Now they seem strange, rare, extraordinary; and whoever feels these powers in himself must nurse, defend, honor, and cultivate them against another world that resists them, until he becomes either a great human being or a mad and eccentric one—or perishes early.

Formerly, these same qualities were common and therefore considered *common*—not distinguished. Perhaps they were demanded or presupposed; in any case, it was impossible to become great through them, if only because they involved no danger of madness or solitude.

It is preeminently in the generations and castes that *conserve* a people that we encounter such recrudescences of old instincts, while such atavisms are improbable wherever races, habits, and valuations change too rapidly. For tempo is as significant for the development of peoples as it is in music: in our case, an andante of development is altogether necessary as the andante of a passionate and slow spirit; and that is after all the value of the spirit of conservative generations.

11

Consciousness.— Consciousness is the last and latest development of the organic and hence also what is most unfinished and unstrong. Consciousness gives rise to countless errors that lead an animal or man to perish sooner than necessary, "exceeding destiny," as Homer puts it. If the conserving association of the instincts were not so very much more powerful, and if it did not serve on the whole as a regulator, humanity would have to perish of its misjudgments and its fantasies with open eyes, of its lack of thoroughness and its credulity—in short, of its consciousness; rather, without the former, humanity would long have disappeared.

Before a function is fully developed and mature it constitutes a danger for the organism, and it is good if during the interval it is subjected to some tyranny. Thus consciousness is tyrannized—not least by our pride in it. One thinks that it constitutes the *kernel* of man; what is abiding, eternal, ultimate, and most original in him. One takes consciousness for a determinate magnitude. One denies its growth and its intermittences. One takes it for the "unity of the organism."

This ridiculous overestimation and misunderstanding of consciousness has the very useful consequence that it prevents an all too fast development of consciousness. Believing that they possess consciousness, men have not exerted themselves very much to acquire it; and things haven't changed much in this respect. To this day the task of *incorporating* knowledge and making it instinctive is only beginning to dawn on the human eye and is not yet clearly discernible; it is a task that is seen only by those who have comprehended that so far we have incorporated only our errors and that all our consciousness relates to errors.

12

On the aim of science.— What? The aim of science should be to give men as much pleasure and as little displeasure as possible? But what if pleasure and displeasure were so tied together that whoever *wanted* to have as much as possible of one *must* also have as much as possible of the other—that whoever wanted to learn to "jubilate up to the heavens" would also have to be prepared for "depression unto death"?[9] And that is how things may well be. At least the Stoics believed that this was how things were, and they were consistent when they also desired as little pleasure as possible, in order to get as

[9] An allusion to Clärchen's song in Goethe's *Egmont*, Act III, Scene 2, set to music by Beethoven.

little displeasure as possible out of life. (When they kept saying "The virtuous man is the happiest man," this was both the school's eye-catching sign for the great mass and a casuistic subtlety for the subtle.)

To this day you have the choice: either *as little displeasure as possible,* painlessness in brief—and in the last analysis socialists and politicians of all parties have no right to promise their people more than that—or *as much displeasure as possible* as the price for the growth of an abundance of subtle pleasures and joys that have rarely been relished yet. If you decide for the former and desire to diminish and lower the level of human pain, you also have to diminish and lower the level of their *capacity for joy.* Actually, *science* can promote either goal. So far it may still be better known for its power of depriving man of his joys and making him colder, more like a statue, more stoic. But it might yet be found to be the *great dispenser of pain.* And then its counterforce might be found at the same time: its immense capacity for making new galaxies of joy flare up.

13

On the doctrine of the feeling of power.[10]— Benefiting and hurting others are ways of exercising one's power upon others; that is all one desires in such cases. One hurts those whom one wants to feel one's power, for pain is a much more efficient means to that end than pleasure; pain always raises the question about its origin while pleasure is inclined to stop with itself without looking back. We benefit and show benevolence to those who are already dependent on us in some way (which means that they are used to thinking of us as causes); we want to increase their power because in that way we increase ours, or we want to show them how advantageous it is to be in our power; that way they will become more satisfied with their condition and more hostile to and willing to fight against the enemies of *our* power.

---

[10] This was written while Nietzsche was developing his doctrine of "the will to power," which he proclaimed a year later in *Zarathustra.*

Whether benefiting or hurting others involves sacrifices for us does not affect the ultimate value of our actions. Even if we offer our lives, as martyrs do for their church, this is a sacrifice that is offered for *our* desire for power or for the purpose of preserving our feeling of power. Those who feel "I possess Truth"—how many possessions would they not abandon in order to save this feeling! What would they not throw overboard to stay "on top"—which means, *above* the others who lack "the Truth"!

Certainly the state in which we hurt others is rarely as agreeable, in an unadulterated way, as that in which we benefit others; it is a sign that we are still lacking power, or it shows a sense of frustration in the face of this poverty;[11] it is accompanied by new dangers and uncertainties for what power we do possess, and clouds our horizon with the prospect of revenge, scorn, punishment, and failure. It is only for the most irritable and covetous devotees of the feeling of power that it is perhaps more pleasurable to imprint the seal of power on a recalcitrant brow—those for whom the sight of those who are already subjected (the objects of benevolence) is a burden and boredom. What is decisive is how one is accustomed to *spice* one's life: it is a matter of taste whether one prefers the slow or the sudden, the assured or the dangerous and audacious increase of power; one seeks this or that spice depending on one's temperament.

An easy prey is something contemptible for proud natures. They feel good only at the sight of unbroken men who might become their enemies and at the sight of all possessions that are hard to come by. Against one who is suffering they are often hard because he is not worthy of their aspirations and pride; but they are doubly obliging toward their *peers* whom it would be honorable to fight if the occasion should ever arise. Spurred by the good feeling of *this* perspective, the members of the knightly caste became accustomed to treating each other with exquisite courtesy.

Pity is the most agreeable feeling among those who have little pride and no prospects of great conquests; for them easy

---

[11] Hurting others is a sign that one lacks power!

prey—and that is what all who suffer are—is enchanting. Pity is praised as the virtue of prostitutes.[12]

14

The things people call love.— Avarice and love: what different feelings these two terms evoke! Nevertheless it could be the same instinct that has two names—once deprecated by those who *have*, in whom the instinct has calmed down to some extent, and who are afraid for their "possessions," and the other time seen from the point of view of those who are not satisfied but still thirsty and who therefore glorify the instinct as "good." Our love of our neighbor—is it not a lust for new *possessions*? And likewise our love of knowledge, of truth, and altogether any lust for what is new? Gradually we become tired of the old, of what we safely possess, and we stretch out our hands again. Even the most beautiful scenery is no longer assured of our love after we have lived in it for three months, and some more distant coast attracts our avarice: possessions are generally diminished by possession.

Our pleasure in ourselves tries to maintain itself by again and again changing something new *into ourselves*; that is what possession means. To become tired of some possession means tiring of ourselves. (One can also suffer of an excess—the lust to throw away or to distribute can also assume the honorary name of "love.") When we see somebody suffer, we like to exploit this opportunity to take possession of him; those who become his benefactors and pity him, for example, do this and call the lust for a new possession that he awakens in them "love"; and the pleasure they feel is comparable to that aroused by the prospect of a new conquest.

Sexual love betrays itself most clearly as a lust for possession: the lover desires unconditional and sole possession of the person for whom he longs; he desires equally unconditional power over the soul and over the body of the beloved; he alone wants to be loved and desires to live and rule in the other soul

---

[12] The critique of pity is developed more fully in *Zarathustra*. For a detailed exposition and discussion see Kaufmann, 363–71.

as supreme and supremely desirable. If one considers that this means nothing less than *excluding* the whole world from a precious good, from happiness and enjoyment; if one considers that the lover aims at the impoverishment and deprivation of all competitors and would like to become the dragon guarding his golden hoard as the most inconsiderate and selfish of all "conquerors" and exploiters; if one considers, finally, that to the lover himself the whole rest of the world appears indifferent, pale, and worthless, and he is prepared to make any sacrifice, to disturb any order, to subordinate all other interests—then one comes to feel genuine amazement that this wild avarice and injustice of sexual love has been glorified and deified so much in all ages—indeed, that this love has furnished the concept of love as the opposite of egoism while it actually may be the most ingenuous expression of egoism.

At this point linguistic usage has evidently been formed by those who did not possess but desired. Probably, there have always been too many of these. Those to whom much possession and satiety were granted in this area have occasionally made some casual remark about "the raging demon," as that most gracious and beloved of all Athenians, Sophocles, did; but Eros has always laughed at such blasphemers; they were invariably his greatest favorites.

Here and there on earth we may encounter a kind of continuation of love in which this possessive craving of two people for each other gives way to a new desire and lust for possession —a *shared* higher thirst for an ideal above them. But who knows such love? Who has experienced it? Its right name is *friendship*.

15

From a distance.— This mountain makes the landscape it dominates charming and significant in every way. Having said this to ourselves a hundred times, we become so unreasonable and grateful that we suppose that whatever bestows so much charm must also be the most charming thing around—and we climb the mountain and are disappointed. Suddenly the mountain itself and the whole landscape around us, below us, have lost their magic. We had forgotten that some greatness, like some goodness, wants to be beheld only from a distance and by all means only from below, not from above; otherwise it makes no impression. Perhaps you know some people near you who must look at themselves only from a distance in order to find themselves at all tolerable or attractive and invigorating. Self-knowledge is strictly inadvisable for them.

16

Over the footbridge.— In our relations with people who are bashful about their feelings, we must be capable of dissimulation; they feel a sudden hatred against anyone who catches them in a tender, enthusiastic, or elevated feeling, as if he had seen their secrets. If you want to make them feel good at such moments, you have to make them laugh or voice some cold but witty sarcasm; then their feeling freezes and they regain power over themselves. But I am giving you the moral before telling the story.

There was a time in our lives when we were so close that nothing seemed to obstruct our friendship and brotherhood, and only a small footbridge separated us. Just as you were about to step on it, I asked you: "Do you want to cross the footbridge to me?" —Immediately, you did not want to any more; and when I asked you again, you remained silent. Since then mountains and torrential rivers and whatever separates and alienates have been cast between us, and even if we wanted to get together, we couldn't. But when you now think of that little footbridge, words fail you and you sob and marvel.

17

Finding motives for our poverty.— There is no trick that enables us to turn a poor virtue into a rich and overflowing one; but we can reinterpret its poverty into a necessity so that it no longer offends us when we see it and we no longer sulk at fate on its account. That is what a wise gardener does when he places the poor little stream in his garden in the arms of a nymph and thus finds a motive for its poverty; and who does not need nymphs as he does?[13]

18

The pride of classical antiquity.— We lack the classical coloring of nobility because our feelings no longer know the slaves of classical antiquity. A Greek of noble descent found such tremendous intermediary stages and such distance between his own height and that ultimate baseness that he could scarcely see the slave clearly; even Plato could not really see him anymore. It is different with us, who are accustomed to the *doctrine* of human equality, though not to equality itself. One who is not at his own disposal and who lacks leisure does not by any means seem contemptible to us for that reason; perhaps too much that is slavish in this sense sticks to each of us,[14] in accordance with the conditions of our social order and activities, which are utterly different from those of the ancients.

The Greek philosophers went through life feeling secretly that there were far more slaves than one might think—meaning that everybody who was not a philosopher was a slave. Their pride overflowed at the thought that even the most powerful men on earth belonged among their slaves. This pride, too, is alien and impossible for us; not even metaphorically does the word "slave" possess its full power for us.

19

Evil.— Examine the lives of the best and most fruitful people and peoples and ask yourselves whether a tree that is supposed to grow to a proud height can dispense with bad weather and storms; whether misfortune and external resistance, some kinds of hatred, jealousy, stubbornness, mistrust, hardness, avarice, and violence do not belong among the *favorable* conditions without which any great growth even of virtue is

---

[13] Cf. section 290.
[14] In this sense, "slavish" is the antonym of "liberated" or "autonomous."

scarcely possible. The poison of which weaker natures perish strengthens the strong[15]—nor do they call it poison.

20

The dignity of folly.— A few millennia further along on the road of the last century—and everything men do will exhibit the highest prudence; but that way prudence will lose all of its dignity. By then it will be necessary to be prudent, but it will also be so common and vulgar that a disgusted taste will experience this necessity as a *vulgarity.* And just as a tyranny of truth and science could increase esteem for the lie, a tyranny of prudence could spur the growth of a new kind of nobility. To be noble might then come to mean: to entertain follies.

21

To the teachers of selfishness.— A man's virtues are called *good* depending on their probable consequences not for him but for us and society: the praise of virtues has always been far from "selfless," far from "unegoistic." Otherwise one would have had to notice that virtues (like industriousness, obedience, chastity, filial piety, and justice) are usually harmful for those who possess them, being instincts that dominate them too violently and covetously and resist the efforts of reason to keep them in balance with their other instincts. When you have a virtue, a real, whole virtue (and not merely a mini-instinct for some virtue), you are its *victim.* But your neighbor praises your virtue precisely on that account. One praises the industrious even though they harm their eyesight or the spontaneity and freshness of their spirit. One honors and feels sorry for the youth who has worked himself into the ground because one thinks: "For society as a whole the loss of even the best individual is merely a small sacrifice. Too bad that such sacrifices are needed! But it would be far worse if the individual would think otherwise and considered his preservation and develop-

---

[15] Cf. *Twilight of the Idols,* Ch. 1, section 8 (VPN, 467). Also *Ecce Homo,* Ch. 1, section 2 (BWN, 680).

ment more important than his work in the service of society."
Thus one feels sorry for the youth not for his own sake but
because a devoted *instrument*, ruthless against itself—a so-called
"good man"—has been lost to society by his death.

Perhaps one gives some thought to the question whether it
would have been more useful for society if he had been less
ruthless against himself and had preserved himself longer. One
admits that there would have been some advantage in that, but
one considers the other advantage—that a sacrifice has been
made and that the attitude of the sacrificial animal has once
again been confirmed for all to see—greater and of more lasting
significance.

Thus what is really praised when virtues are praised is, first,
their instrumental nature and, secondly, the instinct in every
virtue that refuses to be held in check by the over-all advantage
for the individual himself—in sum, the unreason in virtue that
leads the individual to allow himself to be transformed into
a mere function of the whole. The praise of virtue is the praise
of something that is privately harmful— the praise of instincts
that deprive a human being of his noblest selfishness and the
strength for the highest autonomy.[16]

To be sure, for educational purposes and to lead men to
incorporate virtuous habits one emphasizes effects of virtue
that make it appear as if virtue and private advantage were
sisters; and some such relationship actually exists. Blindly raging industriousness, for example—this typical virtue of an instrument—is represented as the way to wealth and honor and as
the poison that best cures boredom and the passions, but one
keeps silent about its dangers, its extreme dangerousness. That
is how education always proceeds: one tries to condition an
individual by various attractions and advantages to adopt a way
of thinking and behaving that, once it has become a habit,
instinct, and passion, will dominate him *to his own ultimate
disadvantage* but "for the general good."

How often I see that blindly raging industriousness does
create wealth and reap honors while at the same time depriving
the organs of their subtlety, which alone would make possible

---

[16] *Obhut über sich selbst.*

the enjoyment of wealth and honors; also that this chief anti-
dote to boredom and the passions at the same time blunts the
senses and leads the spirit to resist new attractions. (The most
industrious of all ages—ours—does not know how to make
anything of all its industriousness and money, except always
still more money and still more industriousness; for it requires
more genius to spend than to acquire. —Well, we shall have
our "grandchildren"!)

If this education succeeds, then every virtue of an individual
is a public utility and a private disadvantage, measured against
the supreme private goal—probably some impoverishment of
the spirit and the senses or even a premature decline. Consider
from this point of view, one by one, the virtues of obedience,
chastity, filial piety, and justice.

The praise of the selfless, the self-sacrificial, the virtuous—
that is, of those who do not apply their whole strength and
reason to their own preservation, development, elevation, promotion, and the expansion of their power, but rather live, in
relation to themselves, modestly and thoughtlessly, perhaps even
with indifference or irony—this praise certainly was not born
from the spirit of selflessness. The "neighbor" praises selflessness *because it brings him advantages.* If the neighbor himself
were "selfless" in his thinking, he would repudiate this diminu-
tion of strength, this mutilation for *his* benefit; he would work
against the development of such inclinations, and above all he
would manifest his selflessness by *not* calling it *good!*

This indicates the fundamental contradiction in the morality
that is very prestigious nowadays: the *motives* of this morality
stand opposed to its *principle.* What this morality considers its
proof is refuted by its criterion of what is moral. In order not
to contravene its own morality, the demand "You shall renounce
yourself and sacrifice yourself" could be laid down only by
those who thus renounced their own advantage and perhaps
brought about their own destruction through the demanded
sacrifice of individuals. But as soon as the neighbor (or society)
recommends altruism *for the sake of its utility,* it applies the
contradictory principle. "You shall seek your advantage even
at the expense of everything else"—and thus one preaches, in
the same breath, a "Thou shalt" and "Thou shalt not."

22

L'ordre du jour pour le roi.[17]— The day begins: let us begin to order for this day the business and the festivals of our most merciful master who is still deigning to rest. His majesty has bad weather today: we shall be careful not to call it bad; we shall not speak of the weather—but we shall be a little more solemn about our business than would otherwise be necessary and a little more festive about the festivals. Perhaps his majesty will even be ill: at breakfast we shall present the latest good news of the preceding evening, the arrival of M. Montaigne who jokes so agreeably about his illness; he suffers from a stone. We shall receive a few persons (persons! what would that puffed-up old frog say, who will be among them, if he heard this word! "I am not a person," he would say, "but always the substance itself")—and this reception will take longer than anybody finds agreeable. That is reason enough to tell of the poet who wrote on his door: "Whoever enters here, honors me; whoever does not—pleases me." What a courteous way of expressing a discourtesy! And perhaps this poet is altogether right to be discourteous: it is said that his poems are better than the poet. Let him write many more then and withdraw from the world as much as possible—which is, after all, the meaning of his civil incivility. Conversely, a prince is always worth more than his "verse," even if—but what am I saying? We are chatting and the whole court thinks that we are already at work and racking our brains: there is no window in which anyone ever sees a light burn before ours.

Listen! Wasn't that the bell? Damn! the day and the dance begin and we don't know the schedule! We have to improvise —all the world improvises its day. Let us proceed today as all the world does!

At that, my strange morning dream vanished, probably a victim of the hard strokes of the tower clock which announced the fifth hour with all of its accustomed gravity. It seems to me that on this occasion the god of dreams was pleased to make fun of my habit of beginning the day by ordering it and making

---

[17] The order of the day for the king.

it tolerable *for myself*; and it is possible that I have sometimes done this too formally, as if I were a prince.

23

The signs of corruption.— Consider the following signs of those states of society which are necessary from time to time and which are designated with the word "corruption." As soon as corruption sets in anywhere superstition[18] becomes rank, and the previous common faith[19] of a people becomes pale and powerless against it. For superstition is second-order free spirit: those who surrender to it choose certain forms and formulas that they find congenial and permit themselves some freedom of choice. Whoever is superstitious is always, compared with the religious human being, much more of a person; and a superstitious society is one in which there are many individuals and much delight in individuality. In this perspective, superstition always appears as *progress* and as a sign that the intellect is becoming more independent and demands its rights. Those who then complain of corruption are the adherents of the old religion and religiosity, and they have also determined linguistic usage hitherto and given superstition a bad reputation even among the freest spirits. Let us realize that it is actually a symptom of *enlightenment.*

Second, a society in which corruption spreads is accused of exhaustion; and it is obvious that the esteem for war and the pleasure in war diminish, while the comforts of life are now desired just as ardently as warlike and athletic honors were formerly. But what is generally overlooked is that the ancient national energy and national passion that became gloriously visible in war and warlike games have now been transmuted into countless private passions and have merely become less visible. Indeed, in times of "corruption" the power and force of the national energies that are expended are probably greater than ever and the individual squanders them as lavishly as he could not have formerly when he was simply not yet rich enough. Thus it is precisely in times of "exhaustion" that tragedy runs

---

[18] *Aberglaube.*
[19] *Glaube.*

through houses and streets, that great love and great hatred are born, and that the flame of knowledge flares up into the sky.

Third, it is usually said, as if one wanted to make up for the reproaches of superstition and exhaustion, that such times of corruption are gentler and that cruelty declines drastically, compared with the older, stronger age that was more given to faith. But this praise I cannot accept any more than those reproaches. All I concede is that cruelty now becomes more refined and that its older forms henceforth offend the new taste; but the art of wounding and torturing others with words and looks reaches its supreme development in times of corruption: it is only now that *malice* and the delight in malice are born. The men of corruption are witty and slanderous; they know of types of murder that require neither daggers nor assault; they also know that whatever is *said well* is believed.

Fourth, when "morals decay" those men emerge whom one calls tyrants: they are the precursors and as it were the precocious harbingers of *individuals*. Only a little while later this fruit of fruits hangs yellow and mellow from the tree of a people—and the tree existed only for the sake of these fruits.[20] Once decay has reached its climax along with the infighting of all sorts of tyrants, the Caesar always appears, the final tyrant who puts an end to the weary struggle for sole rule—by putting weariness to work for himself. In his age the individual is usually ripest and culture therefore in its highest and most fruitful stage—but not for his sake or on account of him, although the men of the highest culture like to flatter their Caesar by pretending to be *his* creation. But in truth they merely need peace from outside because they have enough unrest and work inside themselves.

In these ages bribery and treason reach their peak, for the love of the newly discovered ego is much more powerful now than the love of the old, used-up "fatherland," which has been touted to death; and the need to achieve some security from the terrifying ups and downs of fortune opens even nobler hands as soon as anyone who is powerful and rich shows that he is ready to pour gold into them. There is hardly any secure future left; one lives for today, and this state of the soul makes

---

[20] Cf. *Beyond Good and Evil*, section 126 (BWN, 277).

the game easy for all seducers, for one allows oneself to be seduced and bribed only "for today" while reserving the future and one's virtue.

Individuals—being truly in-and-for-themselves[21]— care, as is well known, more for the moment than do their opposites, the herd men, for they consider themselves no less incalculable than the future. They also like to attach themselves to violent men because they credit themselves with the capacity for actions and for information that the mass of men would neither understand nor forgive, while the tyrant or Caesar understands the rights of the individual even in his excesses and has a personal interest in advocating and even abetting a bolder private morality. For he thinks of himself and would like others to think of him in the way Napoleon once expressed in his classical manner: "I have the right to answer all accusations against me with an eternal 'That's me.' I am apart from all the world and accept conditions from nobody. I demand subjection even to my fancies, and people should find it quite natural when I yield to this or that distraction." That is how Napoleon once replied to his wife when she had reasons to question the marital fidelity of her husband.

The times of corruption are those when the apples fall from the tree: I mean the individuals, for they carry the seeds of the future and are the authors of the spiritual colonization and origin of new states and communities. Corruption is merely a nasty word for the autumn of a people.

24

Diverse dissatisfaction.— The weak and quasi feminine type of the dissatisfied has a sensitivity for making life more beautiful and profound; the strong or masculine type, to stick to this metaphor, has a sensitivity for making life better and safer. The former type manifests its weakness and femininity

---

[21] *diese wahren An-und Für-sich's*: a deliberate solecism. In colloquial German "an und für sich" (in and for itself) is little more than a way of stalling; but Hegel had made much of the contrast between "in itself" (sometimes "potentially," "implicitly," sometimes closer to Sartre's *en soi*), "for itself" (sometimes "separately," sometimes "for its own consciousness"), and "in and for itself" (meaning what has realized itself and realizes it).

by gladly being deceived occasionally and settling for a little intoxication and effusive enthusiasm, although it can never be satisfied altogether and suffers from the incurability of its dissatisfaction. Moreover, this type promotes all those who know how to provide opiates and narcotic consolations, and it resents all who esteem physicians above priests: thus it assures the *continuation* of real misery. If this type had not been superabundant in Europe since the Middle Ages, the celebrated European capacity for constant *change* might never have come into existence, for the requirements of the strong among the dissatisfied are too crude and at bottom so undemanding that eventually they can surely be brought to rest.

China, for example, is a country in which large-scale dissatisfaction and the capacity for *change* have become extinct centuries ago; and the socialists and state idolaters of Europe with their measures for making life better and safer might easily establish in Europe, too, Chinese conditions and a Chinese "happiness," if only they could first extirpate the sicklier, tenderer, more feminine dissatisfaction and romanticism that at present are still superabundant here. Europe is sick but owes the utmost gratitude to her incurability and to the eternal changes in her affliction: these constantly new conditions and these no less constantly new dangers, pains, and media of information have finally generated an intellectual irritability that almost amounts to genius and is in any case the mother of all genius.[22]

---

[22] At first glance, Nietzsche seems to contrast the weak and quasi feminine type unfavorably with the strong, male type. But, as often in his work, this initial contrast sets the stage for a surprising reversal. Nietzsche is a dialectical thinker and does not think in black and white.

"The capacity for constant change [*Verwandelung*]" brings to mind the poem that concludes *Beyond Good and Evil*, four years later: *nur wer sich wandelt bleibt mit mir verwandt* (only those who keep changing remain akin to me). Nietzsche possessed and valued this capacity to an extraordinary degree; and "Chinese" stability and "happiness" were to him a terrible prospect—a living death. In the "Prologue" to *Zarathustra*, his next work, such "happiness" is associated with the "last man." Another five years later, in 1888, Kant is called "Chinese"— presumably because he was so rigid and in his moral philosophy considered the passions "pathological."

"State idolaters": In *Zarathustra*, Part I, the chapter on the state is entitled "On the New Idol."

25

Not predestined for knowledge.— There is a stupid humility that is not at all rare, and those afflicted with it are altogether unfit to become devotees of knowledge. As soon as a person of this type perceives something striking, he turns on his heel, as it were, and says to himself: "You have made a mistake. What is the matter with your senses? This cannot, may not, be the truth." And then, instead of looking and listening again, more carefully, he runs away from the striking thing, as if he had been intimidated, and tries to remove it from his mind as fast as he can. For his inner canon says: "I do not want to see anything that contradicts the prevalent opinion. Am *I* called to discover new truths? There are too many old ones, as it is."

26

What is life?— Life—that is: continually shedding something that wants to die. Life—that is: being cruel and inexorable against everything about us that is growing old and weak—and not only about *us.* Life—that is, then: being without reverence for those who are dying, who are wretched, who are ancient? Constantly being a murderer? —And yet old Moses said: "Thou shalt not kill."

27

The man of renunciation.[23]— What does the man of renunciation do? He strives for a higher world, he wants to fly further and higher than all men of affirmation—he throws away much that would encumber his flight, including not a little that he esteems and likes; he sacrifices it to his desire for the heights. This sacrificing, this throwing way, however, is precisely what alone becomes visible and leads people to call him the man of renunciation: it is as such that he confronts us, shrouded in his hood, as if he were the soul of a hairshirt. But he is quite satisfied with the impression he makes on us: he wants to con-

---

[23] *Der Entsagende.* Cf section 285.

ceal from us his desire, his pride, his intention to soar *beyond* us. —Yes, he is cleverer than we thought and so polite to us— this man of affirmation. For that is what he is, no less than we, even in his renunciation.

28

To be harmful with what is best in us.— At times, our strengths propel us so far forward that we can no longer endure our weaknesses and perish from them. We may even foresee this outcome without wishing to have it otherwise. Thus we become hard against everything in us that desires consideration, and our greatness is also our lack of compassion.

Such an experience, for which we must pay in the end with our lives, is a parable for the whole effect of great human beings on others and on their age: precisely with what is best in them, with what only they can do, they destroy many who are weak, unsure, still in the process of becoming, of striving; and thus they are harmful. It can even happen that, everything considered, they are only harmful because what is best in them is accepted and absorbed by those alone whom it affects like a drink that is too strong: they lose their understanding and their selfishness and become so intoxicated that they are bound to break their limbs on all the false paths on which their intoxication leads them astray.

29

Add lies.[24]— When people in France began to attack the Aristotelian unities[25] and others therefore began to defend them, one could see once again what is to be seen so often but what people hate to see: one lied, mendaciously inventing reasons for these laws, simply to avoid admitting that one had become *used* to these laws and no longer wanted things to be different. The same process occurs, and always has occurred, in every

---

[24] *Die Hinzu-Lügner* are those who rationalize, adding lies.
[25] Unity of time, place, and plot in tragedy. Aristotle himself had not demanded the first two.

prevalent morality and religion: the reasons and purposes for habits are always lies that are added only after some people begin to attack these habits and to *ask* for reasons and purposes. At this point the conservatives of all ages are thoroughly dishonest: they add lies.

30

The comedy played by the famous.— Famous men who *need* their fame, like all politicians, for example, never choose allies and friends without ulterior motives: from one they desire the reflected splendor of his virtue; from another the fear inspired by some of the dubious qualities that everybody associates with him; from someone else they steal the reputation of his leisure, his lying in the sun, because it serves their own purposes to appear inattentive and idle at times (this conceals the fact that they actually lie in wait); now they need a dreamer near them, now an expert, now a thinker, now a pedant, as if he were their alter ego; but soon they do not need them any more. Thus the surroundings and exteriors of famous men die continually, even while everybody seems to be pushing to get near them and lend them his own character: in this they resemble great cities. Their reputation keeps changing like their character, for their changing instruments demand these changes and push now this and now that real or fictitious quality out onto the stage. Their friends and allies belong, as I have said, to these stage qualities. What they wish, on the other hand, must stand that much more firmly and unmoved, its splendor visible from a distance; and this, too, occasionally requires a comedy and a stage play.

31

Trade and nobility.— Buying and selling have become common, like the art of reading and writing. Everybody has practiced it even if he is no tradesman, and gets more practice every day—just as formerly, when men were more savage, everybody was a hunter and practiced that art day after day. Then hunting was common; but eventually it became a privilege of the powerful and noble; it lost its everyday character and its commonness because it ceased to be necessary; it became a matter of moods and luxury. The same might happen some day to buying and selling.

One can imagine social conditions in which there is no buying and selling and in which this art gradually ceases to be necessary. Perhaps some individuals who are less subject to the laws of the general condition will then permit themselves to buy and sell as a *luxury of sentiment.* At that point trade would acquire nobility, and the nobility might then enjoy trading as much as they have hitherto enjoyed war and politics, while the esteem for politics might undergo a total change. Even now it is ceasing to be the art of the nobleman, and it is quite possible that some day one may find it so common and even vulgar that, along with all party literature and journalism, one would classify it as "prostitution of the spirit."

32

Undesirable disciples.— What shall I do with these two young men! cried a disgruntled philosopher who "corrupted" youth as Socrates had once done; they are unwelcome students. This one cannot say "No," and that one says to everything "Half and half." Supposing that they adopted my doctrine, the former would *suffer* too much, for my way of thinking requires a warlike soul, a desire to hurt, a delight in saying No, a hard skin; he would slowly die of open and internal wounds. And the other one would make some personal compromise with every cause he represents and thus compromise it;[26] such a disciple I wish my enemy.

---

[26] *der Andere wird sich aus jeder Sache, die er vertritt, eine Mittelmässigkeit zurecht machen und sie dergestalt zur Mittelmässigkeit machen*: while the translation makes the point a little clearer than the original German does, there is no doubt about Nietzsche's meaning. There is no better way to clarify that than to cite his sister as an example. First she wanted to combine Nietzsche and Wagner, "half and half"; later she changed her name to Elisabeth Förster-Nietzsche and tried to fabricate a compromise between the heritage of her late husband, Bernhard Förster, who had been a leading anti-Semite, and the philosophy of her brother, who had detested Förster and anti-Semitism. For the Försters, see Kaufmann, 42ff.

33

Outside the lecture hall.— "In order to prove to you that man is at bottom one of the good-natured animals, I should like to remind you how credulous he has been for such a long time. Only now has he become, very late and after an immense self-conquest, a *mistrustful* animal. Yes, man is now more evil than ever before."

I do not understand this: why should man be more mistrustful and evil now? "Because he now has—and needs—a science."

34

Historia abscondita.[27]— Every great human being exerts a retroactive force: for his sake all of history is placed in the balance again, and a thousand secrets of the past crawl out of their hiding places—into *his* sunshine. There is no way of telling what may yet become part of history. Perhaps the past is still essentially undiscovered! So many retroactive forces are still needed!

35

Heresy and witchcraft.— Thinking in a way that is not customary is much less the result of a superior intellect than it is the result of strong, evil inclinations that detach and isolate one, and that are defiant, nasty, and malicious. Heresy is the pendant of witchcraft and surely no more harmless and least of all anything essentially venerable. Heretics and witches are two species of evil human beings; what they have in common is that they also *feel* that they are evil but are impelled by an unconquerable lust to harm what is dominant (whether people or opinions). The Reformation, which was in a way a redoubled intensification of the medieval spirit, at a time when that was no longer accompanied by a good conscience, produced both in the greatest abundance.

---

[27] Concealed, secret, or unknown history.

36

Last words.— It will be recalled that the Emperor Augustus —that terrible man who had as much self-control and could be as silent as any wise Socrates—became indiscreet at his own expense when he uttered his last words. For the first time he dropped his mask by implying that he had worn a mask and played a comedy: he had played the father of the fatherland and wisdom on the throne—well enough to create the illusion! *Plaudite amici, comoedia finita est!*[28] The idea of the dying Nero—*qualis artifex pereo!*[29]—was also the idea of the dying Augustus: an actor's vanity, an actor's garrulity! Truly the opposite of the dying Socrates!

But Tiberius died silently: this most tormented of all self-tormentors was genuine and no actor. What may have passed through his mind in the end? Perhaps this: "Life—is a long death. Fool that I was to shorten the lives of so many! Was I made to be a benefactor? I should have given them eternal life: then I could have watched them *die* forever. For that I had such good eyes: *qualis spectator pereo!*"[30] When after a long struggle with death he seemed to recover his strength again, it was considered advisable to suffocate him with bed pillows;[31] he died a double death.

37

Owing to three errors.— During the last centuries science has been promoted, partly because it was by means of science that one hoped to understand God's goodness and wisdom best— this was the main motive of the great Englishmen (like Newton); partly because one believed in the absolute utility of

---

[28] Applaud, friends: the comedy is done.
[29] What an artist perishes with me!
[30] What a spectator perishes with me!
[31] Tacitus, *Annals*, VI. 50.
  Another revaluation: Augustus, often praised, is likened to Nero, while Tiberius, a monster, is humanized. As usual, the point is not to substitute one Manichaean simplicity for another but rather to transcend such simplicities by suggesting new perspectives.

knowledge, and especially in the most intimate association of morality, knowledge, and happiness—this was the main motive of the great Frenchmen (like Voltaire);[32] partly because one thought that in science one possessed and loved something unselfish, harmless, self-sufficient, and truly innocent, in which man's evil impulses had no part whatever—the main motive of Spinoza who felt divine when attaining knowledge—in sum, owing to three errors.

38

The explosive ones.— When one considers how much the energy of young men needs to explode, one is not surprised that they decide for this cause or that without being at all subtle or choosy. What attracts them is the sight of the zeal that surrounds a cause—as it were, the sight of the burning fuse, and not the cause itself. Subtle seducers therefore know the art of arousing expectations of an explosion while making no effort to furnish reasons for their cause: reasons are not what wins over such powder kegs.

39

Changed taste.— The change in general taste is more powerful than that of opinions. Opinions, along with all proofs, refutations, and the whole intellectual masquerade, are merely symptoms of the change in taste and most certainly not what they are still often supposed to be, its causes.

What changes the general taste? The fact that some individuals who are powerful and influential announce without any shame, *hoc est ridiculum, hoc est absurdum*,[33] in short, the judgment of their taste and nausea; and then they enforce it tyrannically. Thus they coerce many, and gradually still more develop a new habit, and eventually *all* a new *need*. The reason why these individuals have different feelings and tastes is usually to be found in some oddity of their life style, nutrition,

---

[32] Cf. *Beyond Good and Evil*, section 35 (BWN, 237).
[33] This is ridiculous, this is absurd.

or digestion, perhaps a deficit or excess of inorganic salts in
their blood and brain; in brief, in their *physis*.[34] They have the
courage to side with their *physis* and to heed its demands down
to the subtlest nuances. Their aesthetic and moral judgments
are among these "subtlest nuances" of the *physis*.

40

On the lack of noble manners. — Soldiers and leaders still
have far better relationships with each other than workers and
employers. So far at least, culture that rests on a military basis
still towers above all so-called industrial culture: the latter in
its present shape is altogether the most vulgar form of existence
that has yet existed. Here one is at the mercy of brute need;
one wants to live and has to sell oneself, but one despises those
who exploit this need and *buy* the worker. Oddly, submission
to powerful, frightening, even terrible persons, like tyrants and
generals, is not experienced as nearly so painful as is this submission to unknown and uninteresting persons, which is what
all the luminaries of industry are. What the workers see in the
employer is usually only a cunning, bloodsucking dog of a man
who speculates on all misery; and the employer's name, shape,
manner, and reputation are a matter of complete indifference
to them. The manufacturers and entrepreneurs of business probably have been too deficient so far in all those forms and signs
of a *higher race* that alone make a *person* interesting. If the
nobility of birth showed in their eyes and gestures, there might
not be any socialism of the masses. For at bottom the masses
are willing to submit to slavery of any kind, if only the higher-
ups constantly legitimize themselves as higher, as *born* to command—by having noble manners. The most common man feels
that nobility cannot be improvised and that one has to honor in
it the fruit of long periods of time. But the lack of higher
manners and the notorious vulgarity of manufacturers with
their ruddy, fat hands give him the idea that it is only accident

---

[34] Greek word for nature. For Nietzsche's earlier uses of this term, see
Kaufmann, 154–61, as well as other references listed in the Index. What
is meant above is clearly "physiological make-up."

and luck that have elevated one person above another. Well, then, he reasons: let *us* try accident and luck! let us throw the dice! And thus socialism is born.

41

Against remorse.— A thinker sees his own actions as experiments and questions—as attempts to find out something. Success and failure are for him *answers* above all. To be annoyed or feel remorse because something goes wrong—that he leaves to those who act because they have received orders and who have to reckon with a beating when his lordship is not satisfied with the result.

42

Work and boredom.— Looking for work in order to be paid: in civilized countries today almost all men are at one in doing that. For all of them work is a means and not an end in itself. Hence they are not very refined in their choice of work, if only it pays well. But there are, if only rarely, men who would rather perish than work without any *pleasure* in their work. They are choosy, hard to satisfy, and do not care for ample rewards, if the work itself is not the reward of rewards. Artists and contemplative men of all kinds belong to this rare breed, but so do even those men of leisure who spend their lives hunting, traveling, or in love affairs and adventures. All of these desire work and misery if only it is associated with pleasure, and the hardest, most difficult work if necessary. Otherwise, their idleness is resolute, even if it spells impoverishment, dishonor, and danger to life and limb. They do not fear boredom as much as work without pleasure; they actually require a lot of boredom if *their* work is to succeed. For thinkers and all sensitive spirits, boredom is that disagreeable "windless calm" of the soul that precedes a happy voyage and cheerful winds. They have to bear it and must wait for its effect on them. Precisely this is what lesser natures cannot achieve by any means. To ward off boredom at any cost is vulgar, no less than work without pleasure. Perhaps Asians are distinguished above Europeans by a capacity for longer, deeper calm; even their opiates have a slow effect and require patience, as opposed to the disgusting suddenness of the European poison, alcohol.

43

What laws betray.— It is a serious mistake to study the penal code of a people as if it gave expression to the national character. The laws do not betray what a people are but rather what seems to them foreign, strange, uncanny, outlandish. The laws refer to the exceptions to the morality of *mores*,[35] and the severest penalties are provided for what accords with the *mores* of a neighboring people. Thus the Wahhabis[36] know only two mortal sins: having a god other than the Wahhabi god, and smoking (which they call "the infamous way of drinking"). "And what about murder and adultery?" asked the Englishman who found this out, amazed. "God is gracious and merciful," replied the old chief.

Thus the old Romans had the notion that a woman could incur only two mortal sins: adultery and—drinking wine. Old Cato thought that kissing among relatives had been made part of *mores* only to keep women under control in this matter. The meaning of the kiss? Does she smell of wine? Women caught with wine were actually put to death—certainly not only because women under the influence of alcohol sometimes lose the ability to say No. What the Romans feared above all was the orgiastic and Dionysian cult that afflicted the women of Southern Europe from time to time when wine was still new in Europe: this struck the Romans as a monstrous foreign invasion that overturned the basis of the European sensibility; it seemed treason against Rome, the incorporation of what was foreign.

44

Supposed motives.— Important as it may be to know the motives that actually prompted human conduct so far, it may

---

[35] Cf. BWN, 149f., 154f., 454.
[36] A Muslim sect, founded in Arabia in the eighteenth century by Mohammed ibn Abdul-Wahhab. Their claim that they went back to original Islam is credited by many scholars.

be even more essential to know the fictitious and fanciful motives to which men ascribed their conduct. For their inner happiness and misery has come to men depending on their faith in this or that motive—*not* by virtue of the actual motives. The latter are of second-order interest.

45

Epicurus.— Yes, I am proud of the fact that I experience the character of Epicurus quite differently from perhaps everybody else. Whatever I hear or read of him, I enjoy the happiness of the afternoon of antiquity. I see his eyes gaze upon a wide, white sea, across rocks at the shore that are bathed in sunlight, while large and small animals are playing in this light, as secure and calm as the light and his eyes. Such happiness could be invented only by a man who was suffering continually. It is the happiness of eyes that have seen the sea of existence become calm, and now they can never weary of the surface and of the many hues of this tender, shuddering skin of the sea. Never before has voluptuousness been so modest.[37]

---

[37] Nietzsche's sense of kinship with Epicurus seems plain and brings out a side of Nietzsche that has been ignored totally by most of his interpreters. Cf. the poem "In the South" in the Appendix, and the "Dionysus Dithyramb" "The Sun Sinks" (original and translation on facing pages in Kaufmann, *Twenty German Poets*). Cf. further *Beyond Good and Evil,* section 270 (BWN, 410f.), and the Preface to *The Gay Science,* sections 3 and 4. The last three passages were included by Nietzsche in his *Nietzsche contra Wagner* (VPN, 679–83), which shows how much importance the author attached to this side of himself.

There are also many interesting references to Epicurus in Nietzsche's letters to Peter Gast, who was very much interested in Epicurus. All of these references express admiration and a sense of affinity, although it has often been suggested, falsely, that Nietzsche admired only the *pre*-Socratic philosophers.

"My health is disgustingly rich in pain, as formerly; my life much more severe and lonesome; I myself live on the whole almost like a complete saint, but almost with the outlook of the complete, genuine Epicurus [genuine, as opposed to the popular misconceptions that find expression in the general use of "epicurean"]—with my soul very calm and patient and yet contemplating life with joy" (January 22, 1879).

"I have once again contemplated Epicurus' bust: strength of will and

46

Our amazement.— It is a profound and fundamental good fortune that scientific discoveries stand up under examination and furnish the basis, again and again, for further discoveries. After all, this could be otherwise. Indeed, we are so convinced of the uncertainty and fantasies of our judgments and of the eternal change of all human laws and concepts that we are really amazed how *well* the results of science stand up. Formerly, nothing was known of this fickleness of everything human; the *mores* of morality[38] sustained the faith that all of man's inner life was attached to iron necessity with eternal clamps. Perhaps people then experienced a similarly voluptuous amazement when they listened to fairy tales. The miraculous gave a great deal of pleasure to those who at times grew tired of the rule and of eternity. To lose firm ground for once! To float! To err! To be mad! That was part of the paradise and the debauchery of bygone ages, while our bliss is like that of a man who has suffered shipwreck, climbed ashore, and now stands with both feet on the firm old earth—amazed that it does not waver.

---

spirituality are expressed in the head to the highest degree" (July 1, 1883).

"Epicurus . . . *so far* all the world has *paid him back,* beginning in his own time, for *allowing* himself to be taken for someone else and for taking a light, divinely light view of opinions *about* himself. Already during the last period of his fame [while he was still living] the *pigs* crowded into his gardens . . ." (August 3, 1883; the image of the pigs is derived from Horace, *Epistles* I.4.16). The fact that he himself was even then taken for someone else and was likely to suffer this fate on a much larger scale after his death weighed on Nietzsche and eventually prompted him, first, to write prefaces for the second editions of many of his books, and then to write *Ecce Homo,* in which he says on the first page (BWN, 673): "*Above all, do not mistake me for someone else.*"

For Epicurus see also sections 277, 306, 370, and 375 below; also Nietzsche's last reference to Epicurus, in section 58 of *The Antichrist* (VPN, 649). Nietzsche's reason for finally being dissatisfied with Epicurus is stated most succinctly in *The Will to Power,* note 1029: "I have presented such terrible images to knowledge that any 'Epicurean delight' is out of the question. Only Dionysian joy is sufficient . . ." In the end, Nietzsche was not willing to renounce enthusiasm and passion.
[38] Cf. section 43, note 35.

47

On the suppression of the passions.—If one continually forbids oneself the expression of the passions as if that were something to be left to "common," coarser, bourgeois or peasant
types—desiring to suppress not the passions themselves but only
their language and gestures—the result is nevertheless precisely
what is not desired: the suppression of the passions themselves
or at least their weakening and alteration. The most instructive
example is furnished by the court of Louis XIV and all the
circles that were dependent on the court. The period that *followed,* having been educated to suppress their expression,
lacked the passions themselves and had in their place graceful,
shallow, playful manners. It was an age marked by the incapacity for bad manners: even an insult was accepted and returned
with obliging words. Perhaps our present age furnishes the
most remarkable counterpart: everywhere, in life and on the
stage, and not least of all in everything that is written, I see the
delight in all the *coarser* eruptions and gestures of passion. What
is demanded nowadays is a certain convention of passionate-
ness—anything but genuine passion! Nevertheless, eventually
passion itself will be reached this way, and our descendants
will not only indulge in savage and unruly forms, but will be
really savage.

48

Knowledge of misery.— Perhaps there is nothing that separates men or ages more profoundly than a difference in their
knowledge of misery: misery of the soul as well as the body.
Regarding the latter we moderns may well be, all of us, in
spite of our frailties and infirmities, tyros who rely on fantasies,
for lack of any ample firsthand experience—compared to the
age of fear, the longest of all ages, in which individuals had to
protect themselves. In those days, one received ample training
in bodily torments and deprivations and one understood even
a certain cruelty against oneself and a voluntary habituation to
pain as a necessary means of self-preservation. In those days,
one educated those close to one to endure pain; in those days,
one enjoyed inflicting pain and saw the worst things of this

kind happen to others without feeling anything but—one's own safety. But regarding misery of the soul, I now look at every person to see whether he knows this from experience or only from descriptions; whether he still considers it necessary to simulate this knowledge, say, as a sign of refinement, or whether at the bottom of his soul he no longer believes in great pains of the soul and has much the same experience when they are mentioned that he has at the mention of great physical sufferings, which make him think of his own toothaches and stomachaches. But that is how matters seem to me to stand with most people today.

The general lack of experience of pain of both kinds and the relative rarity of the sight of anyone who is suffering have an important consequence: pain is now hated much more than was the case formerly; one speaks much worse of it; indeed, one considers the existence of the mere *thought* of pain scarcely endurable and turns it into a reproach against the whole of existence.

The emergence of pessimistic philosophies[39] is by no means a sign of great and terrible misery. No, these question marks about the value of all life are put up in ages in which the refinement and alleviation of existence make even the inevitable mosquito bites of the soul and the body seem much too bloody and malignant and one is so poor in real experiences of pain that one would like to consider *painful general ideas*[40] as suffering of the first order.

There is a recipe against pessimistic philosophers and the excessive sensitivity that seems to me the real "misery of the present age"—but this recipe may sound too cruel and might itself be counted among the signs that lead people to judge that "existence is something evil." Well, the recipe against this "misery" is: *misery.*[41]

---

[39] Above all, Schopenhauer's.

[40] *Vorstellungen*—the word Schopenhauer had used, in the singular, in the title of his main work.

[41] Or: Schopenhauer might have been cured of his pessimism if he had experienced real misery—like Nietzsche. In *Beyond Good and Evil*, section 186 (BWN, 289), Nietzsche questions whether Schopenhauer really was a pessimist.

49

Magnanimity and related matters.— Those paradoxical phenomena, like the sudden chill in the behavior of an emotional person, or the humor of a melancholic, and above all *magnanimity* as a sudden renunciation of revenge or of the satisfaction of envy, appear in people who harbor a powerful centrifugal force and experience sudden satiety and sudden nausea. Their satisfactions are so quick and strong that they are followed instantly by weariness and aversion and a flight into the opposite taste. In this opposite, the cramp of feeling is resolved— in one person by a sudden chill, in another by laughter, in a third person by tears of self-sacrifice.

The magnanimous person—or at least the type of magnanimity that has always been considered most impressive— appears to me as an extremely vengeful person who beholds satisfaction so close at hand and who drains it so fully and thoroughly to the last drop, in *anticipation,* that a tremendous and quick nausea follows this quick orgy, and he now rises "above himself," as they say, and forgives his enemy, and even blesses and honors him. With this violence against himself, with this scorn for his lust for revenge that a moment ago was still so powerful, he merely yields to a new impulse that has now attained power over him (nausea), and he does this just as impatiently and orgiastically as he *anticipated* a moment earlier the delight in revenge, draining it in his imagination. Magnanimity contains the same degree of egoism as does revenge, but egoism of a different quality.

50

The argument of growing solitude.— The reproaches of conscience are weak even in the most conscientious people compared to the feeling: "This or that is against the morals of *your* society." A cold look or a sneer on the face of those among whom and for whom one has been educated is feared even by the strongest. What is it that they are really afraid of? Growing solitude! This is the argument that rebuts even the best arguments for a person or cause. —Thus the herd instinct speaks up in us.

51

Truthfulness.— I favor any *skepsis* to which I may reply: "Let us try it!" But I no longer wish to hear anything of all those things and questions that do not permit any experiment. This is the limit of my "truthfulness"; for there courage has lost its right.[42]

52

What others know about us.—What we know about ourselves and remember is not so decisive for the happiness of our life as people suppose. One day that which *others* know about us (or think they know) assaults us—and then we realize that this is more powerful. It is easier to cope with a bad conscience than to cope with a bad reputation.

53

Where the good begins.—Where the poor power of the eye can no longer see the evil impulse as such because it has become too subtle, man posits the realm of goodness; and the feeling that we have now entered the realm of goodness excites all those impulses which had been threatened and limited by the evil impulses, like the feeling of security, of comfort, of benevolence. Hence, the duller the eye, the more extensive the good. Hence the eternal cheerfulness of the common people and of children. Hence the gloominess and grief—akin to a bad conscience—of the great thinkers.[43]

---

[42] For an extended discussion of Nietzsche's "experimentalism" see Kaufmann, 85–95 (the last two sections of the chapter on "Nietzsche's Method").

[43] In *Beyond Good and Evil*, section 212, Nietzsche suggests that the philosophers "have found their task, their hard, unwanted, inescapable task ... in being the bad conscience of their time."

54

The consciousness of appearance.—How wonderful and new and yet how gruesome and ironic I find my position vis-à-vis the whole of existence in the light of my insight! I have discovered for myself that the human and animal past, indeed the whole primal age and past of all sentient being continues in me to invent, to love, to hate, and to infer. I suddenly woke up in the midst of this dream, but only to the consciousness that I am dreaming and that I must go on dreaming lest I perish—as a somnambulist must go on dreaming lest he fall. What is "appearance" for me now? Certainly not the opposite of some essence: what could I say about any essence except to name the attributes of its appearance! Certainly not a dead mask that one could place on an unknown x or remove from it!

Appearance is for me that which lives and is effective and goes so far in its self-mockery that it makes me feel that this is appearance and will-o'-the-wisp and a dance of spirits and nothing more—that among all these dreamers, I, too, who "know," am dancing my dance; that the knower is a means for prolonging the earthly dance and thus belongs to the masters of ceremony of existence; and that the sublime consistency and interrelatedness of all knowledge perhaps is and will be the highest means to *preserve* the universality of dreaming and the mutual comprehension of all dreamers and thus also *the continuation of the dream.*[44]

---

[44] In other words: The world of our experience is shaped by our prerational past and may be likened to a dream. But even when we realize how the world of our experience lacks objectivity and independent reality, we still "must go on dreaming." What we experience is "appearance"; but there is no "essence" behind it that is somehow falsified. "Appearance" is not a mask that we might hope to remove from the face of an unknown x. There is no objective reality, no thing-in-itself; there is only appearance in one or another perspective.

These ideas are developed further in sections 57–59, then in Book III, and much later in the third and fourth chapters of *Twilight of the Idols* (VPN, 484–86). There are also many relevant notes in *The Will to Power.*

55

The ultimate noblemindedness.— What makes a person "noble"? Certainly not making sacrifices, for those frantic with lust also make sacrifices. Certainly not following some passion, for there are contemptible passions. Certainly not doing something for others, without selfishness: perhaps nobody is more consistently selfish than those who are noble. Rather: the passion that attacks those who are noble is peculiar, and they fail to realize this. It involves the use of a rare and singular standard and almost a madness: the feeling of heat in things that feel cold to everybody else; the discovery of values for which no scales have been invented yet; offering sacrifices on altars that are dedicated to an unknown god;[45] a courage without any desire for honors; a self-sufficiency that overflows and gives to men and things. Hitherto, it was rarity and a lack of awareness of this rarity that made a person noble. But we should note that this standard involved an unfair judgment concerning everything usual, near, and indispensable—in short, that which most preserves the species and was the *rule* among men hitherto: all this was slandered on the whole in favor of the exceptions. To become the advocate of the rule—that might be the ultimate form and refinement in which noblemindedness reveals itself on earth.[46]

56

The craving for suffering.—When I think of the craving to do something, which continually tickles and spurs those millions of young Europeans who cannot endure their boredom and themselves, then I realize that they must have a craving to suffer and to find in their suffering a probable reason for action, for deeds. Neediness is needed![47] Hence the politicians' clamor,

---

[45] Cf. Nietzsche's early poem, "To the Unknown God," in Kaufmann, *Twenty German Poets.*
[46] Cf. section 76.
[47] *Not ist nötig.*

hence the many false, fictitious, exaggerated "conditions of distress" of all sorts of classes and the blind readiness to believe in them. These young people demand that—not happiness but unhappiness should approach *from the outside* and become visible; and their imagination is busy in advance to turn it into a monster so that afterward they can fight a monster. If these people who crave distress felt the strength inside themselves to benefit themselves and to do something for themselves internally, then they would also know how to create for themselves, internally, their very own authentic distress.[48] Then their inventions might be more refined and their satisfactions might sound like good music, while at present they fill the world with their clamor about distress and all too often introduce into it the *feeling of distress.* They do not know what to do with themselves—and therefore paint the distress of others on the wall; they always need others! And continually other others! —Pardon me, my friends, I have ventured to paint my *happiness* on the wall.

---

[48] Like Nietzsche, for example. This sentence and the first half of the next sentence explain the last sentence of this section. The basic contrast revolves around self-sufficiency. Anyone lacking that tends to project into others needs and conditions of distress that he can then exert himself to alleviate. Having no project of his own, he can thus give his life some purpose.

BOOK TWO

57

To the realists.— You sober people who feel well armed against passion and fantasies and would like to turn your emptiness into a matter of pride and an ornament: you call yourselves realists and hint that the world really is the way it appears to you. As if reality stood unveiled before you only, and you yourselves were perhaps the best part of it—O you beloved images of Sais![1] But in your unveiled state are not even you still very passionate and dark creatures compared to fish, and still far too similar to an artist in love? And what is "reality" for an artist in love? You are still burdened with those estimates of things that have their origin in the passions and loves of former centuries. Your sobriety still contains a secret and inextinguishable drunkenness. Your love of "reality," for example—oh, that is a primeval "love." Every feeling and sensation contains a piece of this old love; and some fantasy, some prejudice, some unreason, some ignorance, some fear, and ever so much else has contributed to it and worked on it. That mountain there! That cloud there! What is "real" in that? Subtract the phantasm and every human *contribution* from it, my sober friends! If you *can*! If you can forget your descent, your past, your training—all of your humanity and animality. There is no "reality" for us—not for you either, my sober friends. We are not nearly as different as you think, and perhaps our good will to transcend intoxication is as respectable as your faith that you are altogether incapable of intoxication.

58

Only as creators!— This has given me the greatest trouble and still does: to realize that what things *are called* is incomparably more important than what they are. The reputation, name, and appearance, the usual measure and weight of a thing,

---

[1] Another allusion to Schiller's great ballad, "The Veiled Image at Sais." (Cf. the final section of Nietzsche's Preface, above.)

what it counts for—originally almost always wrong and arbitrary, thrown over things like a dress and altogether foreign to their nature and even to their skin—all this grows from generation unto generation, merely because people believe in it, until it gradually grows to be part of the thing and turns into its very body. What at first was appearance becomes in the end, almost invariably, the essence and is effective as such. How foolish it would be to suppose that one only needs to point out this origin and this misty shroud of delusion in order to *destroy* the world that counts for real, so-called *"reality."* We can destroy only as creators. —But let us not forget this either: it is enough to create new names and estimations and probabilities in order to create in the long run new "things."

59

We artists.— When we love a woman, we easily conceive a hatred for nature on account of all the repulsive natural functions to which every woman is subject. We prefer not to think of all this; but when our soul touches on these matters for once, it shrugs as it were and looks contemptuously at nature: we feel insulted; nature seems to encroach on our possessions, and with the profanest hands at that. Then we refuse to pay any heed to physiology and decree secretly: "I want to hear nothing about the fact that a human being is something more than *soul and form.*" "The human being under the skin" is for all lovers a horror and unthinkable, a blasphemy against God and love.

Well, as lovers still feel about nature and natural functions, every worshiper of God and his "holy omnipotence" formerly felt: everything said about nature by astronomers, geologists, physiologists, or physicians, struck him as an encroachment into his precious possessions and hence as an attack—and a shameless one at that. Even "natural law" sounded to him like a slander against God; really he would have much preferred to see all of mechanics derived from acts of a moral will or an arbitrary will. But since nobody was able to render him this service, he *ignored* nature and mechanics as best he could and lived in a dream. Oh, these men of former times knew how to *dream* and did not find it necessary to go to sleep first. And we men of today still master this art all too well, despite all of our good will toward the day and staying awake. It is quite enough to love, to hate, to desire, simply to feel—and right away the spirit and power of the dream overcome us, and with our eyes open, coldly contemptuous of all danger, we climb up on the most hazardous paths to scale the roofs and spires of fantasy—without any sense of dizziness, as if we had been born to climb, we somnambulists of the day! We artists! We ignore what is natural. We are moonstruck and God-struck. We wander, still as death, unwearied, on heights that we do not see as heights but as plains, as our safety.[2]

60

Women and their action at a distance.— Do I still have ears? Am I all ears and nothing else? Here I stand in the flaming surf whose white tongues are licking at my feet; from all sides I hear howling, threats, screaming, roaring coming at me, while the old earth-shaker sings his aria in the lowest depths, deep as a bellowing bull, while pounding such an earth-shaking beat that the hearts of even these weather-beaten rocky monsters are trembling in their bodies. Then, suddenly, as if born out of nothing, there appears before the gate of this hellish labyrinth, only a few fathoms away—a large sailboat, gliding along as silently as a ghost. Oh, what ghostly beauty! How magically it touches me! Has all the calm and taciturnity of the world embarked on it? Does my happiness itself sit in this quiet place—my happier ego, my second, departed self? Not to be dead and yet no longer alive? A spiritlike intermediate being: quietly observing, gliding, floating? As the boat that with its white sails moves like an immense butterfly over the dark sea. Yes! To move *over* existence! That's it! That would be something!

It seems as if the noise here had led me into fantasies. All great noise leads us to move happiness into some quiet distance.

[2] The comparison in the first paragraph of this section leads Nietzsche to offer observations about women in sections 60–75.

When a man stands in the midst of his own noise, in the midst of his own surf of plans and projects, then he is apt also to see quiet, magical beings gliding past him and to long for their happiness and seclusion: *women*. He almost thinks that his better self dwells there among the women, and that in these quiet regions even the loudest surf turns into deathly quiet, and life itself into a dream about life. Yet! Yet! Noble enthusiast, even on the most beautiful sailboat there is a lot of noise, and unfortunately much small and petty noise. The magic and the most powerful effect of women is, in philosophical language, action at a distance, *actio in distans*; but this requires first of all and above all—*distance*.

61

In honor of friendship.— In antiquity the feeling of friendship was considered the highest feeling, even higher than the most celebrated pride of the self-sufficient sage—somehow as the sole and still more sacred sibling of this pride. This is expressed very well in the story of the Macedonian king who gave an Athenian philosopher, who despised the world, a talent[3] as a present—and promptly got it back. "How is that?" asked the king; "has he no friend?" He meant: "I honor the pride of this independent sage, but I should honor his humanity even more if the friend in him had triumphed over his pride. The philosopher has lowered himself before me by showing that he does not know one of the two highest feelings—and the higher one at that."

62

Love.— Love forgives the lover even his lust.

63

Woman in music.— Why is it that warm, rainy winds inspire a musical mood and the inventive pleasure of melodies? Are

[3] A large sum of money.

they not the same winds that fill the churches and arouse thoughts of love in women?

64

Skeptics.—I am afraid that old women are more skeptical in their most secret heart of hearts than any man: they consider the superficiality of existence its essence, and all virtue and profundity is to them merely a veil over this "truth," a very welcome veil over a pudendum—in other words, a matter of decency and shame, and no more than that.

65

Devotion.— There are noble women who are afflicted with a certain poverty of the spirit, and they know no better way to *express* their deepest devotion than to offer their virtue and shame. They own nothing higher. Often this present is accepted without establishing as profound an obligation as the donors had assumed. A very melancholy story!

66

The strength of the weak.— All women are subtle in exaggerating their weaknesses; they are inventive when it comes to weaknesses in order to appear as utterly fragile ornaments who are hurt even by a speck of dust. Their existence is supposed to make men feel clumsy, and guilty on that score. Thus they defend themselves against the strong and "the law of the jungle."

67

Simulating—oneself.— Now she loves him and looks ahead with quiet confidence—like a cow. Alas, what bewitched him was precisely that she seemed utterly changeable and unfathomable. Of steady weather he found too much in himself. Wouldn't she do well to simulate her old character? To simulate a lack of love? Is this not the counsel of—love? *Vivat comoedia.*[4]

68

Will and willingness.— Someone took a youth to a sage and said: "Look, he is being corrupted by women." The sage shook his head and smiled. "It is men," said he, "that corrupt women; and all the failings of women should be atoned by and improved in men. For it is man who creates for himself the image of woman, and woman forms herself according to this image."[5]

"You are too kindhearted about women," said one of those present; "you do not know them." The sage replied: "Will is the manner of men; willingness that of women. That is the law of the sexes—truly, a hard law for women. All of humanity is innocent of its existence; but women are doubly innocent. Who could have oil and kindness enough for them?"

"Damn oil! Damn kindness!" someone else shouted out of the crowd; "women need to be educated better!" —"Men need to be educated better," said the sage and beckoned to the youth to follow him. —The youth, however, did not follow him.

69

Capacity for revenge.— If someone cannot defend himself and therefore does not want to, we do not consider this a disgrace; but we have little respect for anyone who lacks both the capacity and the good will for revenge—regardless of whether it is a man or a woman. Would a woman be able to hold us (or, as they say, "enthral" us) if we did not consider it quite possible that under certain circumstances she could wield a dagger (any kind of dagger) *against us*? Or against herself—which in certain cases would be a crueler revenge (Chinese revenge).

---

[4] Long live comedy!
[5] Nietzsche's comments on women generally do him little credit. See Kaufmann, 22, 42ff., and 84. But here he makes a point that was not widely accepted until more than eighty years later: that women have lost out by modeling themselves on man's image of women. This point is developed further in section 71.

70

Women who master the masters.[6]— A deep and powerful
alto voice of the kind one sometimes hears in the theater can
suddenly raise the curtain upon possibilities in which we
usually do not believe. All at once we believe that somewhere
in the world there could be women with lofty, heroic, and royal
souls, capable of and ready for grandiose responses, resolutions,
and sacrifices, capable of and ready for rule over men because
in them the best elements of man apart from his sex have
become an incarnate ideal. The intention of the theater, to be
sure, is not at all that such voices should create this notion of
women; what they are supposed to represent is usually the
ideal male lover such as Romeo. But to judge by my experience,
the theater regularly miscalculates at that point, as does the
composer who expects that kind of effect from such a voice.
Such lovers are unconvincing: such voices always retain some
motherly and housewifely coloration—most of all when they
make one think of love.

71

On female chastity.— There is something quite amazing and
monstrous about the education of upper-class women. What
could be more paradoxical? All the world is agreed that they
are to be brought up as ignorant as possible of erotic matters,
and that one has to imbue their souls with a profound sense of
shame in such matters until the merest suggestion of such things
triggers the most extreme impatience and flight. The "honor"
of women really comes into play only here: what else would
one not forgive them? But here they are supposed to remain
ignorant even in their hearts; they are supposed to have neither
eyes nor ears, nor words, nor thoughts for this—their "evil";
and mere knowledge is considered evil. And then to be hurled,
as by a gruesome lightning bolt, into reality and knowledge, by
marriage—precisely by the man they love and esteem most! To
catch love and shame in a contradiction and to be forced to
experience at the same time delight, surrender, duty, pity,

---

[6] *Die Herrinnen der Herren.*

terror, and who knows what else, in the face of the unexpected neighborliness of god and beast!

Thus a psychic knot has been tied that may have no equal. Even the compassionate curiosity of the wisest student of humanity is inadequate for guessing how this or that woman manages to accommodate herself to this solution of the riddle, and to the riddle of a solution, and what dreadful, far-reaching suspicions must stir in her poor, unhinged soul—and how the ultimate philosophy and skepsis of woman casts anchor at this point!

Afterward, the same deep silence as before. Often a silence directed at herself, too. She closes her eyes to herself.

Young women try hard to appear superficial and thoughtless. The most refined simulate a kind of impertinence.

Women easily experience their husbands as a question mark concerning their honor, and their children as an apology or atonement. They need children and wish for them in a way that is altogether different from that in which a man may wish for children.

In sum, one cannot be too kind about women.[7]

72

Mothers.— Animals do not think about females[8] as men do; they consider the female the productive being. Paternal love

---

[7] The conclusion returns to the first sentence of the second paragraph in section 68. But there the German word used was *Weiber*; here it is *Frauen*, which sounds much more respectful. Schopenhauer, whose diatribe *"Ueber die Weiber"* ("On Women," in his *Parerga und Paralipomena*, vol. II, 1851) is the most notorious attack on women in the German language, had argued at length that *Frau* ought to be used only in the sense of "wife" (*Aus Arthur Schopenhauer's handschrift-lichem Nachlass*, ed. J. Frauenstädt, 1864, p. 90f.). He had realized that *Weib* sounds disrespectful and added deliberately: "Just so, Jews want to be called *Israelites*, and the tailors *dressmakers* . . . But when an intrinsically innocuous name is discredited, this is not due to the name but to what is named. Hence the new name will soon share the fate of the old one."

[8] *Weiber*. In the next half-sentence, *Weibchen*, which is the usual term for the female *animal*.

does not exist among them; merely something like love for the children of a beloved and a kind of getting used to them.[9] The females find in their children satisfaction for their desire to dominate, a possession, an occupation, something that is wholly intelligible to them and can be chattered with: the sum of all this is what mother love is; it is to be compared with an artist's love for his work.[10] Pregnancy has made women kinder, more patient, more timid, more pleased to submit;[11] and just so does spiritual pregnancy produce the character of the contemplative type, which is closely related to the feminine character: it consists of male mothers. —Among animals the male sex is considered the beautiful sex.

73

Holy cruelty.— A man who held a newborn child in his hands approached a holy man. "What shall I do with this child?" he asked; "it is wretched, misshapen, and does not have life enough to die." "Kill it!" shouted the holy man with a terrible voice; "and then hold it in your arms for three days and three nights to create a memory for yourself: never again will you beget a child this way when it is not time for you to beget." —When the man had heard this, he walked away, disappointed, and many people reproached the holy man because he had counseled cruelty; for he had counseled the man to kill the child. "But is it not crueler to let it live?" asked the holy man.

74

Failures.— Those poor women always fail who in the presence of the man they love become restless and unsure of them-

---

[9] This is surely empirically false.

[10] This comparison recurs in Nietzsche's works but is usually made the other way around, in discussions of the artist or creator or, occasionally, himself.

[11] Nietzsche does not explain all feminine characteristics sociologically (see sections 68 and 71) but gives some weight to biological factors as well.

selves and talk too much. For what seduces men most surely
is a certain secretive and phlegmatic tenderness.

75

The third sex.— "A small man is a paradox but still a man;
but small females seem to me to belong to another sex than
tall women," said an old dancing master. A small woman is
never beautiful—said old Aristotle.[12]

76

The greatest danger.— If the majority of men had not always
considered the discipline of their minds—their "rationality"—
a matter of pride, an obligation, and a virtue, feeling insulted
or embarrassed by all fantasies and debaucheries of thought
because they saw themselves as friends of "healthy common
sense," humanity would have perished long ago. The greatest
danger that always hovered over humanity and still hovers over
it is the eruption of madness—which means the eruption of
arbitrariness in feeling, seeing, and hearing, the enjoyment of
the mind's lack of discipline, the joy in human unreason.[13]
Not truth and certainty are the opposite of the world of the
madman, but the universality and the universal binding force
of a faith; in sum, the non-arbitrary character of judgments.
And man's greatest labor so far has been to reach agreement
about very many things and to submit to a *law of agreement*—
regardless of whether these things are true or false. This is the
discipline of the mind that mankind has received; but the contrary impulses are still so powerful that at bottom we cannot

---

[12] Aristotle actually says: "Greatness of soul implies greatness, as beauty
implies a good-sized body, and small people may be neat and well-
proportioned but cannot be beautiful" (*Nicomachean Ethics*, 1123b).
For the influence of Aristotle's discussion of the great-souled man on
Nietzsche's ethics see Kaufmann, 382–84.

  With this absurd aphorism the pages on women (sections 60–75)
reach their nadir and end. The rest of Book II (through section 107)
deals with art.

[13] *Menschen-Unverstand* is contrasted with *gesunder Menschenverstand*
(healthy common sense).

speak of the future of mankind with much confidence. The image of things still shifts and shuffles continually, and perhaps even more so and faster from now on than ever before. Continually, precisely the most select spirits bristle at this universal binding force—the explorers of *truth* above all. Continually this faith, as *everybody's* faith, arouses nausea and a new lust in subtler minds; and the slow tempo that is here demanded for all spiritual processes, this imitation of the tortoise, which is here recognized as the norm, would be quite enough to turn artists and thinkers into apostates:[14] It is in these impatient spirits that a veritable delight in madness erupts because madness has such a cheerful tempo. Thus the virtuous intellects are needed—oh, let me use the most unambiguous word—what is needed is *virtuous stupidity*, stolid metronomes for the slow spirit, to make sure that the faithful of the great shared faith stay together and continue their dance. It is a first-rate need that commands and demands this. *We others are the exception and the danger*—and we need eternally to be defended. —Well, there actually are things to be said in favor of the exception, *provided that it never wants to become the rule.*[15]

77

The animal with a good conscience.— The vulgar element in everything that gives pleasure in Southern Europe—whether it be Italian opera (for example, Rossini and Bellini) or the Spanish novel of adventure (most readily accessible for us in the French disguise of Gil Blas[16]) does not escape me, but it does not offend me anymore than does the vulgarity that one

---

[14] Cf. *Beyond Good and Evil*, sections 27 and 28 (BWN, 229ff.).

[15] As a rule, Nietzsche extols the exception; but occasionally he adds expressly that the rule should be preserved, as above; and sometimes he defends the rule, as in section 55 above. All three points are obviously compatible, but those who note only the first point—a very common error—seriously misunderstand Nietzsche.

[16] *Gil Blas* is a picaresque romance, published in four volumes, 1715–35, by Alain René Lesage (1668–1747), a French novelist and dramatist. The son of humble Spanish parents, Gil Blas, the hero, is sent off at seventeen with little money, and after many adventures becomes rich and influential. Cf. section 361.

encounters as one walks through Pompeii and, actually, also as one reads any ancient book. How come? Is it because there is no sense of shame and everything vulgar appears as poised and self-assured as anything noble, lovely, and passionate in the same sort of music or novel? "The animal has as much right as any human being; let it run about freely. And you, my dear fellow man, are also still an animal in spite of everything!" That seems to me to be the moral of this story and the peculiarity of Southern humanity. Bad taste has its rights no less than good taste, and even a prior right if it corresponds to a great need, provides certain satisfaction and, as it were, a universal language, an absolutely intelligible mask and gesture. Compared to that, good, elegant taste always seems somewhat deliberate and contrived[17] and not altogether sure how it will be understood: it never is or has been popular. What is and remains popular is the *mask*. Hence there is no point in objecting to the element of masquerade in the melodies and cadenzas, in the leaps and jollities that mark the rhythms of these operas. And as for ancient life! What can we understand of that as long as we do not understand the delight in masks and the good conscience in using any kind of mask![18] Here is the bath and the recreation of the ancient spirit; and perhaps the rare and sublime characters of the ancient world needed this bath even more than the vulgar.

A vulgar turn in Northern works, on the other hand, in German music, for example, offends me unspeakably. Here there is a sense of shame; the artist has lowered himself in his own eyes and could not even help blushing: we are ashamed with him and feel so offended because we sense that he considered it necessary to lower himself for our sake.

78

What should win our gratitude.— Only artists, and especially those of the theater, have given men eyes and ears to see and

---

[17] *etwas Suchendes, Versuchtes*: Nietzsche loved plays on *suchen, versuchen, Versuch, Versuchung,* etc. Cf. Kaufmann, 85f.
[18] For Nietzsche's own use of masks, see the many passages in *Beyond Good and Evil* listed in the Index of BWN, 817.

hear with some pleasure what each man *is* himself, experiences himself, desires himself; only they have taught us to esteem the hero that is concealed in everyday characters; only they have taught us the art of viewing ourselves as heroes—from a distance and, as it were, simplified and transfigured—the art of staging and watching ourselves. Only in this way can we deal with some base details in ourselves. Without this art we would be nothing but foreground and live entirely in the spell of that perspective which makes what is closest at hand and most vulgar appear as if it were vast, and reality itself.

Perhaps one should concede a similar merit to the religion that made men see the sinfulness of every single individual through a magnifying glass, turning the sinner into a great, immortal criminal. By surrounding him with eternal perspectives, it taught man to see himself from a distance and as something past and whole.

79

The attraction of imperfection.—Here I see a poet who, like many a human being, is more attractive by virtue of his imperfections than he is by all the things that grow to completion and perfection under his hands. Indeed, he owes his advantages and fame much more to his ultimate incapacity than to his ample strength. His works never wholly express what he would like to express and what he would *like to have seen*: it seems as if he had had the foretaste of a vision and never the vision itself; but a tremendous lust for this vision remains in his soul, and it is from this that he derives his equally tremendous eloquence of desire and craving. By virtue of this lust he lifts his listeners above his work and all mere "works" and lends them wings to soar as high as listeners had never soared. Then, having themselves been transformed into poets and seers, they lavish admiration upon the creator of their happiness, as if he had led them immediately to the vision of what was for him the holiest and ultimate—as if he had attained his goal and had really *seen* and communicated his vision. His fame benefits from the fact that he never reached his goal.

80

Art and nature.— The Greeks (or at least the Athenians)
liked to hear people speak well. Nothing distinguishes them so
thoroughly from non-Greeks as does this truly greedy craving.
Even of passion on the stage they demanded that it should
speak well, and they endured the unnaturalness of dramatic
verse with rapture. In nature, passion is so poor in words, so
embarrassed and all but mute; or when it finds words, so confused and irrational and ashamed of itself. Thanks to the
Greeks, all of us have now become accustomed to this unnatural
stage convention just as we tolerate, and tolerate gladly, thanks
to the Italians, that other unnatural convention: passion that
sings.

We have developed a need that we cannot satisfy in reality:
to hear people in the most difficult situations speak well and
at length; we are delighted when the tragic hero still finds
words, reasons, eloquent gestures, and altogether intellectual
brightness, where life approaches abysses and men in reality
usually lose their heads and certainly linguistic felicity. This
kind of *deviation from nature* is perhaps the most agreeable
repast for human pride: for its sake man loves art as the
expression of a lofty, heroic unnaturalness and convention. We
rightly reproach a dramatic poet if he does not transmute everything into reason and words but always retains in his hands a
residue of *silence*—just as we are dissatisfied with the operatic
composer who cannot find melodies for the highest sentiments
but only a sentimental "natural" stammering and screaming. At
this point nature is *supposed to be* contradicted. Here the
vulgar attraction of illusion is *supposed to* give way to a higher
attraction.

The Greeks went far, very far in this respect—alarmingly
far. Just as they made the stage as narrow as possible and
denied themselves any effects by means of deep backgrounds;
just as they made facial expressions and easy movements impossible for the actor and transformed him into a solemn, stiff,
masked bogey—they also deprived passion itself of any deep
background and dictated to it a law of beautiful speeches.
Indeed, they did everything to counteract the elementary effect

of images that might arouse fear and pity—for *they did not want fear and pity*. Giving all honor—and the highest honors—to Aristotle, he certainly did not hit the nail, much less on the head, when he discussed the ultimate end of Greek tragedy.[19] Just look at the Greek tragic poets to see what it was that most excited their industry, their inventiveness, their competition: certainly not the attempt to overwhelm the spectator with sentiments. The Athenian went to the theater *in order to hear beautiful speeches*. And beautiful speeches were what concerned Sophocles: pardon this heresy!

It is very different with *serious opera*. All of its masters take pains to prevent anyone from understanding their characters. Occasionally picking up a word must help the inattentive listener, but on the whole the situation must explain itself, and the speeches do not matter! That is what all of them think, and hence they have their fun with the words. Perhaps they merely lacked the courage to express fully their ultimate lack of regard for words. With just a little more impertinence, Rossini would have had everybody sing nothing but la-la-la-la—and that would have made good, rational sense. Confronted with the characters in an opera, we are not supposed to take their word for it, but the sound! That is the difference, that is the beautiful *unnaturalness* for whose sake one goes to the opera. Even the *recitativo secco* really is not meant to be heard as words and text: this kind of half-music is only supposed, first, to give the musical ear a little rest (rest from the *melody* as the most sublime but therefore also most strenuous enjoyment of this art) and then very soon also something else: namely, a growing impatience, a growing irritation, a new desire for *whole* music, for melodies.

How are things with Richard Wagner's art, when we consider it in this perspective? Different perhaps? Often it has seemed to me as if one had to memorize the words *and* the music of his creations before the performance; otherwise, it seemed to me, one *heard* neither the words nor even the music.

---

[19] Aristotle's *Poetics*, Chapter 6, 1449b. For a full discussion of "pity and fear" see Kaufmann, *Tragedy and Philosophy*, 1968, section 11.

81

Greek taste.— "What is beautiful in it?" asked the surveyor
after a performance of *Iphigenia*; "nothing is proved in it!"
Were the Greeks really so far from sharing this taste? In
Sophocles at any rate "everything is proved."

82

Esprit as un-Greek.— The Greeks were exceedingly logical
and plain in all of their thinking. They never wearied of that,
at least during their long good period, as the French so often
do, who just love to take a little leap into the opposite and
really can endure the spirit of logic only if, owing to a lot of
such little leaps into the opposite, it betrays its sociable readiness for pleasantry, its sociable self-denial. Logic they considered necessary, like bread and water—but also, like these, as
the kind of nourishment that is fit for prisoners if it is to be
taken straight, with nothing added. In good society one must
never wish to be solely and entirely right, which is what all
pure logic aims at; hence the small dose of unreason in all
French *esprit*.

The sociability of the Greeks was far less developed than
that of the French has been and still is. That is why we find so
little *esprit* even in their most spirited men, so little wit even
in their wittiest men, and—alas, even these sentences will
meet with disbelief, and how many more of that sort I am
tempted to add! —*Est res magna tacere*[20]—said Martial, like all
garrulous people.

83

Translations.— The degree of the historical sense of any age
may be inferred from the manner in which this age makes

---

[20] It is a big thing to remain silent. Martial (40–104), a Spanish-born
Roman poet, is remembered chiefly for his *Epigrams*. (See *The Epigrams
of Martial*, Selected and Translated by James Michie, Random House
and Vintage paperback, 1973.)

translations and tries to absorb former ages and books. In the age of Corneille and even of the Revolution,[21] the French took possession of Roman antiquity in a way for which we would no longer have courage enough—thanks to our more highly developed historical sense. And Roman antiquity itself: how forcibly and at the same time how naively it took hold of everything good and lofty of Greek antiquity, which was more ancient! How they translated things into the Roman present! How deliberately and recklessly they brushed the dust off the wings of the butterfly that is called moment! Thus Horace now and then translated Alcaeus or Archilochus; and Propertius did the same with Callimachus and Philetas (poets of the same rank as Theocritus, if we *may* judge).[22] What was it to them that the real creator had experienced this and that and written the signs of it into his poem? As poets, they had no sympathy for the antiquarian inquisitiveness that precedes the historical sense; as poets, they had no time for all those very personal things and names and whatever might be considered the costume and mask of a city, a coast, or a century: quickly, they replaced it with what was contemporary and Roman. They seem to ask us: "Should we not make new for ourselves what is old and find ourselves in it? Should we not have the right to breathe our own soul into this dead body? For it is dead after all; how ugly is everything dead!" They did not know the delights of the historical sense; what was past and alien was an embarrassment for them; and being Romans, they saw it as an incentive for a Roman conquest. Indeed, translation was a form of conquest. Not only did one omit what was historical; one also added allusions to the present and, above all, struck out the name of the poet and replaced it with one's own—not with any

---

[21] The great dramatist was born in 1606 and died in 1684. The French Revolution: 1789.
[22] The dates of the Roman poets: Horace (65–8 B.C.) and Propertius (fl. ca. 50–15 B.C.). The Greek poets: Alcaeus (620–580 B.C.), Archilochus (seventh century B.C.); Callimachus, Philetas, and Theocritus (all early third century B.C.).

sense of theft but with the very best conscience of the *imperium Romanum*.[23]

84

On the origin of poetry.— Those who love the fantastic side of man and at the same time champion the notion of instinctive morality, argue as follows: "If we assumed that utility had always been venerated as the supreme deity, how could we possibly account for poetry? After all, this rhythmic speech does anything but promote the clarity of communication, and yet it has shot up all over the earth, and still does, as if it meant to mock expediency and utility. The wild and beautiful irrationality of poetry refutes your utilitarianism. It was precisely the desire to get away from utility for once that elevated man and furnished the inspiration for morality and art."

Well, in this case I have to side with the utilitarians. After all, they are right so rarely that it is really pitiful. In those ancient times in which poetry came into existence, the aim *was* utility, and actually a very great utility. When one lets rhythm permeate speech—the rhythmic force that reorders all the atoms of a sentence, bids one choose one's words with care, and gives one's thoughts a new color, making them darker, stranger, and more remote—the utility in question was *superstitious*. Rhythm was meant to impress the gods more deeply with a human petition, for it was noticed that men remember a verse much better than ordinary speech. It was also believed that a rhythmic ticktock was audible over greater distances; a rhythmical prayer was supposed to get closer to the ears of the gods. Above all, men desired the utility of the elemental and overpowering effect

---

[23] The English tradition in translation has always been much closer to Roman practice than the German, for in Germany the art of translation came into its own together with the historical sense. The fountainhead of the modern German tradition is J. H. Voss's translation of Homer's *Odyssey* into German dactylic hexameters (1781). In the twentieth century, American translators have gone to the opposite, the Roman, extreme. Here the fountainhead was Ezra Pound's *Homage to Sextus Propertius* (1917); and appropriately Pound mentioned Callimachus and Philetas in the very first line.

that we experience in ourselves as we listen to music: rhythm is a compulsion; it engenders an unconquerable urge to yield and join in; not only our feet follow the beat but the soul does, too—probably, one surmised, the soul of the gods as well! Thus one tried to *compel* the gods by using rhythm and to force their hand: poetry was thrown at them like a magical snare.

There was an even stranger notion that may have contributed most of all to the origin of poetry. Among the Pythagoreans it appears as a philosophical doctrine and an artifice in education; but long before there were any philosophers, music was credited with the power of discharging the emotions, of purifying the soul, of easing the *ferocia animi*[24]—precisely by means of rhythm. When the proper tension and harmony of the soul had been lost, one had to *dance*, following the singer's beat: that was the prescription of this therapy. That is how Terpander[25] put an end to a riot, how Empedocles[26] soothed a raging maniac, and how Damon[27] purified a youth who was pining away, being in love; and this was also the cure one tried to apply to the gods when the desire for revenge had made them rabid. Above all, one sought to push the exuberance and giddiness of the emotions to the ultimate extreme, making those who were in a rage entirely mad; and the vengeful, frenzied with lust for revenge. All orgiastic cults aim at discharging the *ferocia* of some deity all at once, turning it into an orgy, in order that the deity should feel freer and calmer afterward and leave man in peace. Etymologically, *melos*[28] is a tranquilizer, not because it is tranquil itself but because its aftereffects make one tranquil. It is not only in the cult song but also in worldly songs of the most ancient times that it is assumed that rhythm has a magical power. As one draws water or rows, for example, a

---

[24] Ferocity of the mind.
[25] Greek lyrical poet of the early seventh century B.C.
[26] Greek philosopher and poet of the fifth century B.C.
[27] Athenian writer on music, mentioned in Plato's *Republic* 400 and 424, and discussed here and there in Nietzsche's early philological writings. In Nietzsche's notes for his lectures on "History of Greek Literature" (1875–76) all three incidents are mentioned together as above (*Werke*, Musarion edition, vol. V, p. 220).
[28] Greek word for melody.

song is supposed to cast a spell over the demons that one imagines at work in such cases; it makes them pliant and unfree so that they become man's instruments. Every action provides an occasion for song: *every* action depends on the assistance of spirits, and the magical song and the spell seem to be the primeval form of poetry.

Verse also had a function in oracles—the Greeks claimed that the hexameter was invented at Delphi—because here, too, rhythm was supposed to effect a compulsion. Asking for a prophecy meant originally (according to the etymology of the word that seems most probable to me) to get something determined: one thought that one could compel the future by gaining the favor of Apollo, who was originally taken to be much more than a prescient god. As the formula is pronounced, with literal and rhythmical precision, it binds the future. But the formula is the invention of Apollo who, being the god of rhythm, can bind even the goddesses of fate.

In sum: What could have been more useful for the ancient, superstitious type of man than rhythm? It enabled one to do anything—to advance some work magically; to force a god to appear, to be near, and to listen; to mold the future in accordance with one's will; to cleanse one's own soul from some excess (of anxiety, mania, pity, or vengefulness)—and not only one's own soul but also that of the most evil demon: without verse one was nothing; by means of verse one almost became a god. Such a fundamental feeling can never be erased entirely; and even now, after men have fought against such superstitions for thousands of years, the wisest among us are still occasionally fooled by rhythm—if only insofar as we sometimes consider an idea truer simply because it has a metrical form and presents itself with a divine skip and jump. Isn't it rather amusing that to this day the most serious philosophers, however strict they may be in questions of certainty, still call on what poets have said in order to lend their ideas force and credibility? And yet it is more dangerous for a truth when a poet agrees than when he contradicts it. For as Homer says: "Many lies tell the poets."[29]

---

[29] The irony of ending with an illustration of the very habit that has just been criticized is, of course, deliberate. Cf. the chapter "On Poets"

85

The good and the beautiful.— Artists continually *glorify*—
they do nothing else—all those states and things that are reputed
to give man the opportunity to feel good for once, or great, or
intoxicated, or cheerful, or well and wise. These select things
and states, whose value for human happiness is considered safe
and assured, are the artists' objects. Artists always lie in wait
to discover such objects and draw them into the realm of art.
What I mean is that they are not themselves the appraisers of
happiness; rather they try to get close to those who make the
appraisals, with the utmost curiosity and the urge to utilize
these appraisals immediately. Since they have, in addition to
this impatience, also the big lungs of heralds and the feet of
runners, they are also always among the first to glorify the
new good; and they therefore *appear* to be the first to call it
good, to appraise it as good. But this is, as I have said, an
error: they are merely quicker and louder than the real appraisers. —But who *are* the real appraisers?—The rich and
the idle.

86

Of the theater.— I had strong and elevated feelings again
today, and if I could have music and art in the evening, I know
very well what sort of music and art I do *not* want—namely,
the kind that tries to intoxicate the audience and to force it to
the height of a moment of strong and elevated feelings. This
kind is designed for those everyday souls who in the evening
are not like victors on their triumphal chariots but rather like
tired mules who have been whipped too much by life. What
would men of this type know of "higher moods" if there were

---

in *Zarathustra* (VPN, 239): " 'But what was it that Zarathustra once
said to you? That the poets lie too much? But Zarathustra, too, is a
poet. Do you now believe that he spoke the truth here? Why do you
believe that?' The disciple answered, 'I believe in Zarathustra.' But
Zarathustra shook his head and smiled. 'Faith does not make me
blessed," he said, 'especially not faith in me. But suppose somebody
said in all seriousness, the poets lie too much: he would be right; *we*
do lie too much.' "

no intoxicants and idealistic whips? Hence they have those who enthuse them even as they have their wines. But what are their drinks and their intoxication to me? Does he that *is* enthusiastic need wine? Rather he looks with some sort of nausea at the means and mediators that are trying to produce an effect without a sufficient reason—aping the high tide of the soul!

What now? One gives the mole wings and proud conceits— before it is time to go to sleep, before he crawls back into his hole? One sends him off into the theater and places large glasses before his blind and tired eyes? Men whose lives are not an "action" but a business, sit before the stage and observe strange creatures for whom life is no mere business? "That is decent," you say; "that is entertaining; that is culture."

Well, in that case I often lack culture; for much of the time I find this spectacle nauseous. Whoever finds enough tragedy and comedy in himself, probably does best when he stays away from the theater. Or if he makes an exception, the whole process, including the theater, the audience, and the poet, will strike him as the really tragic or comical spectacle, while the play that is performed will mean very little to him by comparison. What are the Fausts and Manfreds of the theater to anyone who is somewhat like Faust and Manfred? But it may give him something to think about that characters of that type should ever be brought upon the stage. The strongest ideas and passions brought before those who are not capable of ideas and passions but only of intoxication! And here they are employed as a means to produce intoxication! Theater and music as the hashish-smoking and betel-chewing of the European! Who will ever relate the whole history of narcotica?—It is almost the history of "culture," of our so-called higher culture.

87

Of the vanity of artists.[30]— I believe that artists often do not know what they can do best, because they are too vain and have fixed their minds on something prouder than those small

---

[30] This section was reprinted, slightly revised, as the first section of *Nietzsche contra Wagner*, under the title "Where I admire" (VPN, 662–64).

plants seem to be that really can grow on their soil to perfection and are new, strange, and beautiful. They do not think much of what is actually good in their own garden or vineyard; and their love and insight are not of the same order.

Here is a musician who, more than any other musician, is a master at discovering the tones out of the realm of suffering, depressed, tormented souls and at giving speech even to dumb animals. Nobody equals him in the colors of late fall, the indescribably moving happiness of the last, very last, very briefest enjoyment; he finds sounds for those secret and uncanny midnights of the soul in which cause and effect appear to be unhinged and any moment something can come into being "out of nothing." More happily than anyone else, he draws from the very bottom of human happiness—as it were, from its drained cup, where the bitterest and most repulsive drops have merged in the end, for better or for worse, with the sweetest. He knows how souls drag themselves along when they can no longer leap and fly, nor even walk; his is the shy glance of concealed pain, of understanding without comfort, of farewells without confessions. As the Orpheus of all secret misery he is greater than anyone, and he has incorporated in art some things that had previously seemed to be inexpressible and even unworthy of art, as if words could only frighten them away, not grasp them—very small, microscopic features of the soul: yes, he is the master of the very small.

But that is not what he *wants* to be. His character prefers large walls and audacious frescoes. He fails to see that his spirit has a different taste and urge and likes best of all to sit quietly in the nooks of houses that have collapsed; there, concealed, concealed from himself, he paints his real masterpieces all of which are very short, often only a single measure in length; there he becomes wholly good, great, and perfect—perhaps only there. —But he does not know it. He is too vain to know it.[31]

---

[31] What is said beautifully here in general terms is applied to Wagner in section 7 of *The Case of Wagner* (BWN, 626f.). In NCW Nietzsche omitted the last two sentences, above, and added instead: "Wagner is one who has suffered deeply—that is his *distinction* above other musicians. I admire Wagner wherever he puts himself to music."

88

Being serious about truth.— Being serious about truth: what
very different ideas people associate with these words! The
very same views and types of proof and scrutiny that a thinker
may consider a frivolity in himself to which he has succumbed
on this or that occasion to his shame—these very same views
may give an artist who encounters them and lives with them for
a while the feeling that he has now become deeply serious
about truth and that it is admirable how he, although an artist,
has at the same time the most serious desire for the opposite
of mere appearance. Thus it can happen that a man's emphatic
seriousness shows how superficial and modest his spirit has
been all along when playing with knowledge. —And does not
everything that we take *seriously* betray us? It always shows
what has weight for us and what does not.

89

Now and formerly.— What good is all the art of our works
of art if we lose that higher art, the art of festivals? Formerly,
all works of art adorned the great festival road of humanity, to
commemorate high and happy moments. Now one uses works
of art to lure aside from the great *via dolorosa*[32] of humanity
those who are wretched, exhausted, and sick, and to offer them
a brief lustful moment—a little intoxication and madness.

90

Lights and shadows.— Books and drafts mean something
quite different for different thinkers. One collects in a book
the lights that he has been able to steal and carry home swiftly
out of the rays of some insight that suddenly dawned on him,
while another thinker offers us nothing but shadows—images
in black and gray of what had built up in his soul the day
before.

---

[32] *Leidensstrasse*: road of suffering.

91

Caution.— As is well known, Alfieri[33] told a great many lies when he told his surprised contemporaries the story of his life. What prompted these lies was the same despotic attitude toward himself that he also manifested in the way in which he created his own language and tyrannically forced himself to become a poet: he had finally found a severe form of sublimity into which he then pressed his life and his memory. No doubt, there was much agony in all of this. —I also would not believe a biography of Plato, written by himself—anymore than Rousseau's or the *Vita Nuova* of Dante.

92

Prose and poetry.— It is noteworthy that the great masters of prose have almost always been poets, too—if not publicly than at least secretly, in the "closet." Good prose is written only face to face with poetry. For it is an uninterrupted, well-mannered war with poetry: all of its attractions depend on the way in which poetry is continually avoided and contradicted. Everything abstract wants to be read as a prank against poetry and as with a mocking voice; everything dry and cool is meant to drive the lovely goddess into lovely despair. Often there are *rapprochements,* reconciliations for a moment—and then a sudden leap back and laughter. Often the curtain is raised and harsh light let in just as the goddess is enjoying her dusks and muted colors. Often the words are taken out of her mouth and sung to a tune that drives her to cover her refined ears with her refined hands. Thus there are thousands of delights in this war, including the defeats of which the unpoetic souls, the so-called prose-men, do not know a thing; hence they write and speak only *bad* prose. *War is the father of all good things;*[34] war is also the father of good prose.

Four very strange and truly poetic human beings in this century have attained mastery in prose, for which this century

---

[33] Count Vittorio Alfieri (1749–1803), Italian dramatist. The *Memoirs of his Life* were published posthumously.
[34] Heraclitus' fragment 53: "War is the father of all."

was not made otherwise—for lack of poetry, as I have suggested. Not including Goethe, who may fairly be claimed by the century that produced him, I regard only Giacomo Leopardi, Prosper Mérimée, Ralph Waldo Emerson, and Walter Savage Landor, the author of *Imaginary Conversations*, as worthy of being called masters of prose.[35]

93

But why do you write?— A: I am not one of those who think with an inky pen in their hand, much less one of those who in front of an open inkwell abandon themselves to their passions while they sit in a chair and stare at the paper. I am annoyed by and ashamed of my writing; writing is for me a pressing and embarrassing need, and to speak of it even in a parable disgusts me.

B: But why, then, do you write? —A: Well, my friend, to be quite frank: so far, I have not discovered any other way of getting rid of my thoughts. —B: And why do you want to get rid of them? —A: Why I want to? Do I want to? I must. —B: Enough! Enough!

94

Growth after death.— Those audacious little words about moral questions that Fontenelle threw out in his immortal

---

[35] Goethe (1749–1832). Leopardi (1798–1837) is best known as perhaps the greatest lyrical poet of Italy. Mérimée (1803–70), is now remembered chiefly as the writer of *Carmen*. Emerson (1803–82) is discussed in the Introduction. Landor (1775–1864) is the only one of these writers who is not mentioned elsewhere in Nietzsche's books. Although two of the four "masters" were born in the eighteenth century, like Goethe, the exclusion of Goethe makes sense because much of his best poetry and prose was written in that century. Still, there is something deliberate in the choice of one Italian, one Frenchman, one American, one Englishman—and no German. Actually, it would have strengthened Nietzsche's case if he had included Heine; but he made up for that omission in *Ecce Homo*: "One day it will be said that Heine and I have been by far the foremost artists of the German language—at an incalculable distance from everything mere Germans have done with it" (BWN, 701)

Dialogues of the Dead[36] were considered in his own time as mere paradoxes and games of a not inconsiderable wit. Even the highest arbiters of taste and spirit found nothing more here, and perhaps Fontenelle himself did not. Now something incredible happens: these thoughts become realities! Science proves them.[37] The game becomes serious. And now we read these

---

[36] 1683. For Fontenelle, see section 3 above.

[37] It is far from obvious what Nietzsche might mean, and his other references to Fontenelle provide no clue. What Nietzsche has in mind is presumably the theme that truth is unobtainable, that errors are required for life, and that the conviction that truth can be discovered by man is itself an error. These ideas turn up in the witty repartee of the *Dialogues* and now seem to Nietzsche to have been proved—to put the point very succinctly—by Kant and Darwin. Kant showed in his *Critique of Pure Reason* (1781) that the world of our experience is not ultimate reality, and Darwin's *Origin of Species* (1859) placed Kant's ideas in a new perspective. (Cf. Kaufmann, 87–89). Nietzsche develops these ideas much more fully in Book III (section 108ff.).

See, for example, the following passages in Fontenelle's *Dialogues*:
Part III, Dialogue 4: "Ah, you don't know yet how folly [*folie*] serves us? It keeps us from knowing ourselves; for the sight of oneself is very sad; and since it is never good to know oneself, it would not do for folly to leave men even for a single moment." "The insane [*frénétiques*] are merely fools of another kind. The follies of all men are of the same nature," so that men have found it easy to adjust to each other and do not consider each other mad; "and one does not call people fools except for certain fools who are, so to say, out of step and whose folly does not accord with that of all the others . . ."
Part V, Dialogue 2: "One must have before one's eyes an imaginary goal that gives one an incentive. . . . One would lose courage if one were not sustained by false ideas. . . . If by some misfortune the truth were to show itself as it is, all would be lost; but it seems to grasp very well the importance of always remaining well concealed."
Part VI, Dialogue 4: "One has some reason for always being deceived by the promises of the philosophers. From time to time they discover some small truths of no consequence that, however, provide some entertainment. But regarding the essentials of philosophy, I submit that there is scarcely any advance. I believe that occasionally one finds the truth about points that matter, but the trouble is that one does not know that one has found it . . ."
These last remarks are put into the mouth of Descartes. These three samples will suffice to give an idea both of Fontenelle's tone and of what Nietzsche had in mind.

dialogues with very different feelings than Voltaire and Helvetius did, and automatically we promote their author to another, much higher rank in the hierarchy of spirits. Rightly? or wrongly?

95

Chamfort.[38]— That a man who understood men and the crowd as well as Chamfort, nevertheless joined the crowd and did not stay aside in philosophical renunciation and resistance, I can explain to myself only in this way: He had one instinct that was even stronger than his wisdom and had never been satisfied—hatred of all nobility by blood. Perhaps it was the old hatred felt by his mother, that was only too easy to explain and had been sanctified by him through his love for her—an instinct of revenge that went back to his boyhood and waited for the hour to revenge his mother. And now life and his genius —and, no doubt, most of all the paternal blood in his veins— had seduced him to join the ranks of this nobility as an equal, for many, many years. Eventually, however, he could no longer endure the sight of himself—the sight of the "old type" under the old regime. He became repentant with a violent passion, and this led him to put on the clothes of the mob, as his kind of hairshirt. He had a bad conscience because he had not taken revenge.

Had Chamfort remained just a little more of a philosopher, the Revolution would have missed out on its tragic wit and its sharpest sting; it would be regarded as a much more stupid event and would not seduce so many spirits. But the hatred and revenge of Chamfort educated a whole generation; and the most illustrious human beings passed through this school. Note that Mirabeau[39] looked up to Chamfort as to his higher and

---

[38] Sébastien Roch Nicolas Chamfort (1741–94). His celebrated collection of aphorisms provided one of the models for Nietzsche's aphoristic works. When the Revolution broke out, he was one of the first of those who stormed the Bastille to enter the building; but later he spoke as sarcastically of the Convention as he had earlier spoken of the royal court. He was arrested, released, and tried to kill himself before being rearrested. He died a few days later.

[39] Honoré Gabriel Riqueti, Comte de Mirabeau (1749–91), French statesman who was prominent during the Revolution.

older self from which he expected and accepted impulses, warnings, and verdicts—Mirabeau who as a human being belongs to an altogether different order of greatness than even the foremost statesmen of yesterday and today.

It is odd that despite such a friend and advocate—after all, we have Mirabeau's letters to Chamfort—this wittiest of all moralists has remained a stranger to the French, no less than Stendhal[40] who may well have had more thoughtful eyes and ears than any other Frenchman of *this* century. Is that because the latter had too many German and English traits to be tolerable for Parisians? While Chamfort, a man who was rich in depths and backgrounds of the soul—gloomy, suffering, ardent —a thinker who needed laughter as a remedy against life and who almost considered himself lost on every day on which he had not laughed—seems much more like an Italian, related to Dante and Leopardi, than like a Frenchman! We know the last words of Chamfort: *"Ah! mon ami,"* he said to Sieyès; *"je m'en vais enfin de ce monde, où il faut que le coeur se brise ou se bronze—."*[41] These are surely not the words of a dying Frenchman.

96

Two speakers.— Of these two speakers, one can show the full rationality of his cause only when he abandons himself to passion; this alone pumps enough blood and heat into his brain to force his high spirituality to reveal itself. The other one may try the same now and then—to present his cause sonorously, vehemently, and to sweep his audience off their feet with the help of passion—but usually with little success. Soon he speaks obscurely and confusedly; he exaggerates; he omits things; and he arouses mistrust about the rationality of his cause. Actually, he himself comes to feel mistrust, and that explains sudden leaps into the coldest and most repugnant tones that lead his audience to doubt whether his passion was genuine. In his case,

---

[40] Pseudonym of Henri Beyle (1783–1842), the great novelist. Nietzsche often refers to him with great admiration.
[41] "Ah, my friend! At last I am about to leave this world where the heart must either break or become hard as bronze." Abbé Emmanuel-Joseph Sieyès was a French political figure (1748–1836).

passion always inundates the spirit, perhaps because it is stronger than in the first speaker. But he is at the height of his powers when he resists the flood of his emotions and virtually derides it; only then does his spirit emerge fully from its hiding place—a logical, mocking, playful, and yet awesome spirit.

97

Of the garrulousness of writers.— There is a garrulousness of wrath—frequently encountered in Luther as well as Schopenhauer. A garrulousness due to a superabundant supply of conceptual formulations, as in Kant. A garrulousness due to the delight in ever new twists of the same thing: to be found in Montaigne. A garrulousness of spiteful characters: anyone who reads contemporary publications will recall two writers of this type. A garrulousness due to the delight in good words and language forms: not at all rare in Goethe's prose. A garrulousness due to an inner pleasure in noise and confused emotions: for example, in Carlyle.

98

In praise of Shakespeare.— I could not say anything more beautiful in praise of Shakespeare *as a human being* than this: he believed in Brutus and did not cast one speck of suspicion upon this type of virtue. It was to him that he devoted his best tragedy—it is still called by the wrong name—to him and to the most awesome quintessence of a lofty morality. Independence of the soul!—that is at stake here. No sacrifice can be too great for that: one must be capable of sacrificing one's dearest friend for it, even if he should also be the most glorious human being, an ornament of the world, a genius without peer—if one loves freedom as the freedom of great souls and he threatens this kind of freedom. That is what Shakespeare must have felt. The height at which he places Caesar is the finest honor that he could bestow on Brutus: that is how he raises beyond measure Brutus's inner problem as well as the spiritual strength that was able to cut *this knot*.

Could it really have been political freedom that led this poet to sympathize with Brutus—and turned him into Brutus's accomplice? Or was political freedom only a symbol for something inexpressible? Could it be that we confront some unknown dark event and adventure in the poet's own soul of which he wants to speak only in signs? What is all of Hamlet's melancholy compared to that of Brutus? And perhaps Shakespeare knew both from firsthand experience. Perhaps he, too, had his gloomy hour and his evil angel, like Brutus.

But whatever similarities and secret relationships there may have been: before the whole figure and virtue of Brutus, Shakespeare prostrated himself, feeling unworthy and remote. His witness of this is written into the tragedy. Twice he brings in a poet, and twice he pours such an impatient and ultimate contempt over him that it sounds like a cry—the cry of self-contempt. Brutus, even Brutus, loses patience as the poet enters —conceited, pompous, obtrusive, as poets often are—apparently overflowing with possibilities of greatness, including moral greatness, although in the philosophy of his deeds and his life he rarely attains even ordinary integrity. "I'll know his humor when he knows his time. / What should the wars do with these jigging fools? / Companion, hence!" shouts Brutus. This should be translated back into the soul of the poet who wrote it.[42]

---

[42] This section calls for comments on several levels. To begin with Shakespeare's treatment of the poet, the quotation is from *Julius Caesar*, 4.3. 136ff. Nietzsche quotes a German translation that is not quite exact, but the deviations do not matter greatly, though it is worth noting that the "jigging fools" become a *Schellen-Hanswurst*, for the *Hanswurst* (buffoon) becomes important in Nietzsche's *Ecce Homo* (II.4 and IV.1, BWN, 702 and 782). The other scene in *Julius Caesar* in which a poet appears is 3.3 where Cinna is torn to pieces. First, the Plebeians mistake him for a conspirator; when he explains, "I am Cinna the poet! I am Cinna the poet!" the retort is: "Tear him for his bad verses! Tear him for his bad verses!" Incidentally, a poet also appears in *Timon of Athens*, 5.1—and is driven away by Timon with utter contempt.

As for Brutus, here is a quotation from Nietzsche's notebooks of this period: "In that which moved Zarathustra, Moses, Mohammed, Jesus, Plato, Brutus, Spinoza, Mirabeau—I live, too." (*Werke*, Musarion edition, XXI, p. 98) It has been noted long ago that in the section "In

99

Schopenhauer's followers.— What happens when barbarians come into contact with a higher culture—the lower culture always accepts first of all the vices, weaknesses, and excesses and only then, on that basis, finds a certain attraction in the higher culture and eventually, by way of the vices and weaknesses that it has acquired, also accepts some of the overflow of what really has value—that can also be observed nearby, without traveling to remote barbarian tribes. Of course, what we see near us is somewhat refined and spiritualized and not quite so palpable.

What do Schopenhauer's German followers generally accept first of all from their master? In comparison with his superior culture, they must surely feel barbarous enough to be initially fascinated and seduced by him like barbarians. Is it his sense for hard facts, his good will for clarity and reason, which so often makes him appear so English and un-German? Or the strength of his intellectual conscience that endured a life-long contradiction between Being and Willing,[43] and also compelled him to contradict himself continually in his writings on almost every point? Or his cleanliness in questions about the church and the Christian god? For here his cleanliness was quite unprecedented among German philosophers, and he lived and

---

praise of Shakespeare" Nietzsche had in mind his own break with Wagner; but it would be folly to trivialize what Nietzsche says by seeing in it no more than a reflection on a particular personal experience. Insofar as this section sheds light on Nietzsche himself, it should at least be noted that in order to retain independence he turned against everything he loved, not only against Wagner. To quote another note: "A very popular error: having the courage of one's convictions; rather it is a matter of having the courage for an *attack* on one's convictions!!!" (*ibid.*, XVI, 318). For further discussion, see Kaufmann, 35f., 244f., 392, and 398; for another striking illustration, see the following section on Schopenhauer.

[43] Although Schopenhauer was very different from what he desired of man, he showed his intellectual conscience by not compromising and by not adjusting his "will" to his "being." Nietzsche also gives credit to Schopenhauer's intellectual conscience for not glossing over contradictions and for not sacrificing insights to harmony.

died "as a Voltairian." Or his immortal doctrines of the intellectuality of intuition, of the a priori nature of the causal law, of the instrumental character of the intellect and the unfreedom of the will? No, none of this enchants his German followers; they do not find it enchanting at all. But Schopenhauer's mystical embarrassments and subterfuges in those places where the factual thinker allowed himself to be seduced and corrupted by the vain urge to be the unriddler of the world; the unprovable doctrine of the *One Will* ("all causes are merely occasional causes of the appearance of the will at this time and at this place" and "the will to life is present, whole and undivided, in every being, including the least—as completely as in all beings that ever have been, are, and shall be, if they were all taken together"); the *denial of the individual* ("all lions are at bottom only one lion"; "the plurality of individuals is mere appearance," even as *development* is mere appearance: he calls Lamarck's idea "an ingenious but absurd error"); his ecstatic reveries about *genius* ("in aesthetic contemplation, the individual is no longer an individual but the pure, will-less, painless, timeless subject of knowledge"; "as the subject is wholly absorbed in the object that it contemplates, it becomes this object itself"); the nonsense about *pity,* about how it makes possible a break through the *principium individuationis,*[44] and how this is the source of all morality; also such claims as "dying is really the purpose of existence" and *"a priori,* one cannot altogether deny the possibility that magical effects might emanate from one who has died"—these and other such *excesses* and vices of the philosopher are always accepted first of all and turned into articles of faith; for vices and excesses are always aped most easily and require no long training.

But let us discuss the most famous living follower of Schopenhauer: Richard Wagner. —What happened to him has happened to many artists: he misinterpreted the characters that he himself had created and misunderstood the philosophy that was implicit in his most characteristic works of art. Until the middle of his life, Richard Wagner allowed himself to be led astray by Hegel. Later, the same thing happened to him a second time

---

[44] Principle of individuation: one of Schopenhauer's central concepts.

when he began to read Schopenhauer's doctrine into his characters and to apply to himself such categories as "will," "genius," and "pity." Nevertheless it will remain true that nothing could be more contrary to the spirit of Schopenhauer than what is distinctively Wagnerian in Wagner's heroes: I mean the innocence of the utmost selfishness, the faith in great passion as the good in itself—in one word, what is Siegfried-like in the countenance of his heroes. "All this smells more even of Spinoza than it does of me," Schopenhauer himself might say.[45]

Although Wagner would have good reasons to look for some other philosopher rather than Schopenhauer, the spell that this thinker has cast over him has blinded him not only to all other philosophies but even to science itself. More and more, his whole art wants to present itself as a companion piece and supplement to Schopenhauer's philosophy, and more and more explicitly it renounces the loftier ambition of becoming a companion piece and supplement to human knowledge and science. Nor is it only the whole mysterious pomp of this philosophy, which would also have attracted a Cagliostro,[46] but the gestures and passions of the philosophers have always been seductive, too.

Wagner is Schopenhauerian, for example, in his exasperation over the corruption of the German language; and if one should applaud his imitation at this point, it should not be overlooked that Wagner's own style suffers rather heavily from all the ulcers and swellings whose sight enraged Schopenhauer; and as for the Wagnerians who write German, Wagnerism is beginning to prove as dangerous as any Hegelisms ever did.

Wagner is Schopenhauerian in his hatred of the Jews to whom he is not able to do justice even when it comes to their greatest deed; after all, the Jews are the inventors of Christianity.

Wagner is Schopenhauerian in his attempts to understand

---

[45] It should be remembered that Spinoza was a Jew and Wagner an impassioned anti-Semite.

[46] The eighteenth-century Italian adventurer, magician, and alchemist who claimed among many other things to have the philosopher's stone. He was a proverbial impostor and died in a dungeon.

Christianity as a seed of Buddhism that has been carried far away by the wind, and to prepare a Buddhistic epoch in Europe, with an occasional *rapprochement* with Catholic-Christian formulas and sentiments.

Wagner is Schopenhauerian when he preaches mercy in our relations with animals. As we know, Schopenhauer's predecessor at this point was Voltaire who may already have mastered the art that we encounter among his successors—to dress up his hatred against certain things and people as mercy for animals. At least Wagner's hatred of science, which finds expression in his preachment, is certainly not inspired by any spirit of kind-heartedness and benignity—nor indeed, as is obvious, by anything meriting the name of *spirit*.[47]

Of course, the philosophy of an artist does not matter much if it is merely an afterthought and does not harm his art. One cannot be too careful to avoid bearing any artist a grudge for an occasional, perhaps very unfortunate and presumptuous masquerade. We should not forget that, without exception, our dear artists are, and have to be to some extent, actors; and without play-acting they would scarcely endure life for any length of time.

Let us remain faithful to Wagner in what is *true* and authentic in him—and especially in this, that we, as his disciples, remain faithful to ourselves in what is true and authentic in us. Let him have his intellectual tempers and cramps. Let us, in all fairness, ask what strange nourishments and needs an art like this may require to be able to live and grow. It does not matter that as a thinker he is so often in the wrong; justice and patience are not for *him*. Enough that his life is justified before itself and remains justified—this life which shouts at everyone of us: "Be a man and do not follow me[48]—but yourself! But yourself!" *Our* life, too, shall remain justified in our

---

[47] *Geist*. Here, as usual—though not earlier in the same sentence—Nietzsche associates *Geist* strongly, but by no means exclusively, with intellect.

[48] Goethe had added these words as an epigraph to later editions of his first novel, *The Sufferings of the Young Werther*, because the hero's suicide had inspired a great many people to commit suicide with the book in their hand or in a pocket. Cf. also poem #7 above.

own eyes! We, too, shall grow and blossom out of ourselves, free and fearless, in innocent selfishness. And as I contemplate such a human being, these sentences still come to my mind today as formerly:

"That passion is better than Stoicism and hypocrisy, that being honest in evil is still better than losing oneself to the morality of tradition, that a free human being can be good as well as evil, but that the unfree human being is a blemish upon nature and has no share in any heavenly or earthly comfort; finally, that everyone who wishes to become free must become free through his own endeavor, and that freedom does not fall into any man's lap as a miraculous gift" (*Richard Wagner in Bayreuth*, p. 94).[49]

100

Learning to pay homage.— Men have to learn to pay homage no less than to feel contempt. Anyone who breaks new paths and who has led many others onto new paths, discovers with some amazement how clumsy and poor these people are in their capacity for expressing gratitude—and how rarely gratitude achieves expression at all. It almost seems that whenever gratitude wants to speak, she begins to gag, clears her throat, and falls silent before she has got out a word. The way in which a thinker gets some notion of the effects of his ideas and

[49] Nietzsche is quoting his own "Untimely Meditation" on Wagner, published in 1876, only six years earlier, but before their break. The page reference is to the first edition; the passage is found less than four pages from the end.

This discussion of "Schopenhauer's followers" exhibits the "independence of the soul" described in the preceding section. Nietzsche's long admiration for Schopenhauer and Wagner did not make it easy for him to sort out their strengths and weaknesses, as he does here. Moreover, Wagner (born in 1813, like Nietzsche's father, who had died when Nietzsche was only four years old) was still alive when *The Gay Science* appeared in 1882 (he died in February 1883). And Wagner craved blind admiration and resented criticism. Hence it really required remarkable "independence of the soul" as well as considerable courage to write and publish this section; and the way in which the section on Brutus prepares the ground for it is remarkable.

of their transforming, revolutionary power, is almost a comedy; at times it seems as if those who have felt this effect actually feel insulted and as if they could express what they consider their threatened self-reliance only by—bad manners. Whole generations are required merely to invent a polite convention for thanks; and it is only very late that we reach the moment when gratitude acquires a kind of spirit and genius. By then, there is usually also someone who becomes the recipient of great gratitude, not only for the good he himself has done but above all for the treasure of what is best and highest that has gradually been accumulated by his predecessors.

101

Voltaire.— Wherever there was a court, there were laws governing good speech and thus also laws about style for all who wrote. But the language of the court is the courtier's language, and since he has *no professional specialty* he does not permit himself, even in conversation about scientific matters, convenient technical expressions; for they smack of professional specialties. In countries with a courtly culture, technical expressions and anything that betrays a specialist are therefore considered *stylistic blemishes.* Now that every court has become a caricature of the past and present, one is amazed to find even Voltaire incredibly prim and fastidious at this point (for example, in his judgments about such stylists as Fontenelle and Montesquieu). For all of us are now emancipated from courtly taste, while Voltaire *perfected* it.

102

A remark for philologists.— That some books are so valuable and so royal that whole generations of scholars are well employed if their labors to preserve these books in a state that is pure and intelligible—philology exists in order to fortify this faith again and again. It presupposes that there is no lack of those rare human beings (even if one does not see them) who really know how to use such valuable books—presumably those who write, or could write, books of the same type. I mean that philology presupposes a noble faith—that for the sake of a very few human beings, who always "will come" but are never there, a very large amount of fastidious and even dirty work needs to be done first: all of it is work *in usum Delphinorum.*[50]

103

Of German music.— Today German music is, more than any other, the music of Europe, if only because it alone has given expression to the transformation of Europe through the Revolution.[51] Only German composers know how to lend expression to an excited mass of people, creating an immense artificial noise that does not even need to be very loud—while Italian opera, for example, features only choruses of servants or soldiers but no "people." Moreover, in all German music we hear a profound bourgeois envy of nobility, especially of *esprit* and *élégance* as expressions of a courtly, knightly, old, self-assured society. This music is not like that of Goethe's singer outside the gate, which is also appreciated in the great hall of the castle, by the king; the idea is not: "The knights had a courageous look, The fair looked at their laps."[52] Even the Graces do not appear in German music without being accompanied by a bad conscience; only with Charm, the rural sister of the Graces, can the Germans begin to feel wholly moral— and from that point on, more and more so, all the way up to their rapturous, scholarly, and often saturnine "sublimity"— à la Beethoven.

---

[50] *In* (or: *ad*) *usum Delphini:* originally, an edition of Greek or Roman classics, prepared especially for the Dauphin, i.e., the crown prince of France. Nietzsche uses the plural to refer, figuratively speaking, to future royalty.

[51] The French Revolution.

[52] These lines are from Goethe's ballad, "The Singer" (*Der Sänger*), which begins with the king's words: "What do I hear outside the gate . . ." The singer sings for his own pleasure, but the king has him brought inside, is delighted with his music, and offers him a splendid golden chain. The singer turns it down, asks for a cup of the best wine instead, drains it, and leaves gratefully, to go on singing "as birds sing."

If you want to imagine the human being that goes with *this* music, merely imagine Beethoven as he appears beside Goethe— say, at their encounter in Teplitz: as semi-barbarism beside culture, as the people beside nobility, as the good-natured human being next to the good—who is more than merely a "good" human being—as the visionary beside the artist, as the man in need of comfort next to the man who *is* comforted, as the man of exaggeration and suspicion next to one who is fairminded, as the mope and self-tormentor, who is foolishly ecstatic, blissfully unhappy, guilelessly extravagant, presumptuous and crude—and in sum, as the "untamed human being": that is what Goethe felt about him and called him—Goethe, the exception among Germans. No music of his rank has yet been found.[53]

Finally, we might ask whether the contempt for melody that is now spreading more and more and the atrophy of the melodic

---

[53] For the basic documents concerning Beethoven's and Goethe's relationship and their encounter in Teplitz, see *Beethoven: Briefe und Gespräche*, ed. Martin Hürlimann (1946), especially pp. 144–57. For a discussion and evaluation, see Kaufmann, *From Shakespeare to Existentialism*, section 5 of the chapter on "Goethe versus Romanticism" (rev. ed., 1960, pp. 83–88).

There was much more to this relationship, and even to the encounter in Teplitz, than the famous incident of the walk during which the two men met the Empress with her court and Beethoven said to Goethe: "Just keep your arm in mine; they have to step aside, not we." But Goethe stood aside and took off his hat, "while Beethoven, his arms crossed in front of his chest, walked on right through the center, between the dukes, and merely moved his hat a little, while they parted on both sides to make room for him, and all of them greeted him cordially."

Beethoven, who all but worshiped Goethe, lectured him not only on this occasion; but Goethe, who would scarcely have taken that kindly from anyone else, wrote his wife, July 19, 1812: "More concentrated, more energetic, more inwardly, I have never yet found any artist." To his friend, Karl Friedrich Zelter, a composer, he wrote on September 2: "His talent amazes me; but his personality is unfortunately quite untamed. He is, no doubt, quite right in finding the world detestable, but this scarcely makes it more enjoyable either for himself, or for others. But many excuses and much compassion are in order because he is losing his hearing, which may harm his musical nature less than his social character."

sense in Germany should be understood as democratic bad manners and an aftereffect of the Revolution. For melody delights so openly in lawfulness and has such an antipathy for everything that is still becoming, still unformed and arbitrary, that it sounds like an echo of the *old* order in Europe and like a seduction to go back to that.

104

Of the sound of the German language.— We now know where the language comes from that for a few centuries has been accepted as literary German. The Germans, with their reverence for everything that came from the *court*, have studiously modeled their style on officialdom whenever they had to *write* anything, such as letters, documents, wills, and so forth. To write chancery German meant writing like the court and government and was elegant compared to the German of the city in which one happened to live. Eventually one drew the consequence of also speaking as one wrote; that way one became still more elegant in the forms of the words used, in the choice of words and phrases, and ultimately also in sound. One affected the tone of the court when one spoke, and in the end this affectation became second nature.

Perhaps nothing quite like this has happened anywhere else —the triumph of the written style over speech, and the affectation and snobbery of a whole people as the basis for a common language that transcended dialects. I believe that the sound of the German language during the Middles Ages and especially after that was profoundly rustic and vulgar. During the last few centuries it has become a little more elegant primarily because one was compelled to imitate so many French, Italian, and Spanish sounds, which was especially true of the German (and Austrian) nobility who simply could not manage with their mother tongue. But in spite of this practice, German must have sounded intolerably vulgar to Montaigne or, even more so, Racine; and to this day, German travelers in the midst of an Italian mob still sound very rude, woodsy, and hoarse, as if they came from smoky rooms and impolite regions.

Now I note that once again the former admirers of officialdom are succumbing rapidly to a similar craving for an elegant tone, and the Germans are submitting to a most peculiar "acoustic spell" that in the long run could become a real danger to the German language—for one would seek in vain all over Europe to find more abhorrent sounds. Something scornful, cold, indifferent, and careless in one's voice—that is what the Germans now consider elegant. I hear the good will to achieve such elegance in the voices of young officials, teachers, women, merchants; even little girls are beginning to imitate this officers' German. For it is the officers—specifically Prussian officers— who have set this tone, although as military men and specialists these same officers possess an admirably tactful modesty from which all Germans could learn something (including German professors and composers!). But as soon as he speaks and moves, the German officer is the most immodest and distasteful figure in old Europe—quite unselfconsciously, no doubt. Nor are our dear Germans aware of this when they admire him as the paragon of the highest and most elegant society and gladly let him "set the tone." And that is precisely what he does. First of all, the sergeants and noncommissioned officers imitate and coarsen his tone. Just listen to the sound of the commands whose roar surrounds the German cities now that they drill outside all gates[54]: what arrogance, what raging sense of authority, what scornful coldness speak out of this roaring! Could the Germans really be a musical people?

Unquestionably, the Germans are becoming militarized in the sound of their language. Probably, once they are accustomed to *speaking* in a military tone they will eventually also write that way. Becoming accustomed to certain sounds has a profound effect on character; soon one acquires the words and phrases and eventually also the ideas that go with these sounds. Perhaps the Germans have already begun to write like officers; perhaps I merely read too little of what is now written in Germany—but there is one thing I know much more certainly: the public German proclamations that are heard in other countries, too, are not inspired by German music but by this new

---

[54] Whether Nietzsche himself was conscious of this or not, there is a nice contrast here to Goethe's singer outside the gate.

sound of distasteful arrogance. In almost every speech of the foremost German statesman,[55] even when he is heard only through his imperial mouthpiece,[56] we hear an accent that repels and disgusts the ears of foreigners. But the Germans tolerate it—they tolerate themselves.

105

The Germans as artists.— When the Germans really work up a passion (and not merely the good will to feel a passion, as they usually do), they behave as they cannot help but behave and do not give any thought to their conduct. Actually, their behavior at such times is very clumsy and ugly, as if it were totally lacking in tact and melody, and the spectators merely feel pained or touched—unless the Germans rise into the sphere of rapture and sublimity of which some passions are capable. When that happens, even Germans become *beautiful*. A vague sense of the heights that are required before beauty pours her magic even upon Germans drives German artists into heights and superheights and into excesses of passion—in other words, a really deep craving to rise beyond, or at least look beyond, ugliness and clumsiness toward a better, lighter, more southern, sunnier world. Thus their cramps are often no more than signs that they would like to *dance*—these poor bears in whom hidden nymphs and sylvan gods are carrying on—and at times even higher deities!

106

Music as an advocate.— "I am thirsting for a composer," said an innovator to his disciple, "who would learn my ideas from me and transpose them into his language; that way, I should reach men's ears and hearts far better. With music one can seduce men to every error and every truth: who could refute a tone?" —"Then you would like to be considered irrefutable?" said his disciple.

The innovator replied: "I wish for the seedling to become a

---

[55] Bismarck.
[56] Wilhelm I, whom it was not unfair to call a mouthpiece in this context.

tree. For a doctrine to become a tree, it has to be believed for a good while; for it to be believed, it has to be considered irrefutable. The tree needs storms, doubts, worms, and nastiness to reveal the nature and the strength of the seedling; let it break if it is not strong enough. But a seedling can only be destroyed —not refuted."

When he had said that, his disciple cried impetuously: "But I believe in your cause and consider it so strong that I shall say everything, everything that I still have in my mind against it."

The innovator laughed in his heart and wagged a finger at him. "This kind of discipleship," he said then, "is the best; but it is also the most dangerous, and not every kind of doctrine can endure it."

107

Our ultimate gratitude to art.— If we had not welcomed the arts and invented this kind of cult of the untrue, then the realization of general untruth and mendaciousness that now comes to us through science—the realization that delusion and error are conditions of human knowledge and sensation—would be utterly unbearable. *Honesty* would lead to nausea and suicide. But now there is a counterforce against our honesty that helps us to avoid such consequences: art as the *good* will to appearance. We do not always keep our eyes from rounding off something and, as it were, finishing the poem; and then it is no longer eternal imperfection that we carry across the river of becoming—then we have the sense of carrying a *goddess*, and feel proud and childlike as we perform this service. As an aesthetic phenomenon existence is still *bearable* for us,[57] and

---

[57] This is an allusion to *The Birth of Tragedy* where Nietzsche said "it is only as an *aesthetic phenomenon* that existence and the world are eternally *justified*" (section 5 and again 24: BWN, 52 and 141). Obviously, *bearable* is not the same as *justified*, and the mood of what follows above is very different from the mood of *The Birth of Tragedy*. Nevertheless, Nietzsche uses similar language to remind us of his first book because it was there that he first raised the problem of the relationship of art to science. But at that time he had still lacked the conception of "gay science."

art furnishes us with eyes and hands and above all the good conscience to be *able* to turn ourselves into such a phenomenon. At times we need a rest from ourselves by looking upon, by looking *down* upon, ourselves and, from an artistic distance, laughing *over* ourselves or weeping *over* ourselves. We must discover the *hero* no less than the *fool* in our passion for knowledge; we must occasionally find pleasure in our folly, or we cannot continue to find pleasure in our wisdom. Precisely because we are at bottom grave and serious human beings—really, more weights than human beings—nothing does us as much good as a *fool's cap*: we need it in relation to ourselves—we need all exuberant, floating, dancing, mocking, childish, and blissful art lest we lose the *freedom above things* that our ideal demands of us. It would mean a *relapse* for us, with our irritable honesty, to get involved entirely in morality and, for the sake of the over-severe demands that we make on ourselves in these matters, to become virtuous monsters and scarecrows. We should be *able* also to stand *above* morality[58]—and not only to *stand* with the anxious stiffness of a man who is afraid of slipping and falling any moment, but also to *float* above it and *play*. How then could we possibly dispense with art—and with the fool? —And as long as you are in any way *ashamed* before yourselves, you do not yet belong with us.[59]

---

[58] This sentence together with the immediately preceding one illuminates Nietzsche's "immoralism" and his notorious phrase, "beyond good and evil."

[59] The motif sounded here is crucial for an understanding of *The Gay Science*, for an appreciation of the Prelude in rhymes and the Appendix of songs, and for much of Nietzsche's later work, notably including *Zarathustra, The Case of Wagner,* and *Ecce Homo.* Not Nietzsche, but most of his interpreters, commentators, and translators, lacked the ability to laugh at themselves. Cf. section 275 below: Book III ends on the same note.

BOOK THREE

108

New struggles.— After Buddha was dead, his shadow was still shown for centuries in a cave—a tremendous, gruesome shadow. God is dead;[1] but given the way of men, there may still be caves for thousands of years in which his shadow will be shown. —And we—we still have to vanquish his shadow, too.

109

Let us beware.— Let us beware of thinking that the world is a living being. Where should it expand? On what should it feed? How could it grow and multiply? We have some notion of the nature of the organic; and we should not reinterpret the exceedingly derivative, late, rare, accidental, that we perceive only on the crust of the earth and make of it something essential, universal, and eternal, which is what those people do who call the universe an organism. This nauseates me. Let us even beware of believing that the universe is a machine: it is certainly not constructed for one purpose, and calling it a "machine" does it far too much honor.

Let us beware of positing generally and everywhere anything as elegant as the cyclical movements of our neighboring stars;

---

[1] This is the first occurrence of this famous formulation in Nietzsche's books. We encounter it again in section 125 below, which has been anthologized again and again after it was quoted in the chapter on "The Death of God and the Revaluation" in the first edition of Kaufmann (1950), and then included in *The Portable Nietzsche*. It even brought into being a predictably stillborn movement in Christian theology that created a short-lived sensation in the United States. But most of those who have made so much of Nietzsche's pronouncement that "God is dead" have failed to take note of its other occurrences in his works which obviously furnish the best clues to his meaning. The most important passages include section 343 below and seven passages in *Zarathustra* (VPN, pp. 124f., 191, 202, 294, 371–79, 398f., and 426). This list includes only places in which death or dying are mentioned expressly. No less important are sections 109–56.

even a glance into the Milky Way raises doubts whether there are not far coarser and more contradictory movements there, as well as stars with eternally linear paths, etc. The astral order in which we live is an exception; this order and the relative duration that depends on it have again made possible an exception of exceptions: the formation of the organic. The total character of the world, however, is in all eternity chaos—in the sense not of a lack of necessity but of a lack of order, arrangement, form, beauty, wisdom, and whatever other names there are for our aesthetic anthropomorphisms. Judged from the point of view of our reason, unsuccessful attempts are by all odds the rule, the exceptions are not the secret aim, and the whole musical box repeats eternally its tune[2] which may never be called a melody—and ultimately even the phrase "unsuccessful attempt" is too anthropomorphic and reproachful. But how could we reproach or praise the universe? Let us beware of attributing to it heartlessness and unreason or their opposites: it is neither perfect nor beautiful, nor noble, nor does it wish to become any of these things; it does not by any means strive to imitate man. None of our aesthetic and moral judgments apply to it. Nor does it have any instinct for self-preservation or any other instinct; and it does not observe any laws either. Let us beware of saying that there are laws in nature. There are only necessities: there is nobody who commands, nobody who obeys, nobody who trespasses. Once you know that there are no purposes, you also know that there is no accident; for it is only beside a world of purposes that the word "accident" has meaning. Let us beware of saying that death is opposed to life. The living is merely a type of what is dead, and a very rare type.

Let us beware of thinking that the world eternally creates new things. There are no eternally enduring substances; matter is as much of an error as the God of the Eleatics.[3] But when shall we ever be done with our caution and care? When will

---

[2] This is an allusion to the doctrine of the eternal recurrence (see sections 285 and 341 below).

[3] A group of early Greek philosophers who lived in Southern Italy. The most famous among them, Parmenides, was born about 510 B.C.

all these shadows of God cease to darken our minds?[4] When will we complete our de-deification of nature? When may we begin to *"naturalize"* humanity in terms of a pure, newly discovered, newly redeemed nature?[5]

110

Origin of knowledge.— Over immense periods of time the intellect produced nothing but errors. A few of these proved to be useful and helped to preserve the species: those who hit upon or inherited these had better luck in their struggle for themselves and their progeny. Such erroneous articles of faith, which were continually inherited, until they became almost part of the basic endowment of the species, include the following: that there are enduring things; that there are equal things; that there are things, substances, bodies; that a thing is what it appears to be; that our will is free; that what is good for me is also good in itself. It was only very late that such propositions were denied and doubted; it was only very late that truth emerged—as the weakest form of knowledge. It seemed that one was unable to live with it: our organism was prepared for the opposite; all its higher functions, sense perception and every kind of sensation worked with those basic errors which had been incorporated since time immemorial. Indeed, even in the realm of knowledge these propositions became the norms according to which "true" and "untrue" were determined— down to the most remote regions of logic.

Thus the *strength* of knowledge does not depend on its degree of truth but on its age, on the degree to which it has been incorporated, on its character as a condition of life. Where life and knowledge seemed to be at odds there was never any real fight, but denial and doubt were simply considered madness. Those exceptional thinkers, like the Eleatics, who never-

---

[4] Here, if not earlier, it becomes clear how continuous this section is with 108 and what has been *the central motif of section 109:* what Nietzsche goes on to call the "de-deification" of nature.

[5] "Naturalize" is here used in the sense of naturalism, as opposed to supernaturalism. Man is to be reintegrated into nature.

theless posited and clung to the opposites of the natural errors,
believed that it was possible to *live* in accordance with these
opposites: they invented the sage as the man who was unchangeable and impersonal, the man of the universality of intuition who was One and All at the same time, with a special
capacity for his inverted knowledge: they had the faith that
their knowledge was also the principle of *life*. But in order to
claim all of this, they had to *deceive* themselves about their
own state: they had to attribute to themselves, fictitiously, impersonality and changeless duration; they had to misapprehend
the nature of the knower; they had to deny the role of the
impulses in knowledge; and quite generally they had to conceive of reason as a completely free and spontaneous activity.
They shut their eyes to the fact that they, too, had arrived at
their propositions through opposition to common sense, or
owing to a desire for tranquillity, for sole possession, or for
dominion. The subtler development of honesty and skepticism
eventually made these people, too, impossible; their ways of
living and judging were seen to be also dependent upon the
primeval impulses and basic errors of all sentient existence.

This subtler honesty and skepticism came into being wherever
two contradictory sentences appeared to be *applicable* to life
because *both* were compatible with the basic errors, and it was
therefore possible to argue about the higher or lower degree of
utility for life; also wherever new propositions, though not useful for life, were also evidently not harmful to life: in such
cases there was room for the expression of an intellectual play
impulse, and honesty and skepticism were innocent and happy
like all play. Gradually, the human brain became full of such
judgments and convictions, and a ferment, struggle, and lust for
power[6] developed in this tangle. Not only utility and delight but
every kind of impulse took sides in this fight about "truths."
The intellectual fight became an occupation, an attraction, a
profession, a duty, something dignified—and eventually knowledge and the striving for the true found their place as a need
among other needs. Henceforth not only faith and conviction

---

[6] *Machtgelüst.* Written before Nietzsche's proclamation of "the will to
power."

but also scrutiny, denial, mistrust, and contradiction became a *power*; all "evil" instincts were subordinated to knowledge, employed in her service, and acquired the splendor of what is permitted, honored, and useful—and eventually even the eye and innocence of the *good*.

Thus knowledge became a piece of life itself, and hence a continually growing power—until eventually knowledge collided with those primeval basic errors: two lives, two powers, both in the same human being. A thinker is now that being in whom the impulse for truth and those life-preserving errors clash for their first fight, after the impulse for truth has proved to be also a life-preserving power. Compared to the significance of this fight, everything else is a matter of indifference: the ultimate question about the conditions of life has been posed here, and we confront the first attempt to answer this question by experiment. To what extent can truth endure incorporation? That is the question; that is the experiment.

111

Origin of the logical.— How did logic come into existence in man's head? Certainly out of illogic, whose realm originally must have been immense. Innumerable beings who made inferences in a way different from ours perished; for all that, their ways might have been truer. Those, for example, who did not know how to find often enough what is "equal" as regards both nourishment and hostile animals—those, in other words, who subsumed things too slowly and cautiously—were favored with a lesser probability of survival than those who guessed immediately upon encountering similar instances that they must be equal. The dominant tendency, however, to treat as equal what is merely similar—an illogical tendency, for nothing is really equal—is what first created any basis for logic.

In order that the concept of substance could originate—which is indispensable for logic although in the strictest sense nothing real corresponds to it— it was likewise necessary that for a long time one did not see nor perceive the changes in things. The beings that did not see so precisely had an advantage over those that saw everything "in flux." At bottom, every high degree of caution in making inferences and every skeptical tendency constitute a great danger for life. No living beings would have survived if the opposite tendency—to affirm rather than suspend judgment, to err and *make up* things rather than wait, to assent rather than negate, to pass judgment rather than be just—had not been bred to the point where it became extraordinarily strong.[7]

The course of logical ideas and inferences in our brain today corresponds to a process and a struggle among impulses that are, taken singly, very illogical and unjust. We generally experience only the result of this struggle because this primeval mechanism now runs its course so quickly and is so well concealed.

112

Cause and effect.— "Explanation" is what we call it, but it is "description" that distinguishes us from older stages of knowledge and science. Our descriptions are better—we do not explain any more than our predecessors. We have uncovered a manifold one-after-another where the naive man and inquirer of older cultures saw only two separate things. "Cause" and "effect" is what one says; but we have merely perfected the image of becoming without reaching beyond the image or behind it. In every case the series of "causes" confronts us much more completely, and we infer: first, this and that has to precede in order that this or that may then follow—but this does not involve any *comprehension*. In every chemical process, for example, quality appears as a "miracle," as ever; also, every locomotion; nobody has "explained" a push. But how could we possibly explain anything? We operate only with things that do not exist: lines, planes, bodies, atoms, divisible time spans, divisible spaces. How should explanations be at all possible when we first turn everything into an *image*, our image! It will do to consider science as an attempt to humanize

---

[7] This section illuminates Nietzsche's insistence that, as he put it in an often quoted note in *The Will to Power* (#493), "Truth is the kind of error without which a certain species could not live."

things as faithfully as possible; as we describe things and their one-after-another, we learn how to describe ourselves more and more precisely. Cause and effect: such a duality probably never exists; in truth we are confronted by a continuum out of which we isolate a couple of pieces, just as we perceive motion only as isolated points and then infer it without ever actually seeing it. The suddenness with which many effects stand out misleads us; actually, it is sudden only for us. In this moment of suddenness there is an infinite number of processes that elude us. An intellect that could see cause and effect as a continuum and a flux and not, as we do, in terms of an arbitrary division and dismemberment, would repudiate the concept of cause and effect and deny all conditionality.

113

On the doctrine of poisons.— So many things have to come together for scientific thinking to originate; and all these necessary strengths had to be invented, practiced, and cultivated separately. As long as they were still separate, however, they frequently had an altogether different effect than they do now that they are integrated into scientific thinking and hold each other in check. Their effect was that of poisons; for example, that of the impulse to doubt, to negate, to wait, to collect, to dissolve. Many hecatombs of human beings were sacrificed before these impulses learned to comprehend their coexistence and to feel that they were all functions of one organizing force within one human being. And even now the time seems remote when artistic energies and the practical wisdom of life will join with scientific thinking to form a higher organic system in relation to which scholars, physicians, artists, and legislators—as we know them at present—would have to look like paltry relics of ancient times.

114

How far the moral sphere extends.— As soon as we see a new image, we immediately construct it with the aid of all our previous experiences, *depending on the degree* of our honesty and justice. All experiences are moral experiences, even in the realm of sense perception.[8]

115

The four errors.[9]— Man has been educated by his errors. First, he always saw himself only incompletely; second, he endowed himself with fictitious attributes; third, he placed himself in a false order of rank in relation to animals and nature; fourth, he invented ever new tables of goods and always accepted them for a time as eternal and unconditional: as a result of this, now one and now another human impulse and state held first place and was ennobled because it was esteemed so highly. If we removed the effects of these four errors, we should also remove humanity, humaneness, and "human dignity."

116

Herd instinct.— Wherever we encounter a morality, we also encounter valuations and an order of rank of human impulses and actions. These valuations and orders of rank are always expressions of the needs of a community and herd: whatever benefits it most—and second most, and third most—that is also considered the first standard for the value of all individuals. Morality trains the individual to be a function of the herd and to ascribe value to himself only as a function. The conditions for the preservation of different communities were very different; hence there were very different moralities. Considering essential changes in the forms of future herds and communi-

---

[8] This is the transition from the first part of Book III, which is cosmological-epistemological, to the second part, which deals with morality. Section 108 is best seen as a prologue to Book III. But it should be noted how the final sentences of sections 109, 110, and 113 point to Nietzsche's central concern with what is to become of man—a concern that is moral in the broad sense of that word although Nietzsche's views may seem "immoral" to some apologists for traditional morality.

[9] *Twilight of the Idols* contains a chapter with the title, "The Four Great Errors" (VPN, 492–501). Nietzsche does not repeat himself there, but there is a striking continuity in his thought.

ties, states and societies, we can prophesy that there will yet be very divergent moralities. Morality is herd instinct in the individual.

117

Herd remorse.— During the longest and most remote periods of the human past, the sting of conscience was not at all what it is now. Today one feels responsible only for one's will and actions, and one finds one's pride in oneself. All our teachers of law start from this sense of self and pleasure in the individual as if this had always been the fount of law. But during the longest period of the human past nothing was more terrible than to feel that one stood by oneself. To be alone, to experience things by oneself, neither to obey nor to rule, to be an individual—that was not a pleasure but a punishment; one was sentenced "to individuality."[10] Freedom of thought was considered discomfort itself. While we experience law and submission as compulsion and loss, it was egoism that was formerly experienced as something painful and as real misery. To be a self and to esteem oneself according to one's own weight and measure—that offended taste in those days. An inclination to do this would have been considered madness; for being alone was associated with every misery and fear. In those days, "free will" was very closely associated with a bad conscience; and the more unfree one's actions were and the more the herd instinct rather than any personal sense found expression in an action, the more moral one felt. Whatever harmed the herd, whether the individual had wanted it or not wanted it, prompted the sting of conscience in the individual—and in his neighbor, too, and even in the whole herd. —There is no point on which we have learned to think and feel more differently.

118

Benevolence.— Is it virtuous when a cell transforms itself into a function of a stronger cell? It has no alternative. And

---

[10] *verurteilt zum Individuum*: In German, Jean-Paul Sartre's celebrated dictum that man is "condemned to be free" (*L'être et le Néant*, 1943, p. 515; *Being and Nothingness*, transl. Hazel E. Barnes, 1956, p. 439) is rendered and often quoted as *zur Freiheit verurteilt.*

is it evil when the stronger cell assimilates the weaker? It also has no alternative; it follows necessity, for it strives for super-abundant substitutes and wants to regenerate itself. Hence we should make a distinction in benevolence between the impulse to appropriate and the impulse to submit, and ask whether it is the stronger or the weaker that feels benevolent. Joy and desire appear together in the stronger that wants to transform something into a function; joy and the wish to be desired appear together in the weaker that wants to become a function.

Pity is essentially of the former type: an agreeable impulse of the instinct for appropriation at the sight of what is weaker. But it should be kept in mind that "strong" and "weak" are relative concepts.

119

No altruism!— In many people I find an overwhelmingly forceful and pleasurable desire to be a function: they have a very refined sense for all those places where precisely *they* could "function" and push in those directions. Examples include those women who transform themselves into some function of a man that happens to be underdeveloped in him, and thus become his purse or his politics or his sociability. Such beings preserve themselves best when they find a fitting place in another organism; if they fail to do this, they become grumpy, irritated, and devour themselves.

120

Health of the soul.— The popular medical formulation of morality that goes back to Ariston of Chios,[11] "virtue is the health of the soul," would have to be changed to become useful, at least to read: *"your* virtue is the health of *your* soul." For there is no health as such, and all attempts to define a

---

[11] A pupil of Zeno, the founder of Stoicism. Ariston founded an independent branch of this school and had great influence in Athens around 250 B.C. Nietzsche probably had in mind Plutarch's *Moralia*, 440: "Ariston of Chios also considered virtue *one* in its essential nature and called it health . . ." But well over a hundred years earlier, Plato had suggested in his *Republic*, 444, that justice is the health of the soul; and it is odd that Nietzsche overlooked this.

thing that way have been wretched failures. Even the determination of what is healthy for your *body* depends on your goal, your horizon, your energies, your impulses, your errors, and above all on the ideals and phantasms of your soul. Thus there are innumerable healths of the body; and the more we allow the unique and incomparable to raise its head again, and the more we abjure the dogma of the "equality of men," the more must the concept of a *normal* health, along with a normal diet and the normal course of an illness, be abandoned by medical men. Only then would the time have come to reflect on the health and illness of the *soul*,[12] and to find the peculiar virtue of each man in the health of his soul. In one person, of course, this health could look like its opposite in another person.

Finally, the great question would still remain whether we can really dispense with illness—even for the sake of our virtue— and whether our thirst for knowledge and self-knowledge in particular does not require the sick soul as much as the healthy, and whether, in brief, the will to health alone, is not a prejudice, cowardice, and perhaps a bit of very subtle barbarism and backwardness.[13]

121

Life no argument.— We have arranged for ourselves a world in which we can live—by positing bodies, lines, planes, causes and effects, motion and rest, form and content; without these articles of faith nobody now could endure life. But that does not prove them. Life is no argument. The conditions of life might include error.[14]

---

[12] *Seele* was the word also used by Freud where translators speak of the soul, the *psyche* or, in compounds, use "psychic."

[13] Freud's quest for self-knowledge may furnish an even more obvious example than Nietzsche's of the fact that such a search is typically prompted by a sickness of the soul, at least in the case of the great pioneers.

[14] Cf. the first sections of *Beyond Good and Evil*, especially "untruth as a condition of life" in section 4. What kind of error is meant is explained in section 110 (first paragraph) and in sections 111, 112, and 115.

122

Moral skepticism in Christianity.— Christianity, too, has made a great contribution to the enlightenment, and taught moral skepticism very trenchantly and effectively, accusing and embittering men, yet with untiring patience and subtlety; it destroyed the faith in his "virtues" in every single individual; it led to the disappearance from the face of the earth of all those paragons of virtue of whom there was no dearth in antiquity—those popular personalities who, imbued with faith in their own perfection, went about with the dignity of a great matador.

When we today, trained in this Christian school of skepticism, read the moral treatises of the ancients—for example, Seneca and Epictetus—we have a diverting sense of superiority and feel full of secret insights and over-sights: we feel as embarrassed as if a child were talking before an old man, or an over-enthusiastic young beauty before La Rochefoucauld[15]: we know better what virtue is.

In the end, however, we have applied this same skepticism also to all *religious* states and processes, such as sin, repentance, grace, sanctification, and we have allowed the worm to dig so deep that now we have the same sense of subtle superiority and insight when we read any Christian book: we also know religious feelings better! And it is high time to know them well and to describe them well, for the pious people of the old faith are dying out, too. Let us save their image and their type at least for knowledge.

123

Knowledge as more than a mere means.— *Without* this new passion—I mean the passion to know—science would still be promoted; after all, science has grown and matured without it

---

[15] François de La Rochefoucauld (1613–80) whose *Maxims* are among the treasures of French literature. Their literary form and perfection as well as their unsentimental psychological penetration clearly made an impression on Nietzsche. Most of them (there are about seven hundred in all) are no more than two or three lines long; few, more than half a page. Without being at all mechanical or even deductive in manner, the author continually calls attention to the motive of human self-interest.

until now. The good faith in science, the prejudice in its favor that dominates the modern state (and formerly dominated even the church) is actually based on the fact that this unconditional urge and passion has manifested itself so rarely and that science is considered *not* a passion but a mere condition or an "ethos." Often mere *amour-plaisir*[16] of knowledge (curiosity) is felt to be quite sufficient, or *amour-vanité*,[17] being accustomed to it with the ulterior motive of honors and sustenance; for many people it is actually quite enough that they have too much leisure and do not know what to do with it except to read, collect, arrange, observe, and recount—their "scientific impulse" is their boredom.

Pope Leo X once sang the praises of science (in his brief to Beroaldo[18]): he called it the most beautiful ornament and the

---

[16] Love based on pleasure.

[17] Loved based on vanity.

[18] Having purchased a manuscript of the hitherto unpublished first five books of Tacitus's *Annals* (later divided into six) as well as a copy of a printed volume that contained the last six books and the first five books of Tacitus's *History*, Pope Leo X "determined to give to the world as complete an edition as possible; for which purpose he entrusted the manuscript to the younger Filippo Beroaldo, with directions to correct the text, and to superintend the printing of it in an elegant and useful form. In order to reward the editor for his trouble on this occasion, Leo proposed to grant to him an exclusive privilege for the reprinting and sale of the work; and . . . the brief in which this privilege is conceded contains a kind of justification on the part of the pontiff for devoting so much of his attention to the promotion of profane learning . . .

" 'we have considered those pursuits as not the least important which lead to the promotion of literature and useful arts; for we have been accustomed even from our early years to think, that nothing more excellent or more useful has been given by the Creator to mankind, if we except only the knowledge and true worship of himself, than these studies, which not only lead to the ornament and guidance of human life, but are applicable and useful to every particular situation; in adversity consolatory, in prosperity pleasing and honourable; insomuch, that without them we should be deprived of all the grace of life and all the polish of society.' " (William Roscoe, *The Life and Pontificate of Leo the Tenth*, 5th ed., London 1846, vol. I, p. 355f.).

It will be noted that Nietzsche's "quotation" is rather free, and that the pope did not really keep silent about "the knowledge and true worship" of God. But these criticisms do not undermine Nietzsche's point which he actually understates.

greatest pride of our life and a noble occupation in times of happiness as well as unhappiness; and finally he said: "without it all human endeavors would lack any firm foothold—and even with it things are changeable and insecure enough." But this tolerably skeptical pope keeps silent, like all other ecclesiastical eulogists of science, about his ultimate judgment. From his words one might infer, although this is strange enough for such a friend of the arts, that he places science above art; but in the end it is nothing but good manners when he does not speak at this point of what he places high above all of the sciences, too: "revealed truth" and the "eternal salvation of the soul." Compared to that, what are ornaments, pride, entertainment, and the security of life to him? "Science is something second-class, not anything ultimate, unconditional, not an object of passion"—this judgment Leo retained in his soul: the truly Christian judgment about science.

In antiquity the dignity and recognition of science were diminished by the fact that even her most zealous disciples placed the striving for *virtue* first, and one felt that knowledge had received the highest praise when one celebrated it as the best means to virtue. It is something new in history that knowledge wants to be more than a mere means.

124

In the horizon of the infinite.— We have left the land and have embarked. We have burned our bridges behind us— indeed, we have gone farther and destroyed the land behind us. Now, little ship, look out! Beside you is the ocean: to be sure, it does not always roar, and at times it lies spread out like silk and gold and reveries of graciousness. But hours will come when you will realize that it is infinite and that there is nothing more awesome than infinity.[19] Oh, the poor bird that felt free and now strikes the walls of this cage! Woe, when you feel

---

[19] Cf. the poem "Toward New Seas" in the Appendix.

Here the conclusion of the immediately preceding section is seen in a new light. The attempt to vanquish the shadow of God, heralded in section 108, is felt to be awesome—and in the next section the terror is spelled out more fully.

homesick for the land as if it had offered more *freedom*—and there is no longer any "land."

125

The madman.— Have you not heard of that madman who lit a lantern in the bright morning hours, ran to the market place, and cried incessantly: "I seek God! I seek God!" —As many of those who did not believe in God were standing around just then, he provoked much laughter. Has he got lost? asked one. Did he lose his way like a child? asked another. Or is he hiding? Is he afraid of us? Has he gone on a voyage? emigrated? —Thus they yelled and laughed.

The madman jumped into their midst and pierced them with his eyes. "Whither is God?" he cried; "I will tell you. *We have killed him*—you and I. All of us are his murderers. But how did we do this? How could we drink up the sea? Who gave us the sponge to wipe away the entire horizon? What were we doing when we unchained this earth from its sun? Whither is it moving now? Whither are we moving? Away from all suns? Are we not plunging continually? Backward, sideward, forward, in all directions? Is there still any up or down? Are we not straying as through an infinite nothing? Do we not feel the breath of empty space? Has it not become colder? Is not night continually closing in on us? Do we not need to light lanterns in the morning? Do we hear nothing as yet of the noise of the gravediggers who are burying God? Do we smell nothing as yet of the divine decomposition? Gods, too, decompose. God is dead. God remains dead. And we have killed him.

"How shall we comfort ourselves, the murderers of all murderers? What was holiest and mightiest of all that the world has yet owned has bled to death under our knives: who will wipe this blood off us? What water is there for us to clean ourselves? What festivals of atonement, what sacred games shall we have to invent? Is not the greatness of this deed too great for us? Must we ourselves not become gods simply to appear worthy of it? There has never been a greater deed; and whoever is born after us—for the sake of this deed he will belong to a higher history than all history hitherto."

Here the madman fell silent and looked again at his listeners; and they, too, were silent and stared at him in astonishment. At last he threw his lantern on the ground, and it broke into pieces and went out. "I have come too early," he said then; "my time is not yet. This tremendous event is still on its way, still wandering; it has not yet reached the ears of men. Lightning and thunder require time; the light of the stars requires time; deeds, though done, still require time to be seen and heard. This deed is still more distant from them than the most distant stars—*and yet they have done it themselves.*"

It has been related further that on the same day the madman forced his way into several churches and there struck up his *requiem aeternam deo.* Led out and called to account, he is said always to have replied nothing but: "What after all are these churches now if they are not the tombs and sepulchers of God?"[20]

126

Mystical explanations.— Mystical explanations are considered deep. The truth is that they are not even superficial.[21]

---

[20] This is one of the most famous sections in this book. See the first note on section 108 above, which calls attention to other passages in Nietzsche that use the same, or similar, imagery. Above all, however, it should be noted how this section fits into its immediate context, and how the de-deification in section 109 and all of the intermediate sections build up to the parable of the madman. It has often been asked what Nietzsche means by saying that "God is dead." One might fairly answer: what he means is what he says in sections 108 through 125— and in the sections after that. The problem is created in large measure by tearing a section out of its context, on the *false* assumption that what we are offered is merely a random collection of "aphorisms" that are intended for browsing.

[21] Cf. *Twilight of the Idols,* Chapter I, section 27 (VPN, 470)—which *is* an aphorism, and a poor one at that. But although the wording is almost the same, section 126 has its place between 125 and 127 as a meaningful transition, and it makes a point: Mystical explanations are not even superficial explanations—because they are not explanations at all. They only *seem* to explain something.

127

Aftereffects of the most ancient religiosity.— Every thought-less person supposes that will alone is effective; that willing is something simple, a brute datum, underivable, and intelligible by itself. He is convinced that when he does something—strike something, for example—it is he that strikes, and that he did strike because he *willed* it. He does not see any problem here; the feeling of *will* seems sufficient to him not only for the assumption of cause and effect but also for the faith that he *understands* their relationship. He knows nothing of the mechanism of what happened and of the hundredfold fine work that needs to be done to bring about the strike, or of the incapacity of the will in itself to do even the tiniest part of this work. The will is for him a magically effective force; the faith in the will as the cause of effects is the faith in magically effective forces.

Now man believed originally that wherever he saw something happen, a will had to be at work in the background as a cause, and a personal, willing being. Any notion of mechanics was far from his mind. But since man believed, for immense periods of time, only in persons (and not in substances, forces, things, and so forth), the faith in cause and effect became for him the basic faith that he applies wherever anything happens—and this is what he still does instinctively: it is an atavism of the most ancient origin.

The propositions, "no effect without a cause," "every effect in turn a cause" appear as generalizations of much more limited propositions: "no effecting without willing"; "one can have an effect only on beings that will"; "no suffering of an effect is ever pure and without consequences, but all suffering consists of an agitation of the will" (toward action, resistance, revenge, retribution). But in the pre-history of humanity both sets of propositions were identical: the former were not generalizations of the latter, but the latter were commentaries on the former.

When Schopenhauer assumed that all that has being is only a willing, he enthroned a primeval mythology. It seems that he never even attempted an analysis of the will because, like everybody else, he had *faith* in the simplicity and immediacy of all willing—while willing is actually a mechanism that is so well practiced that it all but escapes the observing eye.

Against him I posit these propositions: First, for will to come into being an idea of pleasure and displeasure is needed. Second, when a strong stimulus is experienced as pleasure or displeasure, this depends on the *interpretation* of the intellect which, to be sure, generally does this work without rising to our consciousness: one and the same stimulus can be interpreted as pleasure or displeasure. Third, it is only in intellectual beings that pleasure, displeasure, and will are to be found; the vast majority of organisms has nothing of the sort.[22]

128

The value of prayer.— Prayer has been invented for those people who really never have thoughts of their own and who do not know any elevation of the soul or at least do not notice it when it occurs: what are they to do at sacred sites and in all significant situations in life, where calm and some sort of dignity are called for? To keep them at least from *disturbing* others, the wisdom of all founders of religions, small as well as great, has prescribed to them the formulas of prayers—as mechanical work for the lips that takes some time and requires some exertion of the memory as well as the same fixed posture for hands, feet, and eyes. Let them, like the Tibetans, keep chewing the cud of their "om mane padme hum" innumerable

---

[22] Nietzsche's own doctrine of the will to power led to some modification of these claims. In the chapter "On Self-Overcoming" in *Zarathustra*, Part II (VPN, 225–28) he professed to find a will to power in all living beings, and later on not only in *living* beings. See the chapter on "Power versus Pleasure" in Kaufmann. It is arguable that Nietzsche never successfully harmonized these two strains of his thought: the polemic against the will that is directed, e.g., at Schopenhauer, and the requirements of his own later doctrine of the will to power. See *Beyond Good and Evil*, section 36 (BWN, 237f.), and the chapter on "The Four Great Errors" in *Twilight of the Idols* (VPN, 492–501), as well as a great many notes collected in *The Will to Power* (see the table of contents and index of the Kaufmann edition and especially sections 466–715).

times or, as in Benares, count the name of the god off their fingers, Ram-Ram-Ram (and so on, with or without charm), or honor Vishnu with his thousand names, or Allah with his ninety-nine; or let them use prayer mills and rosaries: the main thing is that this work fixes them for a time and makes them tolerable to look at. Their kind of prayer has been invented for the benefit of the pious who do know thoughts and elevations of their own. But even this type has weary hours when a sequence of venerable words and sounds and a pious routine are welcome. But suppose these rare human beings—the religious person is an exception in every religion—know what to do in such cases; the poor in spirit do not know what to do, and if one forbade them their prayer-rattling one would deprive them of their religion—as Protestantism shows us more and more by the day. What religion wants from the masses is no more than that they should *keep still* with their eyes, hands, legs, and other organs; that way they become more beautiful for a while and—look more like human beings.

129

The conditions for God.— "God himself cannot exist without wise people," said Luther with good reason. But "God can exist even less without unwise people"—that our good Luther did not say.

130

A dangerous resolve.— The Christian resolve to find the world ugly and bad has made the world ugly and bad.

131

Christianity and suicide.— When Christianity came into being, the craving for suicide was immense—and Christianity turned it into a lever of its power. It allowed only two kinds of suicide, dressed them up with the highest dignity and the highest hopes, and forbade all others in a terrifying manner. Only martyrdom and the ascetic's slow destruction of his body were permitted.

132

Against Christianity.— What is now decisive against Christianity is our taste, no longer our reasons.

133

Principle.— An inescapable hypothesis to which humanity must have recourse again and again is more powerful in the long run than the most firmly believed faith in an untruth (the Christian faith, for example). In the long run: that means in this context a hundred thousand years.

134

Pessimists as victims.— Wherever a deep discontent with existence becomes prevalent, it is the aftereffects of some great dietary mistake made by a whole people over a long period of time that are coming to light. Thus the *spread* of Buddhism (*not* its *origin*) depended heavily on the excessive and almost exclusive reliance of the Indians on rice which led to a general loss of vigor. Perhaps the modern European discontent is due to the fact that our forefathers were given to drinking through the entire Middle Ages, thanks to the effects on Europe of the Teutonic taste. The Middle Ages meant the alcohol poisoning of Europe. —The German discontent with life is essentially a winter sickness that is worsened by the effects of stuffy cellar air and the poison of stove fumes in German living rooms.[23]

---

[23] The problem Nietzsche poses is how a very *widespread* "discontent with existence" is to be explained. The notion that it might simply reflect an accurate estimate of existence is ruled out, for the problem concerns not the *origin* of pessimistic world views but their wide acceptance. In that case, one might look for a sociological solution, but Nietzsche here carries his anti-idealism to materialistic extremes, which is not unusual for him (cf. the second chapter of *Ecce Homo,* BWN, 692 ff.), and directs our attention, first of all, to diet. Lack of vitality, which makes for a lack of enthusiasm for the world, is due to an almost exclusive reliance on rice. Instead of proceeding to weigh the evidence for this hypothesis, Nietzsche goes on to charge his countrymen with the alcohol poisoning of Europe—and claims that this may account

135

Origin of sin.— Sin, as it is now experienced wherever Christianity holds sway or has held sway, is a Jewish feeling and a Jewish invention. Regarding this background of all Christian morality, Christianity did aim to "Judaize" the world.[24] How far it has succeeded in Europe is brought out by the fact that Greek antiquity—a world without feelings of sin—still seems so very strange to our sensibility, although whole generations as well as many excellent individuals have expended so much good will on attempts to approach and incorporate this world. "Only if you *repent* will God show you grace"—that would strike a Greek as ridiculous and annoying. He would say: "Maybe slaves feel that way." The Christian presupposes a powerful, overpowering being who enjoys revenge. His power is so great that nobody could possibly harm him, except for his honor. Every sin is a slight to his honor, a *crimen laesae majestatis divinae*[25]—and no more. Contrition, degradation, rolling in the dust—all this is the first and last condition of his grace: in sum, the restoration of his divine honor. Whether the sin has done any other harm, whether it has set in motion some profound calamity that will grow and seize one person after another like a disease and strangle them—this honor-craving Ori-

---

for "the modern European discontent," which is not analyzed at all and might have struck many of his original readers as a figment of his imagination. For Schopenhauer's pessimism had exceedingly little influence in Germany in the nineteenth century, as Nietzsche himself insists in section 357. But all of these remarks have a light touch and are meant to evidence Southern *esprit* as opposed to German heaviness. Lest anyone miss this point, the last sentence suggests that it is no wonder that people who spend the winter indoors in German living rooms should mope; Nietzsche spent his winters in more invigorating air.

[24] "did aim": Nietzsche is indicating his partial agreement with a familiar view. "Judaize" (*"verjüdeln"*), placed in quotes in the original, is a nasty word with strong anti-Semitic overtones. In other words: There is indeed a sense in which the Western world has been "Judaized" —namely insofar as it is permeated by the notion of sin; and this was accomplished by—Christianity.

[25] The crime of an affront to the divine majesty. Nietzsche uses the Latin wording; in English, it is customary to use the French form *lèse-majesté*.

ental in heaven could not care less! Sin is an offense against him, not against humanity. Those who are granted his grace are also granted this carelessness regarding the natural consequences of sin. God and humanity are separated so completely that a sin against humanity is really unthinkable: every deed is to be considered *solely with respect to its supernatural consequences*, without regard for its natural consequences; that is what Jewish feeling demands, for whatever is natural is considered ignoble. The Greeks, on the other hand, were rather closer to the notion that sacrilege, too, might have some nobility—even theft, as in the case of Prometheus; even the slaughter of cattle as the expression of insane envy, as in the case of Ajax—and in their desire to invent some dignity for sacrilege and to incorporate nobility in it, they invented *tragedy*—an art form and a pleasure that have remained essentially and profoundly foreign to the Jew, in spite of all his poetic gifts and his sense for the sublime.

136

The chosen people.— The Jews, who feel that they are the chosen people among all the nations because they are the moral genius among the nations (because they had a *more profound contempt* for the human being in themselves than any other people)—the Jews' enjoyment of their divine monarch and saint is similar to that which the French nobility derived from Louis XIV. This nobility had surrendered all of its power and sovereignty and had become contemptible. In order not to feel this, in order to be able to forget this, one required royal splendor, royal authority and plenitude of power *without equal* to which only the nobility had access. By virtue of this privilege, one rose to the height of the court, and from that vantage point one saw everything beneath oneself and found it contemptible —and thus one got over an irritable conscience. Thus the tower of the royal power was built ever higher into the clouds, and one did not hold back even the last remaining stones of one's own power.[26]

---

[26] The remark in parentheses about contempt should be compared with the rhapsody on "the great contempt" in "Zarathustra's Prologue" (VPN,

137

Speaking in a parable.— A Jesus Christ was possible only in a Jewish landscape—I mean one over which the gloomy and sublime thunder cloud of the wrathful Jehovah was brooding continually. Only here was the rare and sudden piercing of the gruesome and perpetual general day-night by a single ray of the sun experienced as if it were a miracle of "love" and the ray of unmerited "grace." Only here could Jesus dream of his rainbow and his ladder to heaven on which God descended to man. Everywhere else good weather and sunshine were considered the rule and everyday occurrences.

138

Christ's error.— The founder of Christianity thought that there was nothing of which men suffered more than their sins. That was his error—the error of one who felt that he was without sin and who lacked firsthand experience. Thus his soul grew full of that wonderful and fantastic compassion for a misery that even among his people, who had invented sin, was rarely a very great misery. —But the Christians have found a way of vindicating their master since then and of sanctifying his error by making it "come true."

139

The color of the passions.— People like St. Paul have an evil eye for the passions: all they know of the passions is what is dirty, disfiguring, and heartbreaking; hence their idealistic tendency aims at the annihilation of the passions, and they find

---

125f.): "What is the greatest experience you can have? It is the hour of the great contempt. . . ."

The final point of this section invites comparison with Ludwig Feuerbach (1804–72), who argued that man strips himself of all virtue to endow God with it. This is an immensely fruitful suggestion but much more applicable to Martin Luther than to the Hebrew prophets. Nietzsche himself paid very perceptive tribute to the Old Testament in passages cited in Kaufmann, 290 and 299–301.

See also the discussion of Germans and Jews in the Introduction.

perfect purity in the divine. Very differently from St. Paul and the Jews, the Greeks directed their idealistic tendency precisely toward the passions and loved, elevated, gilded, and deified them. Evidently, passion made them feel not only happier but also purer and more divine. —And the Christians? Did they want to become Jews in this respect? Did they perhaps succeed?

140

Too Jewish.— If God wished to become an object of love, he should have given up judging and justice first of all; a judge, even a merciful judge, is no object of love. The founder of Christianity was not refined enough in his feelings at this point —being a Jew.[27]

141

Too Oriental.— What? A god who loves men, provided only that they believe in him, and who casts an evil eye and threats upon anyone who does not believe in this love? What? A love encapsuled in if-clauses attributed to an almighty god? A love that has not even mastered the feelings of honor and vindictiveness? How Oriental this is! "If I love you, is that your concern?"[28] is a sufficient critique of the whole of Christianity.

---

[27] See the discussion of Germans and Jews in the Introduction.

[28] This beautiful quotation is from Goethe's *Dichtung und Wahrheit*, Part III (1814), Book 14, p. 442. It is from Goethe's discussion of Spinoza's dictum, in the *Ethics*, "Whoever loves God must not expect God to love him in return"; and it also refers back to Goethe's own *Wilhelm Meisters Lehrjahre*, 4.9. The formulation there differs very slightly from that of 1814.

It is surely ironical, though this point escaped Nietzsche, that the words he opposes to the outlook that is "too Oriental" were construed by Goethe himself as a paraphrase of Spinoza—who was a Jew.

For Nietzsche's view of the Teutons, see sections 134 and 149; for his condemnation of "nationalism and race hatred" as "the national scabies of the heart" and of "the mendacious racial self-admiration and racial indecency . . . in Germany today" see section 377.

The Goethe quotation appears also in *The Case of Wagner*, section 2 (BWN, 615).

142

Frankincense.— Buddha says: "Do not flatter your bene-factor!"[29] Repeat this saying in a Christian church: right away it clears the air of everything Christian.

143

The greatest advantage of polytheism.— For an individual to posit his own ideal and to derive from it his own law, joys, and rights—that may well have been considered hitherto as the most outrageous human aberration and as idolatry itself. The few who dared as much always felt the need to apologize to themselves, usually by saying: "It wasn't I! Not I! But *a god* through me." The wonderful art and gift of creating gods—polytheism—was the medium through which this impulse could discharge, purify, perfect, and ennoble itself; for origi-nally it was a very undistinguished impulse, related to stub-bornness, disobedience, and envy. Hostility against this impulse to have an ideal of one's own was formerly the central law of all morality. There was only one norm, *man*; and every people thought that it possessed this one ultimate norm. But above and outside, in some distant overworld, one was permitted to behold a *plurality of norms*; one god was not considered a denial of another god, nor blasphemy against him. It was here that the luxury of individuals was first permitted; it was here that one first honored the rights of individuals. The invention of gods, heroes, and overmen of all kinds, as well as near-men and

---

[29] Cf. Emerson's *Essays*, "Gifts," the end of the third paragraph from the end: "It is a great happiness to get off without injury and heart-burning, from one who has had the ill luck to be served by you. It is a very onerous business, this of being served, and the debtor naturally wishes to give you a slap. A golden text for these gentlemen is that which I so admire in the Buddhist, who never thanks, and who says, 'Do not flatter your benefactors.' " Hubbard, in his *Nietzsche und Emerson* (p. 130), quotes passages Nietzsche marked in his copy of Emerson's *Versuche* and notes that Nietzsche marked this passage heavily in the margin and underlined the quotation at the end; but Hubbard fails to note that Nietzsche used it.

undermen,[30] dwarfs, fairies, centaurs, satyrs, demons, and devils was the inestimable preliminary exercise for the justification of the egoism and sovereignty of the individual: the freedom that one conceded to a god in his relation to other gods—one eventually also granted to oneself in relation to laws, customs, and neighbors.

Monotheism, on the other hand, this rigid consequence of the doctrine of one normal human type—the faith in one normal god beside whom there are only pseudo-gods—was perhaps the greatest danger that has yet confronted humanity. It threatened us with the premature stagnation that, as far as we can see, most other species have long reached; for all of them believe in one normal type and ideal for their species, and they have translated the morality of mores definitively into their own flesh and blood.[31] In polytheism the free-spiriting and many-spiriting[32] of man attained its first preliminary form—the strength to create for ourselves our own new eyes—and ever again new eyes that are even more our own: hence man alone among all the animals has no eternal horizons and perspectives.

144

Religious wars.— Religious war has signified the greatest progress of the masses hitherto; for it proves that the mass has

---

[30] This is the first appearance of "overmen" (*Uebermenschen,* also known as "supermen") in Nietzsche's books. The term is found in German literature before Nietzsche a few times; Nietzsche's own characteristic use of it is introduced in the Prologue to his next book, *Zarathustra. Untermensch* (underman, for a subhuman man) is not rare; nor is *Unterwelt* (underworld); but overworld (*Ueberwelt*) is most unusual. For further discussion of this passage and of "overman" see Chapter 11 of Kaufmann, 307ff.

[31] In other words: the morality of mores (section 43 above) has become not only their second nature but their nature.

[32] *die Freigeisterei und Vielgeisterei:* The former term, coined by Nietzsche, is used in his letters to refer to his aphoristic works, beginning with *Human, All-too-Human,* and ending with the present book—the works in which he had found himself as a free spirit. In this text, of course, the reference is not obviously autobiographical. The second term, also Nietzsche's, depends on another meaning of "spirit" and is explained in the sentence above.

begun to treat concepts with respect. Religious wars start only after the more refined quarrels between sects have refined reason in general to the point where even the mob becomes subtle and takes trifles seriously, and actually considers it possible that the "eternal salvation of the soul" might hinge on small differences between concepts.

145

Danger for vegetarians.— A diet that consists predominantly of rice leads to the use of opium and narcotics, just as a diet that consists predominantly of potatoes leads to the use of liquor. But it also has subtler effects that include ways of thinking and feeling that have narcotic effects. This agrees with the fact that those who promote narcotic ways of thinking and feelings, like some Indian gurus, praise a diet that is entirely vegetarian and would like to impose that as a law upon the masses. In this way they want to create and increase the need that they are in a position to satisfy.

146

German hopes.— Let us not forget that names of peoples are usually abusive names. The Tartars, for example, are literally "the dogs"; that is what the Chinese called them. "Germans" originally meant "heathen." That is what the Goths after their conversion called the great mass of their unbaptized kindred tribes, in accordance with their translation of the Septuagint which uses for the heathen the word that in Greek means "the nations." See Ulfilas.[33]

---

[33] Ulfilas, "the father of Teutonic literature," was a fourth-century Gothic apostle who translated the Bible into Gothic.

Nietzsche's friend Peter Gast raised a question about section 146 when he read the printer's proofs, and Nietzsche's reply of July 30, 1882, may serve as a commentary here:

"The Septuagint is the *Greek* translation of the *Old* Testament. Here the 'heathen' are mentioned innumerable times ('why do the heathen rage—'). The Greek word used is always *ethnē* ('nations' [a correct translation of the Hebrew *goyim*])—and Ulfilas translates 'nations'

It is not too late for the Germans to turn their abusive name into a name of honor by becoming the first *un-Christian* nation in Europe. Schopenhauer gave them credit for having very pronounced predispositions in that direction. That would be a way of fulfilling the words of *Luther* who taught them to be un-Roman and to say: "Here *I* stand. *I* cannot do otherwise."[34]

147

Question and answer.— What is it that savage tribes today accept first of all from Europeans? Liquor and Christianity, the European narcotics. And of what do they perish most quickly? Of the European narcotics.

148

Where reformations occur.— At the time when the church was most corrupt, the church in Germany was least corrupt. That is why the Reformation occurred here, showing that here even the beginnings of corruption were felt to be intolerable. Relatively speaking, no people has ever been more Christian than the Germans of Luther's time; their Christian civilization was ready to burst into hundreds of blossoms; only one more night was needed—but this night brought the storm that put an end to everything.

149

The failure of reformations.— Among the Greeks several attempts to found new Greek religions failed—which speaks for the higher civilization of the Greeks even in rather early

---

literally as *thiuda, thiudos* [the word from which *deutsch*—the German word for "German"—is derived] (I no longer recall the correct ending). For *thiuda* then *meant* 'nation' ["*Volk*"] (the question of the *etymology* of the word is altogether *independent*!). Now I claim: The Goths came to associate *their* word for nations with the *meaning* 'heathen'—just as the Greek-speaking Christians had done with their *ethnē* [and the ancient Hebrews with *goyim*]."

[34] Luther's words at the Diet of Worms in 1520 when he refused to recant his new doctrines unless refuted from Scripture.

times. It suggests that there must have been in Greece at an early time large numbers of diverse individuals whose diverse needs and miseries could not be taken care of with a single prescription of faith and hope.

Pythagoras and Plato, perhaps also Empedocles, and much earlier yet the Orphic enthusiasts, aimed to found new religions; and the first two had souls and talents that fitted them so obviously for the role of religious founders that one can scarcely marvel enough that they should have failed. Yet all they managed to found were sects. Whenever the reformation of a whole people fails and it is only sects that elevate their leader, we may conclude that the people has become relatively heterogeneous and has begun to move away from rude herd instincts and the morality of mores[35]: they are hovering in an interesting intermediate position that is usually dismissed as a mere decay of morals and corruption, although in fact it proclaims that the egg is approaching maturity and that the eggshell is about to be broken.

That Luther's Reformation succeeded in the North suggests that the north of Europe was retarded compared to the south, and still knew only rather homogeneous and monotonous needs. Indeed, Europe would never have become Christian in the first place if the culture of the ancient world in the south had not gradually been barbarized through an excessive admixture of Teutonic barbarian blood, thus losing its cultural superiority.[36]

The more general and unconditional the influence of an individual or the idea of an individual can be, the more homogeneous and the lower must the mass be that is influenced, while counter-movements give evidence of counter-needs that also want to be satisfied and recognized. Conversely, we may always infer that a civilization is really high when powerful and domineering natures have little influence and create only sects. This applies also to the various arts and the field of knowledge. Where someone rules, there are masses; and where we find masses we also find a need to be enslaved. Where men are

---

[35] Cf. sections 43 and 143.
[36] Cf. section 134 above: another slap in the face of German racism.

enslaved, there are few individuals, and these are opposed by herd instincts and conscience.

150

On the critique of saints.— To have a virtue, must one really wish to have it in its most brutal form—as the Christian saints wished—and needed—it? They could endure life only by thinking that the sight of their virtue would engender self-contempt in anyone who saw them. But a virtue with that effect I call brutal.

151

Of the origin of religion.— The metaphysical need is not the *origin* of religions, as Schopenhauer supposed, but merely a late offshoot. Under the rule of religious ideas, one has become accustomed to the notion of "another world (behind, below, above)"—and when religious ideas are destroyed one is troubled by an uncomfortable emptiness and deprivation. From this feeling grows once again "another world," but now merely a metaphysical one that is no longer religious. But what first led to the positing of "another world" in primeval times was not some impulse or need but an *error* in the interpretation of certain natural events, a failure of the intellect.

152

The greatest change.— The illumination and the color of all things have changed. We no longer understand altogether how the ancients experienced what was most familiar and frequent—for example, the day and waking. Since the ancients believed in dreams, waking appeared in a different light. The same goes for the whole of life, which was illumined by death and its significance; for us "death" means something quite different. All experiences shone differently because a god shone through them. All decisions and perspectives on the remote future, too; for they had oracles and secret portents and believed in prophecy. "Truth" was experienced differently, for the insane could be accepted formerly as its mouthpiece—which makes *us* shudder or laugh.

Every wrong had a different effect on men's feelings; for one feared divine retribution and not merely a civil punishment and dishonor. What was joy in ages when one believed in devils and tempters? What was passion when one saw demons lying in wait nearby? What was philosophy when doubt was experienced as a sin of the most dangerous kind—as sacrilege against eternal love, as mistrust of all that was good, high, pure, and merciful?

We have given things a new color; we go on painting them continually. But what do all our efforts to date avail when we hold them against the colored splendor of that old master—ancient humanity?

153

Homo poeta.— "I myself, having made this tragedy of tragedies all by myself, insofar as it is finished—I, having first tied the knot of morality into existence before I drew it so tight that only a god could untie it (which is what Horace demands)—I myself have now slain all gods in the fourth act, for the sake of morality. Now, what is to become of the fifth act? From where am I to take the tragic solution? —Should I begin to think about a comic solution?"[37]

154

Different types of dangerous lives.— You have no idea what you are living through; you rush through life as if you were drunk and now and then fall down some staircase. But thanks

---

[37] The 122 short aphorisms that follow (154–275) hardly provide "a comic solution," but there is a distinct break at this point, and the tone of the rest of Book III is quite different from the attempt to de-deify the world, in sections 108–152. Section 153 provides what transition there is.

The passage in Horace to which Nietzsche alludes is *Ars Poetica,* line 191f., where the point is that no god should be introduced (i.e., no *deus ex machina*) unless the knot is such that no one else could untie it.

to your drunkenness you never break a limb; your muscles are too relaxed and your brain too benighted for you to find the stones of these stairs as hard as we do. For us life is more dangerous: we are made of glass; woe unto us if we merely *bump* ourselves! And all is lost if we *fall*![38]

155

What we lack.— We love what is *great* in nature, and we have discovered this—because in our heads great human beings are lacking. It was the other way around with the Greeks: their feeling for nature was different from ours.

156

Who is most influential.— When a human being resists his whole age and stops it at the gate to demand an accounting, this *must* have influence. Whether that is what he desires is immaterial; that he *can* do it is what matters.

157

Mentiri.— Watch out! He reflects—in a moment he will be ready with a lie. This is a stage of civilization represented by whole peoples. Just consider what the Romans meant when they used the word *mentiri*![39]

158

An inconvenient trait.— To find everything profound—that is an inconvenient trait. It makes one strain one's eyes all the time, and in the end one finds more than one might have wished.

159

Every virtue has its age.— Anyone who is unyielding nowadays will often have a bad conscience due to his honesty; for

---

[38] Cf. section 283.

[39] To lie or make up something: the word is derived from *mens* (mind), and the root meaning is to think up something.

being unyielding is a virtue that does not belong to the same
age as the virtue of honesty.

160

Dealing with virtues.— In dealing with a virtue, too, one
can lack dignity and fawn.

161

To those who love the age.— The ex-priest and the released
criminal keep making faces: what they desire is a face without
a past. —But have you ever seen people who know that their
faces reflect the future and who are so polite to you who love
the "age" that they make a face without future?

162

Egoism.— Egoism is the law of perspective applied to feelings: what is closest appears large and weighty, and as one
moves farther away size and weight decrease.

163

After a great victory.— What is best about a great victory is
that it liberates the victor from the fear of defeat. "Why not be
defeated some time, too?" he says to himself; "Now I am rich
enough for that."

164

Those who seek rest.— The spirits who seek rest I recognize
by the many *dark* objects with which they surround themselves:
those who want to sleep make their room dark or crawl into a
cave. —A hint for those who do not know what it is that they
seek most, but who would like to know.

165

The happiness of those who have renounced something.—
If one renounces something thoroughly and for a long time and

then accidentally encounters it again, one may almost think that one has discovered it—and how much happiness is there in discovery! Let us be wiser than the serpents who lie too long in the same sunlight.

166

Always in our company.— Whatever in nature and in history is of my own kind, speaks to me, spurs me on, and comforts me; the rest I do not hear or forget right away. We are always only in our own company.

167

Misanthropy and love.— One speaks of being sick of man only when one can no longer digest him and yet has one's stomach full of him. Misanthropy comes of an all too greedy love of man and "cannibalism"; but who asked you to swallow men like oysters, Prince Hamlet?[40]

168

Of a sick man.— "He is in a bad way." —What is wrong?— "He is suffering from the desire for praise and does not find nourishment for it." —Incredible! All the world is celebrating him and pampering him, and he is on everybody's lips.— "Yes, but his hearing for praise is bad. When a friend praises him, it seems to him as if his friend praised himself. When an enemy praises him, it seems to him as if his enemy expected praise for being so generous. And when he is praised by one of the rest— and there are not that many left over because he is so famous— he feels hurt that some people consider him neither a friend nor an enemy, and he says: What are those to me who make a show of their justice toward me?"

---

[40] Throughout, Nietzsche speaks of *Menschen*, including women as well as men. Cf. *Hamlet*, 2.2.330: "Man delights not me—no, nor woman neither ..."

169

Open enemies.— Courage before the enemy is one thing and does not rule out cowardice or indecisiveness and confusion. That is how Napoleon judged "the most courageous person" he knew: Murat.[41] It follows that some people need open enemies if they are to rise to the level of their own virtue, virility, and cheerfulness.

170

With the crowd.— So far, he is still running with the crowd and singing its praises; but one day he will become its enemy. For he is following it in the belief that this will allow his laziness full scope, and he has not yet found out that the crowd is not lazy enough for him, that it always pushes on, that it never allows anyone to stand still. And he loves to stand still.

171

Fame.— When the gratitude of many to one throws away all shame, we behold fame.

172

Spoiling the taste.— A: "You keep spoiling the taste; that is what everybody says." B: "Certainly. I spoil the taste of his party for everyone—and no party forgives that."

173

Being profound and seeming profound.— Those who know that they are profound strive for clarity. Those who would like to seem profound to the crowd strive for obscurity. For the crowd believes that if it cannot see to the bottom of something

---

[41] Joachim Murat (1771–1815), one of the eighteen men whom Napoleon promoted to the rank of Marshal of the Empire in 1804 when he himself was crowned Emperor.

it must be profound. It is so timid and dislikes going into the
water.

174

Apart.— Parliamentarianism—that is, public permission to
choose between five basic political opinions—flatters and wins
the favor of all those who would like to *seem* independent and
individual, as if they fought for their opinions. Ultimately, however, it is indifferent whether the herd is commanded to have
one opinion or permitted to have five. Whoever deviates from
the five public opinions and stands apart will always have the
whole herd against him.[42]

175

Of eloquence.— Who has had the most convincing eloquence
so far? The drum roll; and as long as the kings command that,
they remain the best orators and rabble rousers.

176

Pity.— Poor reigning princes! All of their rights are suddenly changing into claims, and all these claims begin to sound
like presumption. Even if they only say "We" or "my people,"
malicious old Europe begins to smile. Surely, a chief master of
ceremonies in the modern world would waste little ceremony
on them and might well decree: *"les souverains rangent aux
parvenus."*[43]

177

On "the educational establishment."— In Germany, higher
men lack one great means of education: the laughter of higher
men, for in Germany these do not laugh.[44]

---

[42] Note how Nietzsche's contempt for parliamentarianism differs from
the fascists'. Cf. also the next section.
[43] Sovereigns belong with parvenus.
[44] Cf. *Zarathustra*, Part IV (e.g., VPN, 529–31).

178

On moral enlightenment.— One has to talk the Germans out of their Mephistopheles, and their Faust as well. These are two moral prejudices against the value of knowledge.

179

Thoughts.— Thoughts are the shadows of our feelings—always darker, emptier, and simpler.

180

A good age for free spirits.— Free spirits take liberties even with science—and so far get away with it, as long as the church still stands. To that extent this is a good age for them.

181

Following and walking ahead.— A: "Of these two one will always follow and the other always walk ahead, wherever fate may lead them. And yet the former excels the other one in virtue as well as spirit." B: "And yet? And yet? You speak for the benefit of the others, not for me, not for us.—*Fit secundum regulam.*"[45]

182

In solitude.— Those who live alone do not speak too loud nor write too loud, for they fear the hollow echo—the critique of the nymph Echo. And all voices sound different in solitude.

183

The music of the best future.[46]— I should account as the foremost musician one who knew only the sadness of the most

---

[45] This is the rule.
[46] Ten years earlier Nietzsche and others had called Wagner's music "the music of the future."

profound happiness, and no other sadness at all; but such a musician has never existed yet.

184

Justice.— I'd sooner have people steal from me than be surrounded by scarecrows and hungry looks;[47] that is my taste. And this is by all means a matter of taste, nothing more.

185

Poor.— He is poor today, but not because one has taken everything away from him; he has thrown away everything. What is that to him? He is used to finding things. It is the poor who misunderstand his voluntary poverty.

186

Bad conscience.— Everything he is doing now is decent and in order, and yet he has a bad conscience. For the extraordinary in his task.[48]

187

Offensive presentation.— This artist offends me by the manner in which he presents his ideas, although they are very good; his presentation is so broad and emphatic and depends on such crude artifices of persuasion, as if he addressed a mob. Whenever we give some time to his art we are soon as if "in bad company."

188

Work.— How close work and the worker are now even to the most leisurely among us! The royal courtesy of the saying

---

[47] The last four words render *Vogelscheuchen*, which means scarecrows but is also used to refer to terribly thin and undernourished people.
[48] This aphorism depends on the contrast between *ordentlich* (in order) and *das Ausserordentliche* (the extraordinary).

"We are all workers" would have been cynical and indecent as recently as the reign of Louis XIV.

189

The thinker.— He is a thinker; that means, he knows how to make things simpler than they are.[49]

190

Against those who praise.— A: "One is praised only by one's peers." B: "Yes, and whoever praises you says: I am your peer."

191

Against many a defense.— The most perfidious way of harming a cause consists of defending it deliberately with faulty arguments.

192

The good-natured.— What is the difference between those good-natured people whose faces radiate good will, and other people? They are cheered by the sight of another person and quickly fall in love with him; therefore they are well disposed toward him, and their first judgment is: "I like him." What distinguishes these people is a rapid succession of the following states: the wish to appropriate (they do not scruple over the worth of the other person), quick appropriation, delight in their new possession, and action for the benefit of their latest conquest.

193

Kant's joke.— Kant wanted to prove, in a way that would dumfound the common man, that the common man was right:

---

[49] Cf. section 179.

that was the secret joke of this soul. He wrote against the scholars in support of popular prejudice, but for scholars and not for the people.[50]

194

The "openhearted."— That person probably always acts in accordance with secret reasons, for he always has communicable reasons on his lips and practically in his open hand.

195

Laughable!— Look! Look! He is running away from people, but they follow after him because he is running ahead of them: they are herd through and through.

196

Limits of our hearing.— One hears only those questions for which one is able to find answers.

197

Better watch out!— There is nothing we like so much to communicate to others as the seal of secrecy—along with what lies under it.

198

Chagrin of the proud.— The proud feel chagrined even by those who advance them: they are angry with the horses of their carriage.

199

Liberality.— With the rich, liberality is often merely a kind of shyness.

---

[50] The reference is surely to Kant's postulates of God, freedom of the will, and immortality of the soul and to the elaborate and difficult distinction between phenomena and noumena that, in Kant's own words, makes "room for faith."

200

Laughter.— Laughter means: being *schadenfroh*[51] but with a good conscience.

201

Applause.— In applause there is always a kind of noise— even when we applaud ourselves.

202

A squanderer.— As yet he does not have the poverty of the rich[52] who have already counted all their treasures once; he is squandering his spirit with the unreason of squandering nature.

203

Hic niger est.[53]— Usually he has no thought in his head, but in exceptional cases he has nasty thoughts.

204

Beggars and courtesy.— "There is no lack of courtesy in using a stone to knock on a door when there is no bell"; that is how beggars feel and all who suffer some sort of distress; but nobody agrees with them.

205

Need.— Need is considered the cause why something came to be; but in truth it is often merely an effect of what has come to be.

---

[51] The word is famous for being untranslatable; it signifies taking a mischievous delight in the discomfort of another person.

[52] *Armut des Reichen.* One of Nietzsche's late poems (one of the so-called Dionysus Dithyrambs) bears the title *Von der Armut des Reichsten* (On the Poverty of the Richest Person).

[53] Here he is black. Cf. *Genealogy*, I, section 5n (BWN, 466).

206

When it rains.— It is raining, and I think of the poor who now huddle together with their many cares and without any practice at concealing these: each is ready and willing to hurt the other and to create for himself a wretched kind of pleasure even when the weather is bad. That and only that is the poverty of the poor.

207

The envious.— He is envious; let us hope that he will not have children, for he would envy them because he cannot be a child anymore.

208

Great man.— From the fact that somebody is "a big man" we cannot infer that he is a man; perhaps he is merely a boy, or a chameleon of all the ages of life, or a bewitched little female.

209

One way of asking for reasons.— There is a way of asking us for our reasons that leads us not only to forget our best reasons but also to conceive a stubborn aversion to all reasons. This way of asking makes people very stupid and is a trick used by tyrannical people.

210

Moderation in industriousness.— One should not try to excel one's father's industriousness; that makes one sick.

211

Secret enemies.[54]— To be able to afford a secret enemy—that

---

[54] Cf. section 169: "Open enemies."

is a luxury for which the morality of even elevated spirits is usually not rich enough.

212

Not to be deceived.— His spirit has bad manners, is hasty, and so impatient that it always stutters. Hence one scarcely suspects how long the breath and how broad the chest of the soul are in which this spirit is at home.

213

The way to happiness.— A sage asked a fool about the way to happiness. The fool answered instantly as if he had merely been asked about the way to the nearest town: "Admire yourself and live in the street." "No," replied the sage, "you are asking too much; it is quite sufficient to admire oneself." The fool shot back: "But how can one constantly admire without constantly feeling contempt?"[55]

214

Faith makes blessed.— Virtue bestows happiness and a kind of bliss only on those who have not lost their faith in their virtue—not on those subtler souls whose virtue consists in a profound mistrust of themselves and of all virtue. Ultimately, then, *"faith* makes blessed" here, too, and *not*—mark it well—virtue.

215

Ideal and material.— The ideal you envisage is noble, but are you a noble enough stone to be made into such a divine image? Anyway, is your work not that of a barbarous sculptor? Is it not a blasphemy against your ideal?

---

[55] Some contrast is required.

216

Danger in the voice.— Anyone with a very loud voice is almost incapable of thinking subtleties.

217

Cause and effect.— Before the effect one believes in different causes than one does afterward.

218

My antipathy.— I do not love people who have to explode like bombs in order to have any effect at all. When one is near them one is always in danger of suddenly losing one's hearing, if not more than that.

219

The purpose of punishment.— The purpose of punishment is to improve those *who punish*; that is the last resort of the apologists for punishment.

220

Sacrifice.— The sacrificial animal does not share the spectators' ideas about sacrifice, but one has never let it have its say.

221

Consideration.— Fathers and sons have much more consideration for each other than mothers and daughters.

222

Poet and liar.— The poet considers the liar a foster brother whom he did out of his milk. Hence his brother remained weak and wretched and never even attained a good conscience.

223

Vicarious senses.— "Our eyes are also intended for hearing," said an old father confessor who had become deaf; "and among the blind he that has the longest ears is king."

224

Animals as critics.— I fear that the animals consider man as a being like themselves that has lost in a most dangerous way its sound animal common sense; they consider him the insane animal, the laughing animal, the weeping animal, the miserable animal.

225

The natural.— "Evil has always had great effects in its favor. And nature is evil. Let us therefore be natural." That is the secret reasoning of those who have mastered the most spectacular effects, and they have all too often been considered great human beings.

226

Mistrust and style.— We say the strongest things simply, provided only that we are surrounded by people who believe in our strength: such an environment educates one to attain "simplicity of style." The mistrustful speak emphatically; the mistrustful also make others emphatic.

227

Bad reasoning, bad shot.[56]— He cannot control himself, and from that a poor woman infers that it will be easy to control him and casts her net for him. Soon she will be his slave.[57]

---

[56] *Fehlschluss, Fehlschuss.*
[57] This apparently quite unphilosophical aphorism goes well with Nietzsche's view that the desire for power over others is often rooted in a lack of power over oneself.

228

Against mediators.— Those who want to mediate between two resolute thinkers show that they are mediocre; they lack eyes for seeing what is unique. Seeing things as similar and making things the same is the sign of weak eyes.[58]

229

Obstinacy and faithfulness.— Obstinately, he clings to something that he has come to see through; but he calls it "faithfulness."

230

Dearth of silence.— His whole nature fails to persuade; that is because he has never remained silent about any of his good deeds.

231

The "thorough."— Those who are slow to know suppose that slowness is of the essence of knowledge.[59]

232

Dreams.— Either we have no dreams or our dreams are interesting. We should learn to arrange our waking life the same way: nothing or interesting.

233

The most dangerous point of view.— What I do or do not do now is as important for everything that is yet to come as is the

---

[58] Nietzsche may have thought especially of his sister as well as others who sought to mediate between him and Wagner. Cf. section 32 above.
[59] Cf. *Beyond Good and Evil*, section 27; also 28 and 246, and above all section 381 below.

greatest event of the past: in this tremendous perspective of effectiveness all actions appear equally great and small.[60]

234

A musician's comfort.— "Your life does not reach men's ears; your life is silent for them, and all the subtleties of its melody, all tender resolutions about following or going ahead remain hidden from them. True, you do not approach on a broad highway with regimental music, but that does not give these good people any right to say that your way of life lacks music. Let those who have ears hear!"

235

Spirit and character.— Some reach their peak as characters, but their spirit is not up to this height, while with others it happens the other way around.

236

To move the crowd.— Must not anyone who wants to move the crowd be an actor who impersonates himself? Must he not first translate himself into grotesque obviousness and then present his whole person and cause in this coarsened and simplified version?

237

Polite.— "He is so polite." —Yes, he always carries a biscuit for Cerberus[61] and is so timid that he thinks everyone is Cerberus, even you and I. That is his "politeness."

238

Without envy.— He is utterly without envy, but there is no merit in that, for he wants to conquer a country that nobody has possessed and scarcely anyone has even seen.

---

[60] Cf. section 341 below.
[61] The three-headed dog guarding the entrance to Hades.

239

Joyless.— A single joyless person is enough to create constant discouragement and cloudy skies for a whole household, and it is a miracle if there is not one person like that. Happiness is not nearly so contagious a disease. Why?

240

At the sea.— I would not build a house for myself, and I count it part of my good fortune that I do not own a house. But if I had to, then I should build it as some of the Romans did—right into the sea. I should not mind sharing a few secrets with this beautiful monster.

241

Work and artist.— This artist is ambitious, nothing more. Ultimately, his work is merely a magnifying glass that he offers everybody who looks his way.

242

Suum cuique.[62]— However great the greed of my desire for knowledge may be, I still cannot take anything out of things that did not belong to me before; what belongs to others remains behind. How is it possible for a human being to be a thief or robber?

243

Origin of "good" and "bad."— Improvements are invented only by those who can feel that something is not good.[63]

---

[62] To each his own. The point is most readily understood when it is applied to works of art, literature, and philosophy.

[63] Cf. section 24 above as well as the rather different *"Dual pre-history of good and evil"* in *Human, All-Too-Human,* section 45 (BWN, 147f.), *Beyond Good and Evil,* section 260 (BWN, 394–98), and the first essay in *Genealogy of Morals* (BWN, 460–92).

244

Thoughts and words.— Even one's thoughts one cannot reproduce entirely in words.

245

Praise by choice.— An artist chooses his subjects; that is his way of praising.

246

Mathematics.— Let us introduce the refinement and rigor of mathematics into all sciences as far as this is at all possible, not in the faith that this will lead us to know things but in order to *determine* our human relation to things. Mathematics is merely the means for general and ultimate knowledge of man.

247

Habit.— Every habit lends our hand more wit but makes our wit less handy.

248

Books.— What good is a book that does not even carry us beyond all books?

249

The sigh of the search for knowledge.— "Oh, my greed! There is no selflessness in my soul but only an all-coveting self that would like to appropriate many individuals as so many additional pairs of eyes and hands—a self that would like to bring back the whole past, too, and that will not lose anything that it could possibly possess. Oh, my greed is a flame! Oh, that I might be reborn in a hundred beings!" —Whoever does not know this sigh from firsthand experience does not know the passion of the search for knowledge.

250

Guilt.— Although the shrewdest judges of the witches and even the witches themselves were convinced of the guilt of witchery, this guilt nevertheless did not exist. This applies to all guilt.

251

Misunderstood sufferers.— Magnificent characters suffer very differently from what their admirers imagine. They suffer most keenly from the ignoble and petty agitations of some evil moments—briefly, from their doubts about their own magnificence—not from the sacrifices and martyrdoms that their task demands from them. As long as Prometheus feels pity for men and sacrifices himself for them, he is happy and great; but when he becomes envious of Zeus and the homage paid to him by mortals, then he suffers.

252

Better a debtor.— "Better a debtor than pay with a coin that does not bear our image!" says our sovereignty.

253

Always at home.— One day we reach our goal, and now point with pride to the long travels we undertook to reach it. In fact, we were not even aware of traveling. But we got so far because we fancied at every point that we were at home.

254

Against embarrassment.— If you are always profoundly occupied, you are beyond all embarrassment.

255

Imitators.— A: "What? You want no imitators?" B: "I do not want to have people imitate my example; I wish that everybody would fashion his own example, as *I* do." A: "So?"[64]

256

Skin-coveredness.— All people who have depth find happiness in being for once like flying fish, playing on the peaks of waves; what they consider best in things is that they have a surface: their skin-coveredness—*sit venia verbo*.[65]

257

From experience.— Some do not know how rich they are until they experience how rich people steal from them.

258

The denial of chance.— No victor believes in chance.

---

[64] This aphorism is ambiguous. What B says could also mean: "I do not want to have people imitate me; I wish that everybody would deceive themselves, which is what *I* do." The last five words could mean that B deceives himself, or that B deceives others, or preferably both. Taken out of context, the phrase *dass Jeder sich etwas vormache* could hardly mean anything but "that everybody would deceive themselves." But the sharp antithesis of *nachmache* (imitate) and *vormache* jolts the reader into an awareness of another meaning of *vormachen*, which is also quite common and often occurs together with *nachmachen*: to show others how something is done so that they can then imitate the procedure. While this meaning generally precludes the reflexive *sich*, found in Nietzsche's text, it still seems probable that this is the primary meaning he intended. If so, B speaks Nietzsche's mind—and A mocks Nietzsche, saying—in a single word ("So—?"): You make such a point of not wanting others to imitate you; but actually you do want others to imitate your self-reliance and autonomy. Cf. two quatrains above: one on the title page of the second edition, the other one, which is particularly relevant, #7 in the Prelude. Moreover, when A and B converse in *The Gay Science*, B generally speaks Nietzsche's mind.
[65] Forgive the word. The German word Nietzsche coined is *Hautlichkeit* The idea is elaborated in the final section of his Preface for the Second Edition, 38 above.

259

From paradise.— "Good and evil are the prejudices of God" —said the snake.

260

Multiplication table.— One is always wrong, but with two, truth begins.—*One* cannot prove his case, but two are irrefutable.

261

Originality.— What is originality? *To see* something that has no name as yet and hence cannot be mentioned although it stares us all in the face. The way men usually are, it takes a name to make something visible for them. —Those with originality have for the most part also assigned names.

262

Sub specie aeterni.[66]— A: ˙You are moving away faster and faster from the living; soon they will strike your name from their rolls." —B: "That is the only way to participate in the privilege of the dead." —A: "What privilege?" —B: "To die no more."[67]

263

Without vanity.— When we are in love we wish that our defects might remain concealed—not from vanity but to keep the beloved from suffering. Indeed, the lover would like to seem divine—and this, too, not from vanity.

---

[66] From the point of view of eternity (Spinoza's phrase). Cf section 357, n 83, below.
[67] In other words: What is timely will pass away with the time, and untimeliness is the price of immortality. Cf. section 365 below; also the final note on that section.

264

What we do.— What we do is never understood but always only praised or censured.

265

Ultimate skepsis.— What are man's truths ultimately? Merely his *irrefutable* errors.[68]

266

Where cruelty is needed.— Those who have greatness are cruel to their virtues and to secondary considerations.

267

With a great goal.— With a great goal one is superior even to justice, not only to one's deeds and one's judges.

268

What makes one heroic?— Going out to meet at the same time one's highest suffering and one's highest hope.

269

In what do you believe?— In this, that the weights of all things must be determined anew.

270

What does your conscience say?— "You shall become the person you are."[69]

---

[68] Cf. sections 94n and 109ff., above.

[69] Nietzsche derived this motto from Pindar, Pyth. II, 73, and later gave his *Ecce Homo* the subtitle: "How one becomes what one is." Cf. also Hegel's formulation that "spirit . . . makes itself that which it is." Cf. Kaufmann, 159, and *Hegel*, section 60; also section 335 below, near the end.

271

Where are your greatest dangers?— In pity.[70]

272

What do you love in others?— My hopes.

273

Whom do you call bad?— Those who always want to put to shame.

274

What do you consider most humane?— To spare someone shame.

275

What is the seal of liberation?— No longer being ashamed in front of oneself.[71]

---

[70] This brief aphorism illuminates Nietzsche's attacks on pity. The theme introduced here in one line is developed in many other passages, notably section 338 and Part IV of *Zarathustra*.

[71] Cf. the conclusion of Book II, section 107 and the last note on it.

BOOK FOUR

❧

SANCTUS JANUARIUS

> *With a flaming spear you crushed*
> *All its ice until my soul*
> *Roaring toward the ocean rushed*
> *Of its highest hope and goal.*
> *Ever healthier it swells,*
> *Lovingly compelled but free:*
> *Thus it lauds your miracles,*
> *Fairest month of January!**
>
> GENOA, *January 1882.*

---

* For a memorable discussion of the miracle of St. Januarius, see Chapter II of Freud, *Zur Psychopathologie des Alltagslebens.* "In a church in Naples, the blood of the Holy Januarius is kept in a vial, and by virtue of a miracle it becomes liquid again on a certain feast day." Put crudely, Nietzsche calls Book Four "*Sanctus* Januarius" because he feels that his own blood has become liquid again.

For the new year.— I still live, I still think: I still have to live, for I still have to think. *Sum, ergo cogito: cogito, ergo sum.*[1] Today everybody permits himself the expression of his wish and his dearest thought; hence I, too, shall say what it is that I wish from myself today, and what was the first thought to run across my heart this year—what thought shall be for me the reason, warranty, and sweetness of my life henceforth. I want to learn more and more to see as beautiful what is necessary in things; then I shall be one of those who make things beautiful. *Amor fati:*[2] let that be my love henceforth! I do not want to wage war against what is ugly. I do not want to accuse; I do not even want to accuse those who accuse. *Looking away* shall be my only negation.[3] And all in all and on the whole: some day I wish to be only a Yes-sayer.[4]

Personal providence.— There is a certain high point in life: once we have reached that, we are, for all our freedom, once more in the greatest danger of spiritual unfreedom, and no matter how much we have faced up to the beautiful chaos of existence and denied it all providential reason and goodness, we still have to pass our hardest test. For it is only now that the idea of a personal providence confronts us with the most penetrating force, and the best advocate, the evidence of our eyes,

---

[1] I am, therefore I think: I think, therefore I am. The second half of this statement is quoted from Descartes who made this formulation famous.

[2] Love of fate. This important concept is introduced here for the first time. The idea is developed further in Book IV; also in *Zarathustra* and in *Ecce Homo.*

[3] Cf. *Zarathustra* III, "On Passing By" (VPN, 287–90).

[4] Cf. *Zarathustra* III, "Before Sunrise" (VPN, 276–79) and "The Seven Seals (Or: The Yes and Amen Song)" (VPN, 340–43); also *Ecce Homo, passim* (see the Index in BWN under "Yes-saying").

speaks for it—now that we can see how palpably always everything that happens to us turns out for the best. Every day and every hour, life seems to have no other wish than to prove this proposition again and again. Whatever it is, bad weather or good, the loss of a friend, sickness, slander, the failure of some letter to arrive, the spraining of an ankle, a glance into a shop, a counter-argument, the opening of a book, a dream, a fraud—either immediately or very soon after it proves to be something that "must not be missing"; it has a profound significance and use precisely for *us*. Is there any more dangerous seduction that might tempt one to renounce one's faith in the gods of Epicurus who have no care and are unknown, and to believe instead in some petty deity who is full of care and personally knows every little hair on our head[5] and finds nothing nauseous in the most miserable small service?

Well, I think that in spite of all this we should leave the gods in peace as well as the genii who are ready to serve us, and rest content with the supposition that our own practical and theoretical skill in interpreting and arranging events has now reached its high point. Nor should we conceive too high an opinion of this dexterity of our wisdom when at times we are excessively surprised by the wonderful harmony created by the playing of our instrument—a harmony that sounds too good for us to dare to give the credit to ourselves. Indeed, now and then someone plays with us—good old chance; now and then chance guides our hand, and the wisest providence could not think up a more beautiful music than that which our foolish hand produces then.[6]

278

The thought of death.— Living in the midst of this jumble of little lanes, needs, and voices gives me a melancholy happi-

---

[5] This allusion to Matthew 10:30 and Luke 12:7 leaves no doubt that Nietzsche is contrasting the gods of Epicurus with the "petty deity" of the Gospels. Cf. *The Antichrist*, section 58 (VPN, 649).

[6] Cf. *Ecce Homo*, the third section of the discussion of *Zarathustra* (BWN, 756f.).

ness: how much enjoyment, impatience, and desire, how much thirsty life and drunkenness of life comes to light every moment! And yet silence will soon descend on all these noisy, living, life-thirsty people. How his shadow stands even now behind every-one, as his dark fellow traveler! It is always like the last moment before the departure of an emigrants' ship: people have more to say to each other than ever, the hour is late, and the ocean and its desolate silence are waiting impatiently behind all of this noise—so covetous and certain of their prey. And all and everyone of them suppose that the heretofore was little or nothing while the near future is everything; and that is the reason for all of this haste, this clamor, this outshouting and overreaching each other. Everyone wants to be the first in this future—and yet death and deathly silence alone are certain and common to all in this future. How strange it is that this sole certainty and common element makes almost no impression on people, and that nothing is further from their minds than the feeling that they form a brotherhood of death. It makes me happy that men do not want at all to think the thought of death![7] I should like very much to do something that would make the thought of life even a hundred times more appealing to them.

279

Star friendship.— We were friends and have become es-tranged. But this was right, and we do not want to conceal and obscure it from ourselves as if we had reason to feel ashamed. We are two ships each of which has its goal and course; our paths may cross and we may celebrate a feast together, as we did—and then the good ships rested so quietly in one harbor and one sunshine that it may have looked as if they had reached their goal and as if they had one goal. But then the almighty force of our tasks drove us apart again into different

---

[7] The contrast with existentialism should be noted. It is not merely verbal or superficial. The next sentence provides the link to Nietzsche's central orientation, and his relatively few other references to death do not contradict this anti-Christian attitude.

seas and sunny zones, and perhaps we shall never see each other again; perhaps we shall meet again but fail to recognize each other: our exposure to different seas and suns has changed us. That we have to become estranged is the law *above* us; by the same token we should also become more venerable for each other—and the memory of our former friendship more sacred. There is probably a tremendous but invisible stellar orbit in which our very different ways and goals may be *included* as small parts of this path; let us rise up to this thought. But our life is too short and our power of vision too small for us to be more than friends in the sense of this sublime possibility. —Let us then *believe* in our star friendship even if we should be compelled to be earth enemies.[8]

280

Architecture for the search for knowledge.— One day, and probably soon, we need some recognition of what above all is lacking in our big cities: quiet and wide, expansive places for reflection. Places with long, high-ceilinged cloisters for bad or all too sunny weather where no shouting or noise of carriages can reach and where good manners would prohibit even priests from praying aloud—buildings and sites that would altogether

---

[8] Although this aphorism has often been cited as a document concerning Nietzsche's attitude toward Wagner, the image of the two ships (*Schiffe*) brings to mind a much homelier, more unpretentious, and more moving passage in a letter to Franz Overbeck, November 14, 1881:

"My dear friend; what is this our life? A boat [*Kahn*] that swims in the sea, and all one knows for certain about it is that one day it will capsize. Here we are, two good old boats that have been faithful neighbors, and above all your hand has done its best to keep me from 'capsizing'! Let us then continue our voyage—each for the other's sake, *for a long time yet*, a long time! We should miss each other so much! Tolerably calm seas and good winds and above all sun—what I wish for myself, I wish for you, too, and am sorry that my gratitude can find expression only in such a *wish* and has no influence at all on wind or weather."

Much of the rest of this letter is cited in a note on section 316, below. The original is not included in Karl Schlechta's selection of letters in his edition of Nietzsche's *Werke*, but will be found in *Friedrich Nietzsches Briefwechsel mit Franz Overbeck*.

give expression to the sublimity of thoughtfulness and of stepping aside. The time is past when the church possessed a monopoly on reflection, when the *vita contemplativa* always had to be first of all a *vita religiosa*; and everything built by the church gives expression to that idea. I do not see how we could remain content with such buildings even if they were stripped of their churchly purposes. The language spoken by these buildings is far too rhetorical and unfree, reminding us that they are houses of God and ostentatious monuments of some supramundane intercourse; we who are godless could not think *our thoughts* in such surroundings. We wish to see *ourselves* translated into stone and plants, we want to take walks *in ourselves* when we stroll around these buildings and gardens.

281

Knowing how to end.— Masters of the first rank are revealed by the fact that in great as well as small matters they know how to end perfectly, whether it is a matter of ending a melody or a thought, or the fifth act of a tragedy or of an action of state. The best of the second rank always become restless as the end approaches and do not manage to slope into the sea in such proud and calm harmony as, for example, the mountains at Portofino—where the bay of Genoa ends its melody.

282

Gait.— By certain manners of the spirit even great spirits betray that they come from the mob or semi-mob; it is above all the gait and stride of their thoughts that betrays them; they cannot *walk.* Thus Napoleon, too, was unable, to his profound chagrin, to walk like a prince, "legitimately," on occasions when that is really required, such as great coronation processions. Even then he was always only the leader of a column— proud and hasty at the same time, and very conscious of this. There is something laughable about the sight of authors who enjoy the rustling folds of long and involved sentences: they are trying to cover up their *feet.*

283

Preparatory human beings. — I welcome all signs that a more virile, warlike age is about to begin, which will restore honor to courage above all. For this age shall prepare the way for one yet higher, and it shall gather the strength that this higher age will require some day—the age that will carry heroism into the search for knowledge and that will *wage wars* for the sake of ideas and their consequences. To this end we now need many preparatory courageous human beings who cannot very well leap out of nothing, any more than out of the sand and slime of present-day civilization and metropolitanism—human beings who know how to be silent, lonely, resolute, and content and constant in invisible activities; human beings who are bent on seeking in all things for what in them must be *overcome*; human beings distinguished as much by cheerfulness, patience, unpretentiousness, and contempt for all great vanities as by magnanimity in victory and forbearance regarding the small vanities of the vanquished; human beings whose judgment concerning all victors and the share of chance in every victory and fame is sharp and free; human beings with their own festivals, their own working days, and their own periods of mourning, accustomed to command with assurance but instantly ready to obey when that is called for—equally proud, equally serving their own cause in both cases; more endangered human beings, more fruitful human beings, happier beings! For believe me: the secret for harvesting from existence the greatest fruitfulness and the greatest enjoyment is—to *live dangerously!*[9] Build your cities on the slopes of Vesuvius! Send your ships into uncharted seas![10] Live at war with your peers and yourselves! Be robbers and conquerors as long as you cannot be rulers and possessors, you seekers of knowledge! Soon the age will be past when you could be content to live hidden in forests like shy

---

[9] This magnificent formulation is found only in this one place in Nietzsche's works, but the idea is one of his central motifs. For some discussion see the chapter on "Nietzsche and Rilke" in Kaufmann, *From Shakespeare to Existentialism*, especially the final section. Cf. also section 154 above.

[10] Cf. Section 124 above; also 289, 291, and 343 below.

deer. At long last the search for knowledge will reach out for
its due; it will want to *rule* and *possess*, and you with it!

284

Faith in oneself.— Few people have faith in themselves. Of
these few, some are endowed with it as with a useful blindness
or a partial eclipse of their spirit (what would they behold if
they could see to the bottom of themselves!), while the rest
have to acquire it. Everything good, fine, or great they do is
first of all an argument against the skeptic inside them. They
have to convince or persuade *him*, and that almost requires
genius. These are the great self-dissatisfied people.

285

Excelsior.— "You will never pray again, never adore again,
never again rest in endless trust; you do not permit yourself to
stop before any ultimate wisdom, ultimate goodness, ultimate
power, while unharnessing your thoughts; you have no perpetual guardian and friend for your seven solitudes;[11] you live
without a view of mountains with snow on their peaks and
fire in their hearts;[12] there is no avenger for you any more nor

[11] God. Cf. the end of the first paragraph of section 277 above.
[12] This clause may seem out of place here, and the association with
Vesuvius in section 283 does not seem to help. But some earlier passages in
the book help to clarify this problem. Section 9 is entitled "Our eruptions"
and suggests that "we are, all of us, growing volcanoes that approach the
hour of their eruption." Section 15 is called "From a distance" and suggests that some mountains look charming only from a distance and from
below. Section 27 is called "The man of renunciation" (*Der Entsagende*),
and the passage we are trying to interpret builds up to the climax: "Man
of renunciation [*Mensch der Entsagung*], all this you want to renounce
[*entsagen*]?" But the point of section 27 was that it is only in order to
fly higher that the man of renunciation sacrifices so much, and that
what he gives up does not strike him as a negation because it is really
part of his soaring desire for the heights. These images are taken up
again in section 285 where renunciation is the price of "rising higher
and higher."
    If mountain ranges really offered a charming or impressive view only
from below, as suggested in section 15, the clause that seemed puzzling

any final improver; there is no longer any reason in what happens, no love in what will happen to you; no resting place is open any longer to your heart, where it only needs to find and no longer to seek; you resist any ultimate peace; you will the eternal recurrence of war and peace:[13] man of renunciation, all this you wish to renounce? Who will give you the strength for that? Nobody yet has had this strength!"

There is a lake that one day ceased to permit itself to flow off; it formed a dam where it had hitherto flown off; and ever since this lake is rising higher and higher. Perhaps this very renunciation will also lend us the strength needed to bear this renunciation; perhaps man will rise ever higher as soon as he ceases to *flow out* into a god.

286

Interruption.— Here are hopes; but what will you hear and see of them if you have not experienced splendor, ardor, and dawns in your own souls? I can only remind you; more I cannot do. To move stones, to turn animals into men—is that what you want from me? Oh, if you are still stones and animals, then better look for your Orpheus.

287

Delight in blindness.— "My thoughts," said the wanderer to his shadow,[14] "should show me where I stand; but they should

---

would make sense now. Since that assumption is actually false, and one can have a stunning view of snowy mountains from a high peak or during a flight, it helps to invoke sections 9 and 283. If you build your house on the slopes of Vesuvius you give up the charming view of the mountain across the bay; and there is a difference between sitting behind a picture window, enjoying the *view* of a volcano, and *being* a volcano.

[13] This is how Nietzsche first introduces his concept of "the eternal recurrence." Cf. section 341 and, for a detailed discussion not only of these passages but also of Nietzsche's reasons for his "doctrine of the eternal recurrence of the same events" and for its antecedents in earlier thinkers, Kaufmann, Chapter 11 (316–33).

[14] Two years earlier, in 1880, Nietzsche had published *The Wanderer and his Shadow*, which later became part of the second volume of *Human, All-Too-Human*.

not betray to me where I am going. I love my ignorance of the future and do not wish to perish of impatience and of tasting promised things ahead of time."

288

Elevated moods.— It seems to me that most people simply do not believe in elevated moods, unless these last for moments only or at most a quarter of an hour—except for those few who know at firsthand the longer duration of elevated feelings. But to be a human being with one elevated feeling—to be a single great mood incarnate—that has hitherto been a mere dream and a delightful possibility; as yet history does not offer us any certain examples. Nevertheless history might one day give birth to such people, too—once a great many favorable preconditions have been created and determined that even the dice throws of the luckiest chance could not bring together today. What has so far entered our souls only now and then as an exception that made us shudder, might perhaps be the usual state for these future souls: a perpetual movement between high and low, the feeling of high and low, a continual ascent as on stairs and at the same time a sense of resting on clouds.

289

Embark!— Consider how every individual is affected by an overall philosophical justification of his way of living and thinking: he experiences it as a sun that shines especially for him and bestows warmth, blessings, and fertility on him; it makes him independent of praise and blame, self-sufficient, rich, liberal with happiness and good will; incessantly it refashions evil into good, leads all energies to bloom and ripen, and does not permit the petty weeds of grief and chagrin to come up at all. In the end one exclaims: How I wish that many such new suns were yet to be created! Those who are evil or unhappy and the exceptional human being—all these should also have their philosophy, their good right, their sunshine! What is needful is not pity for them. We must learn to abandon this arrogant fancy, however long humanity has hitherto spent learning and practicing it. What these people need is not con-

fession, conjuring of souls, and forgiveness of sins; what is
needful is a new *justice*! And a new watchword. And new
philosophers. The moral earth, too, is round. The moral earth,
too, has its antipodes. The antipodes, too, have the right to
exist. There is yet another world to be discovered—and more
than one. Embark, philosophers![15]

290

One thing is needful.— To "give style" to one's character—
a great and rare art! It is practiced by those who survey all the
strengths and weaknesses of their nature and then fit them into
an artistic plan until every one of them appears as art and
reason and even weaknesses delight the eye. Here a large mass
of second nature has been added; there a piece of original
nature has been removed—both times through long practice and
daily work at it. Here the ugly that could not be removed is
concealed; there it has been reinterpreted and made sublime.
Much that is vague and resisted shaping has been saved and
exploited for distant views; it is meant to beckon toward the
far and immeasurable. In the end, when the work is finished,
it becomes evident how the constraint of a single taste governed
and formed everything large and small. Whether this taste was
good or bad is less important than one might suppose, if only it
was a single taste!

It will be the strong and domineering natures that enjoy
their finest gaiety in such constraint and perfection under a law
of their own; the passion of their tremendous will relents in
the face of all stylized nature, of all conquered and serving
nature. Even when they have to build palaces and design
gardens they demur at giving nature freedom.

Conversely, it is the weak characters without power over

---

[15] The call to embark picks up the Columbus theme of sections 124 and
283. But above all this section leads into the next. The theme of
fashioning evil into good, the garden imagery (bloom, ripen, weeds),
and the discussion of what is not needful and what is—all this is taken
up in the next section. What is ultimately needful is much less than was
claimed here: "only" giving style to one's character.

themselves that *hate* the constraint of style. They feel that if this bitter and evil constraint were imposed upon them they would be demeaned; they become slaves as soon as they serve; they hate to serve. Such spirits—and they may be of the first rank—are always out to shape and interpret their environment as *free* nature: wild, arbitrary, fantastic, disorderly, and surprising. And they are well advised because it is only in this way that they can give pleasure to themselves. For one thing is needful: that a human being should *attain* satisfaction with himself, whether it be by means of this or that poetry and art; only then is a human being at all tolerable to behold. Whoever is dissatisfied with himself is continually ready for revenge, and we others will be his victims, if only by having to endure his ugly sight. For the sight of what is ugly makes one bad and gloomy.[16]

291

Genoa.— For a long while now I have been looking at this city, at its villas and pleasure gardens and the far-flung periphery of its inhabited heights and slopes. In the end I must say: I see faces that belong to past generations; this region is studded with the images of bold and autocratic human beings. They have *lived* and wished to live on: that is what they are telling me with their houses, built and adorned to last for centuries and not for a fleeting hour; they were well-disposed toward life, however ill-disposed they often may have been toward themselves. I keep seeing the builders, their eyes resting on everything near and far that they have built, and also on the city, the sea, and the contours of the mountains, and there is violence and conquest in their eyes. All this they want to fit into *their* plan and ultimately make their *possession* by making it part of their plan. This whole region is overgrown

---

16 This is one of the most important passages Nietzsche ever wrote on moral psychology. It brings out beautifully his close association of power with self-control and style, and of lack of self-control with weakness. Note also the suggestion that resentment is rooted in an inability to accept oneself. Some of the following sections develop Nietzsche's conception of character further; especially sections 295 and 296.

with this magnificent, insatiable selfishness of the lust for possessions and spoils; and even as these people refused to recognize any boundaries in distant lands and, thirsting for what was new, placed a new world beside the old one,[17] each rebelled against each at home, too, and found a way to express his superiority and to lay between himself and his neighbor his personal infinity. Each once more conquered his homeland for himself by overwhelming it with his architectural ideas and refashioning it into a house that was a feast for his eyes.

In the north one is impressed by the law and the general delight in lawfulness and obedience as one contemplates the way cities are built. One is led to guess at the ways in which, deep down, people posited themselves as equal and subordinated themselves; that must have been what was dominant in the souls of all builders. But what you find *here* upon turning any corner is a human being apart who knows the sea, adventure, and the Orient; a human being who abhors the law and the neighbor as a kind of boredom and who measures everything old and established with envious eyes. With the marvelous cunning of his imagination he would like to establish all of this anew at least in thought, and put his hand to it and his meaning into it—if only for the moments of a sunny afternoon when his insatiable and melancholy soul does feel sated for once, and only what is his and nothing alien may appear to his eyes.

292

To those who preach morals.— I do not wish to promote any morality, but to those who do I give this advice: If you wish to deprive the best things and states of all honor and worth, then go on talking about them as you have been doing. Place them at the head of your morality and talk from morning to night of the happiness of virtue, the composure of the soul, of justice and immanent retribution. The way you are going about it, all these good things will eventually have popularity and the clamor of the streets on their side; but at the same time all the gold

---

[17] An allusion to Columbus.

that was on them will have been worn off by so much handling, and all the gold *inside* will have turned to lead. Truly, you are masters of alchemy in reverse: the devaluation of what is most valuable. Why don't you make the experiment of trying another prescription to keep from attaining the opposite of your goal as you have done hitherto? *Deny* these good things, withdraw the mob's acclaim from them as well as their easy currency; make them once again concealed secrets of solitary souls; say *that morality is something forbidden.* That way you might win over for these things the kind of people who alone matter: I mean those who are *heroic.* But to that end there has to be a quality that inspires fear and not, as hitherto, nausea. Hasn't the time come to say of morality what Master Eckhart said: "I ask God to rid me of God."

293

Our air.— We know very well how science strikes those who merely glance at it in passing, as if they were walking by, as women do and unfortunately also many artists: the severity of its service, its inexorability in small as in great matters, and the speed of weighing and judging matters and passing judgment makes them feel dizzy and afraid. Above all they are terrified to see how the most difficult is demanded and the best is done without praise and decorations. Indeed, what one hears is, as among soldiers, mostly reproaches and harsh rebukes; for doing things well is considered the rule, and failure is the exception; but the rule always tends to keep quiet. This "severity of science" has the same effect as the forms and good manners of the best society: it is frightening for the uninitiated. But those who are used to it would never wish to live anywhere else than in this bright, transparent, vigorous, electrified air—in this *virile* air. Anywhere else things are not clean and airy enough for them; they suspect that elsewhere their best art would not really profit others nor give real delight to themselves; that among misunderstandings half of their lives would slip through their fingers; that they would be required to exercise a great deal of caution, conceal things, be inhibited—so many ways of

losing a lot of strength for no good reason. But in this severe
and clear element they have their full strength; here they can
fly. Why, then, go down into those muddy waters where one
has to swim and wade and get one's wings dirty?

No, it is too hard for us to live there. Is it our fault that we
were born for the air, clean air, we rivals of the beams of
light, and that we wish we could ride on ethereal dust specks
like these beams—not away from the sun but *toward the sun*!
That, however, we cannot do. Let us therefore do what alone
we can do: bring light to the earth, be "the light of the earth"!
And to that end we have our wings and our speed and severity;
for this are we virile and even terrible like fire. Let those be
terrified by us who do not know how to gain warmth and
light from us!

294

Against the slanderers of nature.— I find those people disagreeable in whom every natural inclination immediately becomes a sickness, something that disfigures them or is downright
infamous: it is *they* that have seduced us to hold that man's
inclinations and instincts are evil. *They* are the cause of our
great injustice against our nature, against all nature. There are
enough people who *might well* entrust themselves to their instincts with grace and without care; but they do not, from fear
of this imagined "evil character" of nature. That is why we
find so little nobility among men; for it will always be the mark
of nobility that one feels no fear of oneself, expects nothing
infamous of oneself, flies without scruple where we feel like
flying, we freeborn birds. Wherever we may come there will
always be freedom and sunlight around us.

295

Brief habits.— I love brief habits and consider them an
inestimable means for getting to know *many* things and states,
down to the bottom of their sweetness and bitternesses. My
nature is designed entirely for brief habits, even in the needs of

my physical health and altogether *as far* as I can see at all—
from the lowest to the highest. I always believe that here is
something that will give me lasting satisfaction—brief habits,
too, have this faith of passion, this faith in eternity—and that
I am to be envied for having found and recognized it; and now
it nourishes me at noon and in the evening and spreads a deep
contentment all around itself and deep into me so that I desire
nothing else, without having any need for comparisons, contempt, or hatred. But one day its time is up; the good thing parts
from me, not as something that has come to nauseate me but
peacefully and sated with me as I am with it—as if we had
reason to be grateful to each other as we shook hands to say
farewell. Even then something new is waiting at the door, along
with my faith—this indestructible fool and sage!—that this
new discovery will be just right, and that this will be the last
time. That is what happens to me with dishes, ideas, human
beings, cities, poems, music, doctrines, ways of arranging the
day, and life styles.

Enduring habits I hate. I feel as if a tyrant had come near me
and as if the air I breathe had thickened when events take
such a turn that it appears that they will inevitably give rise to
enduring habits; for example, owing to an official position, constant association with the same people a permanent domicile,
or unique good health. Yes, at the very bottom of my soul I feel
grateful to all my misery and bouts of sickness and everything
about me that is imperfect, because this sort of thing leaves me
with a hundred backdoors through which I can escape from
enduring habits.

Most intolerable, to be sure, and the terrible par excellence
would be for me a life entirely devoid of habits, a life that
would demand perpetual improvisation. That would be my exile
and my Siberia.[18]

---

[18] This conclusion qualifies the resolve to live dangerously. But some
stability and temporary equilibrium are needed to permit the concentra-
tion of all mental and emotional resources on the most important problems. One simply cannot question everything at once. The most one can
do is to grant nothing *permanent* immunity.

Cf. sections 3 and 4 of the Preface above.

296

A firm reputation.— A firm reputation used to be extremely useful; and wherever society is still dominated by the herd instinct it is still most expedient for every one to *pretend* that his character and occupation are unchangeable, even if at bottom they are not. "One can depend on him, he remains the same": in all extremities of society this is the sort of praise that means the most. Society is pleased to feel that the virtue of this person, the ambition of that one, and the thoughtfulness and passion of the third provide it with a dependable *instrument* that is always at hand; society honors this *instrumental nature,* this way of remaining faithful to oneself, this unchangeability of views, aspirations, and even faults and lavishes its highest honors upon it. Such esteem, which flourishes and has flourished everywhere alongside the morality of mores,[19] breeds "character" and brings all change, all re-learning, all self-transformation into *ill repute.* However great the advantages of this way of thinking may be elsewhere, for the search after knowledge no general judgment could be more harmful, for precisely the good will of those who seek knowledge to declare themselves at any time dauntlessly *against* their previous opinions and to mistrust everything that wishes to become *firm* in us is thus condemned and brought into ill repute.[20] Being at odds with "a firm reputation," the attitude of those who seek knowledge is considered *dishonorable* while the petrification of opinions is accorded a monopoly on honor! Under the spell of such notions we have to live to this day. How hard it is to live when one feels the opposition of many millennia all around. It is probable that the search after knowledge was afflicted for many millennia with a bad conscience, and that the history of the greatest spirits must have contained a good deal of self-contempt and secret misery.

---

[19] Cf. sections 43, 143, and 149 above.
[20] See the immediately preceding section and the note on that. Cf. also Nietzsche's note: "A very popular error: having the courage of one's convictions; rather it is a matter of having the courage for an *attack* on one's convictions!!!" (Musarion edition, vol. XVI, p. 318.)

297

The ability to contradict.— Everybody knows nowadays that the ability to accept criticism and contradiction is a sign of high culture. Some people actually realize that higher human beings desire and provoke contradiction in order to receive some hint about their own injustices of which they are as yet unaware. But the ability to contradict, the attainment of a good conscience when one feels hostile to what is accustomed, traditional, and hallowed—that is still more excellent and constitutes what is really great, new, and amazing in our culture; this is the step of steps of the liberated spirit: Who knows that?

298

Sigh.— I caught this insight on the way and quickly seized the rather poor words that were closest to hand to pin it down lest it fly away again. And now it has died of these arid words and shakes and flaps in them—and I hardly know any more when I look at it how I could ever have felt so happy when I caught this bird.[21]

299

What one should learn from artists.— How can we make things beautiful, attractive, and desirable for us when they are not? And I rather think that in themselves they never are. Here we could learn something from physicians, when for example they dilute what is bitter or add wine and sugar to a mixture—but even more from artists who are really continually trying to bring off such inventions and feats. Moving away from things until there is a good deal that one no longer sees and there is much that our eye has to add if we are still to see them at all; or seeing things around a corner and as cut out and framed; or to place them so that they partially conceal each other and grant us only glimpses of architectural perspectives;[22]

---

[21] Cf. the final section of *Beyond Good and Evil*, #296 (BWN, 426f.). Sections 295–97 help to explain his meaning.

[22] *oder sie so stellen, dass sie sich teilweise verstellen und nur perspectivische Durchblicke gestatten.*

or looking at them through tinted glass or in the light of the sunset; or giving them a surface and skin that is not fully transparent—all this we should learn from artists while being wiser than they are in other matters. For with them this subtle power usually comes to an end where art ends and life begins; but we want to be the poets of our life—first of all in the smallest, most everyday matters.

300

Preludes of science.— Do you really believe that the sciences would ever have originated and grown if the way had not been prepared by magicians, alchemists, astrologers, and witches whose promises and pretensions first had to create a thirst, a hunger, a taste for *hidden* and *forbidden* powers? Indeed,[23] infinitely more had to be *promised* than could ever be fulfilled in order that anything at all might be fulfilled in the realm of knowledge.

Even as these preludes and preliminary exercises of sciences were not by any means practiced and experienced as such, the whole of *religion* might yet appear as a prelude and exercise to some distant age. Perhaps religion could have been the strange means to make it possible for a few single individuals to enjoy the whole self-sufficiency of a god and his whole power of self-redemption. Indeed—one might ask—would man ever have learned without the benefit of such a religious training and prehistory to experience a hunger and thirst for *himself*, and to find satisfaction and fullness in *himself*? Did Prometheus have to *fancy* first that he had *stolen* the light and then pay for that—before he finally discovered that he had created the light *by coveting the light* and that not only man but also the *god* was the work of his own hands and had been mere clay in his

---

[23] I am omitting "that" at this point as well as a question mark at the end of this sentence because the original construction in German is illogical. The answer to the first question is clearly meant to be: no. But the answer to this second question, which I have not cast in the form of a question, would have to be: yes. See also section 23.

hands? All mere images of the maker—no less than the fancy,
the theft, the Caucasus, the vulture, and the whole tragic
Prometheia of all seekers after knowledge?[24]

301

The fancy of the contemplatives.— What distinguishes the
higher human beings from the lower is that the former see and
hear immeasurably more, and see and hear thoughtfully—and
precisely this distinguishes human beings from animals, and the
higher animals from the lower. For anyone who grows up into
the heights of humanity the world becomes ever fuller; ever
more fishhooks are cast in his direction to capture his interest;
the number of things that stimulate him grows constantly, as
does the number of different kinds of pleasure and displeasure:
The higher human being always becomes at the same time
happier and unhappier. But he can never shake off a *delusion*:
He fancies that he is a *spectator* and *listener* who has been
placed before the great visual and acoustic spectacle that is
life; he calls his own nature *contemplative* and overlooks that
he himself is really the poet who keeps creating this life. Of
course, he is different from the *actor* of this drama, the so-
called active type; but he is even less like a mere spectator and
festive guest in front of the stage. As a poet, he certainly has
vis contemplativa and the ability to look back upon his work,
but at the same time also and above all *vis creativa*,[25] which the
active human being *lacks*, whatever visual appearances and the
faith of all the world may say. We who think and feel at the
same time are those who really continually *fashion* something

---

[24] In the first part of his Prometheus trilogy (*Prometheia*), which is the
only part that has survived, Aeschylus shows us Prometheus "bound,"
chained, or crucified upon a Caucasian rock. The legend says that an
eagle (or vulture?) was dispatched by Zeus to feed on Prometheus's
liver, which was renewed daily so that the titan's torment would not
cease. This was, at least in part, his punishment for defying Zeus and
stealing fire from heaven. Nietzsche's point becomes clearer in the next
section.

[25] Contemplative power; creative power.

that had not been there before: the whole eternally growing world of valuations, colors, accents, perspectives, scales, affirmations, and negations. This poem that we have invented is continually studied by the so-called practical human beings (our actors) who learn their roles and translate everything into flesh and actuality, into the everyday. Whatever has *value* in our world now does not have value in itself, according to its nature —nature is always value-less, but has been *given* value at some time, as a present—and it was *we* who gave and bestowed it. Only we have created the world *that concerns man*! —But precisely this knowledge we lack, and when we occasionally catch it for a fleeting moment we always forget it again immediately; we fail to recognize our best power and underestimate ourselves, the contemplatives, just a little. We are *neither as proud nor as happy* as we might be.

302

The danger of the happiest.— To have refined senses, including the sense of taste; to be accustomed to the most exquisite things of the spirit as if they were simply the right and most convenient nourishment; to enjoy a strong, bold, audacious soul; to go through life with a calm eye and firm step, always prepared to risk all—festively, impelled by the longing for undiscovered worlds and seas, people and gods; to harken to all cheerful music as if it were a sign that bold men, soldiers, seafarers were probably seeking their brief rest and pleasure there—and in the most profound enjoyment of the moment, to be overcome by tears and the whole crimson melancholy of the happy: who would not wish that all this might be *his* possession, his state! This was the *happiness of Homer*! The state of him that gave the Greeks their gods—no, who invented his own gods for himself! But we should not overlook this: With this Homeric happiness in one's soul one is also more capable of suffering than any other creature under the sun. This is the only price for which one can buy the most precious shell that the waves of existence have ever yet washed on the shore. As its owner one becomes ever more refined in pain and ultimately too refined; any small dejection and nausea was quite enough in the end to spoil life for Homer. He had been unable to guess a foolish little riddle posed to him by some fishermen.[26] Yes, little riddles are the danger that confronts those who are happiest.—

303

Two who are happy.— Truly, in spite of his youth, this is a great *improviser of life* who amazes even the subtlest observer; for he never seems to make a mistake although he continually takes the greatest risk. One is reminded of those masters of musical improvisation whose hands the listener would also like to credit with divine *infallibility* although here and there they make a mistake as every mortal does. But they are practiced and inventive and ready at any moment to incorporate into their thematic order the most accidental tone to which the flick of a finger or a mood has driven them, breathing a beautiful meaning and a soul into an accident.

Here is an altogether different person: at bottom, everything he desires and plans goes wrong. What he has occasionally set his heart upon has brought him several times to the edge of the abyss and within a hair of destruction; and if he escaped that, it was certainly not merely "with a black eye."[27] Do you suppose that he feels unhappy about that? He made up his mind long ago not to take his own desires and plans too seriously. "If I do not succeed at *this*," he says to himself, "I may perhaps succeed at that; and on the whole I do not know whether I do not have more reason to be grateful to my failures than to any success.[28] Was I made to be stubborn and to have horns like a bull? What constitutes the value and result of life for *me* lies elsewhere; my pride as well as my misery lie elsewhere. I

---

[26] This was an ancient Greek tradition.

[27] The German idiom "to get away with a black eye" means "to get off lightly."

[28] If there were any doubt that Nietzsche is here thinking of himself, his Preface to the book would dispel it. When he later used parts of this Preface in *Nietzsche contra Wagner*, he added: "I have often asked myself whether I am not more heavily obligated to the hardest years of my life than to any others" (VPN, 680).

know more about life because I have so often been on the verge
of losing it; and precisely for that reason I get more out of life
than any of you."

304

By doing we forego.— At bottom I abhor all those moralities
which say: "Do not do this! Renounce! Overcome yourself!"
But I am well disposed toward those moralities which goad me
to do something and do it again, from morning till evening, and
then to dream of it at night, and to think of nothing except
doing this *well*, as well as *I* alone can do it. When one lives
like that, one thing after another that simply does not belong to
such a life drops off. Without hatred or aversion one sees this
take its leave today and that tomorrow, like yellow leaves that
any slight stirring of the air takes off a tree. He may not even
notice that it takes its leave; for his eye is riveted to his goal—
forward, not sideward, backward, downward. What we do
should determine what we forego; by doing we forego—that is
how I like it, that is my *placitum*.[29] But I do not wish to strive
with open eyes for my own impoverishment; I do not like
negative virtues—virtues whose very essence it is to negate and
deny oneself something.

305

Self-control.— Those moralists who command man first of
all and above all to gain control of himself thus afflict him with
a peculiar disease; namely, a constant irritability in the face of
all natural stirrings and inclinations—as it were, a kind of itch-
ing. Whatever may henceforth push, pull, attract, or impel such
an irritable person from inside or outside, it will always seem
to him as if his self-control were endangered. No longer may he
entrust himself to any instinct or free wingbeat; he stands in a
fixed position with a gesture that wards off, armed against
himself, with sharp and mistrustful eyes—the eternal guardian
of his castle, since he has turned himself into a castle. Of course,

---

[29] principle.

he can achieve *greatness* this way. But he has certainly become insufferable for others, difficult for himself, and impoverished and cut off from the most beautiful fortuities of his soul. Also from all further *instruction*. For one must be able to lose oneself occasionally if one wants to learn something from things different from oneself.

306

Stoics and Epicureans.— The Epicurean selects the situation, the persons, and even the events that suit his extremely irritable, intellectual constitution; he gives up all others, which means almost everything, because they would be too strong and heavy for him to digest. The Stoic, on the other hand, trains himself to swallow stones and worms, slivers of glass and scorpions without nausea; he wants his stomach to become ultimately indifferent to whatever the accidents of existence might pour into it: he reminds one of that Arabian sect of the Assaua whom one encounters in Algiers: like these insensitive people, he, too, enjoys having an audience when he shows off his insensitivity, while the Epicurean would rather dispense with that, having his "garden"![30] For those with whom fate attempts improvisations —those who live in violent ages and depend on sudden and mercurial people—Stoicism may indeed be advisable. But anyone who foresees more or less that fate permits him to spin *a long thread* does well to make Epicurean arrangements. That is what all those have always done whose work is of the spirit.[31] For this type it would be the loss of losses[32] to be deprived of their subtle irritability and be awarded in its place a hard Stoic hedgehog skin.

307

In favor of criticism.— Now something that you formerly loved as a truth or probability strikes you as an error; you shed

---

[30] Epicurus bought a house and garden in Athens, which became the domicile of his school. He taught not in the market place but in his garden.

[31] *alle Menschen der geistigen Arbeit:* artists, scholars, writers.

[32] Superlative, like the song of songs.

it and fancy that this represents a victory for your reason. But perhaps this error was as necessary for you then, when you were still a different person—you are always a different person —as are all your present "truths," being a skin, as it were, that concealed and covered a great deal that you were not yet permitted to see. What killed that opinion for you was your new life and not your reason: *you no longer need it,* and now it collapses and unreason crawls out of it into the light like a worm. When we criticize something, this is no arbitrary and impersonal event; it is, at least very often, evidence of vital energies in us that are growing and shedding a skin. We negate and must negate because something in us wants to live and affirm—something that we perhaps do not know or see as yet. —This is said in favor of criticism.[33]

308

The history of every day.— What is the history of every day in your case? Look at your habits that constitute it: are they the product of innumerable little cowardices and lazinesses or of your courage and inventive reason? However different these two cases are, people might very well praise you equally and you might actually profit them equally this way and that. But praise and profit and respectability may suffice those who merely wish to have a good conscience—but not you who try the heart and reins and make even conscience an object of science![34]

309

From the seventh solitude.— One day the wanderer slammed a door behind himself, stopped in his tracks, and wept. Then he said: "This penchant and passion for what is true, real, non-

---

[33] It might be interesting to compare this section with Hegel's *Phenomenology of the Spirit.*

[34] *der du ein Wissen um das Gewissen hast:* this play on words, which can be salvaged in English only for the eye, occurs a number of times in Nietzsche's works.

apparent,[35] certain[36]—how it aggravates me! Why does this gloomy and restless fellow keep following and driving *me*? I want to rest, but he will not allow it. How much there is that seduces me to tarry! Everywhere Armida's[37] gardens beckon me; everywhere I must keep tearing my heart away and experience new bitternesses. I must raise my feet again and again, weary and wounded though they be; and because I must go on, I often look back in wrath at the most beautiful things that could not hold me—*because* they could not hold me."

310

Will and wave.— How greedily this wave approaches, as if it were after something! How it crawls with terrifying haste into the inmost nooks of this labyrinthine cliff! It seems that it is trying to anticipate someone; it seems that something of value, high value, must be hidden there.—And now it comes back, a little more slowly but still quite white with excitement; is it disappointed? Has it found what it looked for? Does it pretend to be disappointed?—But already another wave is approaching, still more greedily and savagely than the first, and its soul, too, seems to be full of secrets and the lust to dig up treasures. Thus live waves—thus live we who will—more I shall not say.

So? You mistrust me? You are angry with me, you beautiful monsters? Are you afraid that I might give away your whole secret? Well, be angry with me, arch your dangerous green bodies as high as you can, raise a wall between me and the sun—as you are doing now! Truly, even now nothing remains of the world but green twilight and green lightning. Carry on as you like, roaring with overweening pleasure and malice—or

---

[35] *Un-Scheinbaren:* written as one word, without hyphen, this would mean, not looking like much, insignificant. The spelling makes clear that what is meant here is what is not merely apparent.

[36] *Gewissen:* that "certain" is meant is clear from the grammatical context; nevertheless the word echoes the conclusion of section 308 where *Gewissen* (emphasized by Nietzsche) means conscience.

[37] The title and heroine of an opera by Christoph Willibald Gluck, first performed in 1777.

dive again, pouring your emeralds down into the deepest depths, and throw your infinite white mane of foam and spray over them: Everything suits me, for everything suits you so well, and I am so well-disposed toward you for everything; how could I think of betraying you? For—mark my word!—I know you and your secret, I know your kind! You and I—are we not of one kind?—You and I—do we not have *one secret*?[38]

---

[38] This is a prose poem that may *look* "as if it were after something" although in fact it is born of "overweening pleasure and malice." *Uebermut,* literally over-mood or over-courage, has no exact English equivalent but suggests an overweening, exuberant state of mind. Nietzsche was fond of this word, of *Lust* (the one word for pleasure that he liked because it has some overtones of passion), and of *Bosheit* (malice, wickedness—often "sarcasm" comes closest to his meaning).

What he shares with the waves is the overflowing vitality that never comes to a stop—not because it has failed to find what it was looking for but because this constant play is its life. A critic might object: How can one speak of Nietzsche's overflowing vitality when he was sick and in pain much of the time? But neither his doctors' advice to save his half-blind eyes by giving up reading and writing nor his migraine headaches and other torments stopped him, and he might have said with Goethe's Tasso (V.2):

If I may not reflect and fashion poems,
then is my life no longer life to me.
As soon forbid the silkworm to spin on
when he is spinning himself close to death!

Nietzsche's comments on the slogan *l'art pour l'art* (*Beyond Good and Evil,* sections 208 and 254), *Twilight,* IX, section 24, and *The Will to Power,* sections 81 and 808) are consistent with this reading. He applauds the rejection of a moral purpose for art but objects to any claim of "objectivity" and to any repudiation of will, passion, and love. " 'Play,' the useless—as the ideal of him who is overfull of strength, as 'childlike.' The 'childlikeness' of God, *pais paizon*" (*The Will to Power,* section 797). The *pais paizon* (child playing) is one of the central images in Nietzsche, derived from Heraclitus and enriched by Friedrich Schiller's play theory of art. Cf. the first chapter of *Zarathustra* (after the Prologue).

These reflections are relevant to Nietzsche's conception of the eternal recurrence of the same events, which is first presented in this book. The absence of all purpose and meaning, to which one's first reaction may well be nausea or despair, can be experienced as liberating and delightful in what Nietzsche later calls a "Dionysian" perspective.

311

Refracted light.— One is not always bold, and when one grows tired then one of us, too, is apt to moan like this: "It is so hard to hurt people—oh, why is it necessary! What does it profit us to live in seclusion when we refuse to keep to ourselves what gives offense? Would it not be more advisable to live in the swarm and to make up to individuals the sins that should and must be committed against all? To be foolish with fools, vain with the vain, and enthusiastic with enthusiasts? Wouldn't that be fair, given such overweening deviation on the whole? When I hear of the malice of others against me—isn't my first reaction one of satisfaction? Quite right! I seem to be saying to them—I am so ill-attuned to you and have so much truth on my side that you might as well have a good day at my expense whenever you can! Here are my faults and blunders, here my delusion, my bad taste, my confusion, my tears, my vanity, my owlish seclusion, my contradictions. Here you can laugh. Laugh, then, and be merry! I do not resent the law and nature of things according to which faults and blunders cause merriment.

"To be sure, times used to be more 'beautiful' when anyone with a halfway new idea could still feel so *indispensable* that he would go out into the street and shout at everyone: 'Behold, the kingdom of heaven is at hand!' —I should not miss myself if I were not there. All of us are dispensable."

But, to repeat it, that is not how we think when we are bold; then we don't think of this.[39]

312

My dog.— I have given a name to my pain and call it "dog." It is just as faithful, just as obtrusive and shameless, just as

---

[39] This section reveals a great deal about Nietzsche's personality.

Cf. Nietzsche's letter to Gast, August 20, 1880: ". . . To this day, my whole philosophy totters after an hour's sympathetic conversation with total strangers: it seems so foolish to me to wish to be right at the price of love, and not be *able to communicate* what one considers most valuable lest one destroy the sympathy. *Hinc meae lacrimae* [hence my tears]."

entertaining, just as clever as any other dog—and I can scold it and vent my bad mood on it, as others do with their dogs, servants, and wives.

313

No image of torture.— I want to proceed as Raphael did and never paint another image of torture. There are enough sublime things so that one does not have to look for the sublime where it dwells in sisterly association with cruelty; and my ambition also could never find satisfaction if I became a sublime assistant at torture.

314

New domestic animals.— I want to have my lion and eagle near me so that I always have hints and omens that help me to know how great or small my strength is. Must I look down upon them today and feel fear? And will the hour return when they look up to me—in fear?—[40]

315

On the last hour.— Storms are my danger. Will I have my storm of which I will perish, as Oliver Cromwell perished of his storm? Or will I go out like a light that no wind blows out but that becomes tired and sated with itself—a burned-out light? Or finally: will I blow myself out lest I burn out?—[41]

---

[40] This grandiloquent passage contrasts rather sharply with its context. Lion and eagle never turn up again as a pair; but in section 342 below and in Nietzsche's next book, Zarathustra speaks of "my eagle and my serpent," and symbolic lions appear several times in *Zarathustra* (Part I, "On the three Metamorphoses," VPN, 137ff.; Part III, "On Old and New Tablets," section 1, VPN, 308; and Part IV, "The Welcome," "Among Daughters of the Wilderness," and "The Sign," VPN, 395, 420, and 436 ff.).

[41] Professor Lawrence Stone advises me: "Cromwell died just after one of the worst storms of the century: 'Tossed in a furious hurricane/Did Oliver give up his reign.' (S. Butler, *Hudibras*, Pt. III, Canto ii, line 215). The storm was generally taken to be symbolic of the collapse of

316

Prophetic human beings.— You have no feeling for the fact that prophetic human beings are afflicted with a great deal of suffering; you merely suppose that they have been granted a beautiful "gift," and you would even like to have it yourself. But I shall express myself in a parable. How much may animals suffer from the electricity in the air and the clouds! We see how some species have a prophetic faculty regarding the weather; monkeys, for example (as may be observed even in Europe, and not only in zoos—namely, on Gibraltar). But we pay no heed that it is their *pains* that make them prophets. When a strong positive electrical charge, under the influence of an approaching cloud that is as yet far from visible, suddenly turns into negative electricity and a change of the weather is impending, these animals behave as if an enemy were drawing near and prepare for defense or escape; most often they try to hide: They do not understand bad weather as a kind of weather but as an enemy whose hand they already *feel*.[42]

---

all he had stood for."

The last sentence brings to mind Van Gogh's suicide in 1890. Although Nietzsche was in many ways prophetic and the very next section offers some pertinent reflections about that, he did not foresee that his own light would all but go out, that he would fail to blow it out himself while he still could, and that after his mind was gone others would keep him alive for another eleven and a half years—and that his sister would then commission drawings, etchings, and sculptures of his surviving carcass, and that in the twentieth century many of his admirers and publishers would prefer these "portraits" to photographs of Nietzsche during his creative years.

[42] On October 28, 1881 Nietzsche asked Overbeck to have a book sent to him "on account of the terrible effects of atmospheric electricity on me—they will yet drive me over the earth; there *must* be better living conditions for my nature. E.g., in the high plateaus of Mexico, on the Pacific side (Swiss colony 'New Bern'). Very, very much tormented day after day."

On November 14, 1881 in the letter cited in the note on section 279 above, Nietzsche writes Overbeck that he has received the book—by Foissac, on medical meteorology—but found it disappointing. "I should have been at the electricity exhibition in Paris, partly to learn the latest findings, partly as an exhibition; for as one who senses electrical changes and as a so-called weather prophet I am a match for the monkeys and

317

Looking back.— The true pathos of every period of our life rarely becomes clear to us as long as we live in this period; then we always assume that it is the only state that is possible and reasonable for us and—to speak with the Greeks and adopt their distinction—an *ethos* and not a *pathos*.[43] A few musical chords reminded me today of a winter and a house and an extremely solitary life, as well as the feeling in which I lived at that time: I thought that I might go on living that way forever. But now I comprehend that it was wholly pathos and passion and thus comparable to this painful and bold music that was so certain that there was some comfort. That sort of thing one must not have for years or for eternities; otherwise one would become too "supra-terrestrial" for this planet.

318

Wisdom in pain.— There is as much wisdom in pain as there is in pleasure: both belong among the factors that contribute the most to the preservation of the species. If pain did not, it would have perished long ago; that it hurts is no argument against it but its essence. In pain I hear the captain's command: "Take in the sails!" The bold seafarer "man" must have mastered the art of doing a thousand things with his sails; otherwise he would be done for in no time, and the ocean would swallow him. We must learn to live with diminished energies, too: As soon as pain gives its safety signal the time

---

am probably a 'specialty.' Could [Eduard] Hagenbach [Professor of Physics at Basel] possibly tell us what clothing (or chains, rings, etc.) would be the best protection against these excessive effects? After all, I cannot always hang in a silken hammock! Better really hang oneself! Quite radically! . . .

"My eyes fail more and more—the extraordinary pain even after the *briefest* use of my eyes keeps me virtually *away* from science (quite apart from the extreme weakness of my eyesight). For how long now have I been unable to *read*!!"

[43] Pathos is defined as "literally, the more transitory and passive experiences of life, as contrasted with ethos, the more permanent and active disposition and character" (James Mark Baldwin, *Dictionary of Philosophy and Psychology*, vol. II, 1902).

has come to diminish them; some great danger or other, a storm is approaching, and we are well advised to "inflate" ourselves as little as possible.

True, there are people who hear precisely the opposite command when great pain approaches: Their expression is never prouder, more warlike, and happier than it is when a storm comes up; indeed, pain itself gives them their greatest moments. This is the heroic type, the great *pain bringers* of humanity, those few or rare human beings who need the very same apology that pain itself needs—and truly, one should not deny it to them. They contribute immensely to the preservation and enhancement of the species, even if it were only by opposing comfortableness and by not concealing how this sort of happiness nauseates them.[44]

319

As interpreters of our experiences.— One sort of honesty has been alien to all founders of religions and their kind: They have never made their experiences a matter of conscience for knowledge. "What did I really experience? What happened in me and around me at that time? Was my reason bright enough? Was my will opposed to all deceptions of the senses and bold in resisting the fantastic?" None of them has asked such questions, nor do any of our dear religious people ask them even now. On the contrary, they thirst after things that *go against reason*, and they do not wish to make it too hard for themselves to satisfy it. So they experience "miracles" and "rebirths" and hear the voices of little angels! But we, we others who thirst after reason, are determined to scrutinize our experiences as severely as a scientific experiment—hour after hour, day after day. We ourselves wish to be our experiments and guinea pigs.[45]

---

[44] The theme of contempt for comfortableness and "this sort of happiness" receives its classical statement in the Prologue of *Zarathustra*, section 3ff.

[45] This is quintessential Nietzsche. Those who ignore this theme, which is introduced in section 2 above and developed further in Book V below and in *The Antichrist*, sections 50–55, misunderstand him.

The above section is relevant not only to the interpretation of Nietzsche and the evaluation of *religious* experiences but also to non-religious, non-denominational "mystical" experiences.

320

Upon seeing each other again.— A: Do I still understand you well? You are seeking? Where is *your* nook and star in the actual world? Where can *you* lie down in the sun so that you, too, reap an excess of wellbeing and your existence justifies itself? Let everyone do that for himself—you seem to me to be saying—and let everyone put out of his mind generalities and worries about others and about society!

B: What I want is more; I am no seeker. I want to create for myself a sun of my own.

321

New caution.— Let us stop thinking so much about punishing, reproaching, and improving others! We rarely change an individual, and if we should succeed for once, something may also have been accomplished, unnoticed: *we* may have been changed by him. Let us rather see to it that our own influence on *all that is yet to come* balances and outweighs his influence. Let us not contend in a direct fight—and that is what all reproaching, punishing, and attempts to improve others amount to. Let us rather raise ourselves that much higher. Let us color our own example ever more brilliantly. Let our brilliance make them look dark. No, let us not become darker ourselves on their account, like all those who punish others and feel dissatisfied. Let us sooner step aside. Let us look away.[46]

322

Parable.— Those thinkers in whom all stars move in cyclic orbits are not the most profound. Whoever looks into himself as into vast space and carries galaxies in himself, also knows how irregular all galaxies are; they lead into the chaos and labyrinth of existence.[47]

---

[46] Cf. sections 276 and 304.
[47] Cf. Nietzsche's critique of philosophical systems—Kaufmann, 78ff; and the Prologue to *Zarathustra*, section 5: "One must still have chaos in oneself to give birth to a dancing star" (VPN, 129).

323

Good luck in fate.— The greatest distinction that fate can bestow on us is to let us fight for a time on the side of our opponents. With that we are *predestined* for a great victory.[48]

324

In media vita.[49]— No, life has not disappointed me. On the contrary, I find it truer,[50] more desirable and mysterious every year—ever since the day when the great liberator came to me: the idea that life could be an experiment of the seeker for knowledge—and not a duty, not a calamity, not trickery. —And knowledge itself: let it be something else for others; for example, a bed to rest on, or the way to such a bed, or a diversion, or a form of leisure—for me it is a world of dangers and victories in which heroic feelings, too, find places to dance and play. *"Life as a means to knowledge"*—with this principle in one's heart one can live not only boldly but even gaily, and laugh gaily, too. And who knows how to laugh anyway and live well if he does not first know a good deal about war and victory?[51]

325

What belongs to greatness.— Who will attain anything great if he does not find in himself the strength and the will to *inflict* great suffering? Being able to suffer is the least thing; weak women and even slaves often achieve virtuosity in that. But not to perish of internal distress and uncertainty when one inflicts great suffering and hears the cry of this suffering—that is great, that belongs to greatness.[52]

---

[48] Nietzsche himself began his career as a writer as a fighter on Richard Wagner's side.

[49] In mid-life.

[50] *wahrer.* The Musarion edition has richer (*reicher*).

[51] Cf. sections 283, 310, and 319—they furnish the best commentary.

[52] Cf. section 311 above, especially the beginning. The distress that this section caused some of Nietzsche's first readers illustrates his point. He knew how his development and books had pained his mother and sister, Richard and Cosima Wagner, Wagner's admirers, and ever so many others.

326

The physicians of the soul and pain.— All preachers of morals as well as all theologians share one bad habit; all of them try to con men into believing that they are in a very bad way and need some ultimate, hard, radical cure. Because humanity has listened to these teachers much too eagerly for whole centuries, something of this superstition that they are in a very bad way has finally stuck. Now they are only too ready to sigh, to find nothing good in life and to sulk together, as if life were really hard to *endure.* Actually, they are overwhelmingly sure of their life and in love with it, and they know innumerable ruses and subtle tricks to vanquish what is disagreeable and to pull the fangs of pain and misfortune.

It seems to me that people always *exaggerate* when they speak of pain and misfortune, as if it were a requirement of good manners to exaggerate here, while one keeps studiously quiet about the fact that there are innumerable palliatives against pain, such as anaesthesia or the feverish haste of thoughts, or a quiet posture, or good or bad memories, purposes, hopes, and many kinds of pride and sympathy that almost have the same effect as anaesthetics—and at the highest degrees of pain one automatically loses consciousness. We know quite well how to drip sweetnesses upon our bitternesses, especially the bitternesses of the soul; we find remedies in our courage and sublimity as well as the nobler deliria of submission and resignation. A loss is a loss for barely one hour; somehow it also brings us some gift from heaven—new strength, for example, or at least a new opportunity for strength.

What fantasies about the inner "misery" of evil people moral preachers have invented! What *lies* they have told us about the unhappiness of passionate people! "Lies" is really the proper word here; for they knew very well of the over-rich happiness of this kind of human being, but they kept a deadly silence about it because it refuted their theory according to which all happiness begins only after the annihilation of passion and the silencing of the will.[53] Finally, regarding the prescription of all

---

[53] The phrasing here, if not before, makes it clear that Nietzsche had Schopenhauer in mind, among others. The young Nietzsche had admired

these physicians of the soul and their praise of a hard, radical cure, it should be permitted to ask: Is our life really painful and burdensome enough to make it advantageous to exchange it for a Stoic way of life and petrification? We are *not so badly off* that we have to be as badly off as Stoics.

327

Taking seriously.— In the great majority, the intellect is a clumsy, gloomy, creaking machine that is difficult to start. They call it "taking the matter *seriously*" when they want to work with this machine and think well. How burdensome they must find good thinking! The lovely human beast always seems to lose its good spirits when it thinks well; it becomes "serious." And "where laughter and gaiety are found, thinking does not amount to anything": that is the prejudice of this serious beast against all "gay science."   — Well then, let us prove that this is a prejudice.[54]

Schopenhauer for insisting boldly and unfashionably on the suffering in the world; but already in his first book, *The Birth of Tragedy*, Nietzsche had turned his back on Schopenhauer's "Buddhistic negation of the will": The tragic poets of Greece had not shut their eyes to suffering, but they had affirmed life and the world as beautiful in spite of all suffering. This remained a central motif in Nietzsche's work from first to last. Our pains are no excuse for slandering the world.

[54] The conception of "gay science" takes the theme of the preceding section a step further, beyond what we find in Nietzsche's early work. The opposition to gravity remains central in Nietzsche's mature thought but was missed entirely by many of his early interpreters and translators, partly owing to the influence of his sister. In *The Gay Science* this theme is equally pronounced in Nietzsche's verse and in his prose. In *Zarathustra I* we find the words: "Not by wrath does one kill but by laughter. Come, let us kill the spirit of gravity!" ("On Reading and Writing," VPN, 153) In Part III we encounter not only a whole chapter "On the Spirit of Gravity" but also scattered references to "the spirit of gravity, my devil and archenemy" ("On the Vision and the Riddle," VPN, 268; cf. "On Old and New Tablets," section 2, VPN, 309, and "The Awakening" in Part IV, VPN, 422), as well as Zarathustra's celebration of "light feet" and the dance. Listing all the relevant passages, also in Nietzsche's later works, would lead too far afield. But

328

To harm stupidity.— Surely, the faith preached so stubbornly and with so much conviction, that egoism is reprehensible, has on the whole harmed egoism (while *benefiting,* as I shall repeat a hundred times, *the herd instincts!*)—above all, by depriving egoism of its good conscience and bidding us to find in it the true source of all unhappiness. "Your selfishness is the misfortune of your life"—that was preached for thousands of years and harmed, as I have said, selfishness and deprived it of much spirit, much cheerfulness, much sensitivity, much beauty; it made selfishness stupid and ugly and poisoned it.

The ancient philosophers taught that the main source of misfortune was something very different. Beginning with Socrates, these thinkers never wearied of preaching: "Your thoughtlessness and stupidity, the way you live according to the rule, your submission to your neighbor's opinion is the reason why you so rarely achieve happiness; we thinkers, as thinkers, are the happiest of all."

Let us not decide here whether this sermon against stupidity had better reasons on its side than did the sermon against selfishness. What is certain, however, is that it deprived stupidity of its good conscience; these philosophers *harmed* stupidity.

329

Leisure and idleness.— There is something of the American Indians, something of the ferocity peculiar to the Indian blood, in the American lust for gold;[55] and the breathless haste with

---

what is at stake is not merely a group of images.

The point is of considerable philosophical significance. It concerns Nietzsche's view of science. With science he dealt again and again from his first book to his last, and he is widely held to have been "against" it. In fact, he did not repudiate science even in his discussion of "ascetic ideals" in his *Genealogy of Morals,* where science is seen to involve ascetic ideals but Nietzsche, unlike many of his readers, never loses sight of the fact that he himself was an ascetic. Still, the ideal is— gay science. And once this is understood one can even find it announced in Nietzsche's first book, *The Birth of Tragedy,* when Nietzsche envisages "an artistic Socrates" (section 14).

[55] The reference is surely to the great gold rush of 1849, though not only to that.

which they work—the distinctive vice of the new world—is already beginning to infect old Europe with its ferocity and is spreading a lack of spirituality[56] like a blanket. Even now one is ashamed of resting, and prolonged reflection almost gives people a bad conscience. One thinks with a watch in one's hand, even as one eats one's midday meal while reading the latest news of the stock market; one lives as if one always "might miss out on something." "Rather do anything than nothing": this principle, too, is merely a string to throttle all culture and good taste. Just as all forms are visibly perishing by the haste of the workers, the feeling for form itself, the ear and eye for the melody of movements are also perishing. The proof of this may be found in the universal demand for *gross obviousness* in all those situations in which human beings wish to be honest with one another for once—in their associations with friends, women, relatives, children, teachers, pupils, leaders, and princes: One no longer has time or energy for ceremonies, for being obliging in an indirect way, for *esprit* in conversation, and for any *otium*[57] at all. Living in a constant chase after gain compels people to expend their spirit to the point of exhaustion in continual pretense and overreaching and anticipating others. Virtue has come to consist of doing something in less time than someone else. Hours in which honesty is *permitted* have become rare, and when they arrive one is tired and does not only want to "let oneself go" but actually wishes to *stretch out* as long and wide and ungainly as one happens to be. This is how people now write *letters,* and the style and spirit of letters will always be the true "sign of the times."

If sociability and the arts still offer any delight, it is the kind of delight that slaves, weary of their work, devise for themselves. How frugal our educated—and uneducated—people have become regarding "joy"! How they are becoming increasingly suspicious of all joy! More and more, *work* enlists all good conscience on its side; the desire for joy already calls itself a "need to recuperate" and is beginning to be ashamed of itself. "One owes it to one's health"—that is what people say

---

[56] *Geistlosigkeit.*
[57] leisure.

when they are caught on an excursion into the country. Soon we may well reach the point where people can no longer give in to the desire for a *vita contemplativa* (that is, taking a walk with ideas and friends) without self-contempt and a bad conscience.

Well, formerly it was the other way around: it was work that was afflicted with the bad conscience. A person of good family used to conceal the fact that he was working if need compelled him to work. Slaves used to work, oppressed by the feeling that they were doing something contemptible: "doing" itself was contemptible. "Nobility and honor are attached solely to *otium* and *bellum*,"[58] that was the ancient prejudice.

330

Applause.— A thinker needs no applause and clapping of hands, if only he is assured of his own hand-clapping; without that he cannot do. Are there people who can dispense with that also and altogether with every kind of applause? I doubt it. Even about the wisest of men, Tacitus, who did not slander the wise, said: *quando etiam sapientibus gloriae cupido novissima exuitur*[59]—which with him means, never.

331

Better deaf than deafened.— Formerly, one wished to acquire fame and be *spoken* of. Now that is no longer enough because the market has grown too large; nothing less than *screaming* will do. As a consequence, even good voices scream till they are hoarse, and the best goods are offered by cracked voices. Without the screaming of those who want to sell and without hoarseness there no longer is any genius.

This is surely an evil age for a thinker. He has to learn how to find his silence between two noises and to pretend to be deaf

---

[58] war.
[59] *Histories,* IV.6: "Even for the wise the lust for fame is the desire they give up last." Cf. Milton's "Lycidas," line 71: "That last infirmity of noble mind."

until he really becomes deaf. Until he has learned this, to be sure, he runs the risk of perishing of impatience and headaches.[60]

332

The evil hour.— Every philosopher has probably had an evil hour when he thought: What do I matter if one does not accept my bad arguments, too? —And then some mischievous[61] little bird flew past him and twittered: "What do you matter? What do you matter?"

333

The meaning of knowing.— *Non ridere, non lugere, neque detestari, sed intelligere!* says Spinoza[62] as simply and sublimely as is his wont. Yet in the last analysis, what else is this *intelligere* than the form in which we come to feel the other three at once? One result of the different and mutually opposed desires to laugh, lament, and curse? Before knowledge is possible, each of these instincts must first have presented its onesided view of the thing or event; after this comes the fight of these onesided views, and occasionally this results in a mean, one grows calm, one finds all three sides right, and there is a kind of justice and a contract; for by virtue of justice and a contract all these instincts can maintain their existence and assert their rights against each other. Since only the last scenes of reconciliation and the final accounting at the end of this long process rise to our consciousness, we suppose that *intelligere* must be something conciliatory, just, and good—something that stands essentially opposed to the instincts, while it is actually nothing but a *certain behavior of the instincts toward one another.*

---

[60] Partly for the reasons noted here, partly because he was competing with Wagner, and partly because his solitude and the lack of any response to his books became intolerable for him, the tone of Nietzsche's own books grew shrill in the end.

[61] *schadenfrohes.*

[62] "Not to laugh, not to lament, nor to detest, but to understand." *Tractatus Politicus,* I. § 4.

For the longest time, conscious thought was considered thought itself. Only now does the truth dawn on us that by far the greatest part of our spirit's activity remains unconscious and unfelt. But I suppose that these instincts which are here contending against one another understand very well how to make themselves felt by, and how to hurt, *one another.* This may well be the source of that sudden and violent exhaustion that afflicts all thinkers (it is the exhaustion on a battlefield). Indeed, there may be occasions of concealed *heroism* in our warring depths, but certainly nothing divine that eternally rests in itself, as Spinoza supposed. *Conscious* thinking, especially that of the philosopher, is the least vigorous and therefore also the relatively mildest and calmest form of thinking; and thus precisely philosophers are most apt to be led astray about the nature of knowledge.

334

One must learn to love.— This is what happens to us in music: First one has to *learn to hear* a figure and melody at all, to detect and distinguish it, to isolate it and delimit it as a separate life. Then it requires some exertion and good will to *tolerate* it in spite of its strangeness, to be patient with its appearance and expression, and kindhearted about its oddity. Finally there comes a moment when we are *used* to it, when we wait for it, when we sense that we should miss it if it were missing; and now it continues to compel and enchant us relentlessly until we have become its humble and enraptured lovers who desire nothing better from the world than it and only it.

But that is what happens to us not only in music. That is how we have *learned to love* all things that we now love. In the end we are always rewarded for our good will, our patience, fairmindedness, and gentleness with what is strange; gradually, it sheds its veil and turns out to be a new and indescribable beauty. That is its *thanks* for our hospitality. Even those who love themselves will have learned it in this way; for there is no other way. Love, too, has to be learned.

335

Long live physics!— How many people know how to observe
something? Of the few who do, how many observe themselves?
"Everybody is farthest away—from himself";[63] all who try the
reins know this to their chagrin, and the maxim "know thy-
self!" addressed to human beings by a god, is almost malicious.
That the case of self-observation is indeed as desperate as that
is attested best of all by the manner in which *almost everybody*
talks about the essence of moral actions—this quick, eager,
convinced, and garrulous manner with its expression, its smile,
and its obliging ardor! One seems to have the wish to say to
you: "But my dear friend, precisely this is my specialty. You
have directed your question to the one person who is entitled
to answer you. As it happens, there is nothing about which I am
as wise as about this. To come to the point: when a human
being judges '*this is right*' and then infers '*therefore it must be
done,*' and then proceeds to *do* what he has thus recognized as
right and designated as necessary—then the essence of his
action is *moral.*"

But my friend, you are speaking of three actions instead of
one. When you judge "this is right," that is an action, too.
Might it not be possible that one could judge in a moral and in
an immoral manner? *Why* do you consider this, precisely this,
right?

"Because this is what my conscience tells me; and the voice
of conscience is never immoral, for it alone determines what is
to be moral."

But why do you *listen* to the voice of your conscience? And
what gives you the right to consider such a judgment true and
infallible? For this *faith*—is there no conscience for that? Have
you never heard of an intellectual conscience?[64] A conscience
behind your "conscience"? Your judgment "this is right" has a
pre-history in your instincts, likes, dislikes, experiences, and

---

[63] "*Jeder ist sich selber der Fernste.*" *Der Fernste* (the farthest) is the
opposite of *der Nächste* (the nearest), which is the word used in the
German Bible where the English versions have the "neighbor."
[64] Cf. sections 2, 319, and 344.

lack of experiences. "*How* did it originate there?" you must ask, and then also: "What is it that impels me to listen to it?" You can listen to its commands like a good soldier who hears his officer's command. Or like a woman who loves the man who commands. Or like a flatterer and coward who is afraid of the commander. Or like a dunderhead who obeys because no objection occurs to him. In short, there are a hundred ways in which you can listen to your conscience. But that you take this or that judgment for the voice of conscience—in other words, that you feel something to be right—may be due to the fact that you have never thought much about yourself and simply have accepted blindly that what you had been *told* ever since your childhood was right; or it may be due to the fact that what you call your duty has up to this point brought you sustenance and honors—and you consider it "right" because it appears to you as your own "condition of existence" (and that you have a *right* to existence seems irrefutable to you).

For all that, the *firmness* of your moral judgment could be evidence of your personal abjectness, of impersonality; your "moral strength" might have its source in your stubbornness— or in your inability to envisage new ideals. And, briefly, if you had thought more subtly, observed better, and learned more, you certainly would not go on calling this "duty" of yours and this "conscience" of yours duty and conscience. Your understanding *of the manner in which moral judgments have originated* would spoil these grand words for you, just as other grand words, like "sin" and "salvation of the soul" and "redemption" have been spoiled for you. —And now don't cite the categorical imperative, my friend! This term tickles my ear and makes me laugh despite your serious presence. It makes me think of the old Kant who had obtained the "thing in itself" *by stealth*—another very ridiculous thing!—and was punished for this when the "categorical imperative" crept stealthily into his heart and led him *astray—back* to "God," "soul," "freedom," and "immortality," like a fox who loses his way and goes astray back into his cage. Yet it had been *his* strength and cleverness that had *broken open* the cage![65]

---

[65] Like most philosophers after Kant, Nietzsche believes that Kant was not entitled to the "thing in itself" and that this notion contradicts the

What? You admire the categorical imperative within you? This "firmness" of your so-called moral judgment? This "unconditional" feeling that "here everyone must judge as I do"? Rather admire your *selfishness* at this point. And the blindness, pettiness, and frugality of your selfishness. For it is selfish to experience one's own judgment as a universal law; and this selfishness is blind, petty, and frugal because it betrays that you have not yet discovered yourself nor created for yourself an ideal of your own, your very own—for that could never be somebody else's and much less that of all, all!

Anyone who still judges "in this case everybody would have to act like this" has not yet taken five steps toward self-knowledge. Otherwise he would know that there neither are nor can be actions that are the same; that every action that has ever been done was done in an altogether unique and irretrievable way, and that this will be equally true of every future action; that all regulations about actions relate only to their coarse exterior (even the most inward and subtle regulations of all moralities so far) ; that these regulations may lead to some semblance of sameness, *but really only to some semblance*; that as one contemplates or looks back upon *any* action at all, it is and remains impenetrable; that our opinions about "good" and "noble" and "great" can never be *proved true* by our actions because every action is unknowable; that our opinions, valuations, and tables of what is good certainly belong among the most powerful levers in the involved mechanism of our actions, but that in any particular case the law of their mechanism is indemonstrable.

Let us therefore *limit* ourselves to the purification of our opinions and valuations and to the *creation of our own new*

---

central tenets of Kant's theory of knowledge. Most philosophers since Kant would also agree with Nietzsche that the doctrine of the categorical imperative, the core of Kant's ethics, is untenable; and in his ethics—specifically, in his *Critique of Practical Reason*—Kant "postulates" God, freedom, and immortality, after having shown in his *Critique of Pure Reason* that all three are indemonstrable. While few philosophers have followed Kant at these points, Nietzsche's discussion is distinguished by its irreverent wit, which recalls the tone of Heine's *On the History of Religion and Philosophy in Germany* (German 1st ed. 1835, 2nd ed. 1852).

tables of what is good, and let us stop brooding about the "moral value of our actions"! Yes, my friends, regarding all the moral chatter of some about others it is time to feel nauseous. Sitting in moral judgment should offend our taste. Let us leave such chatter and such bad taste to those who have nothing else to do but drag the past a few steps further through time and who never live in the present—which is to say the many, the great majority. We, however, *want to become those we are*[66]—human beings who are new, unique, incomparable, who give themselves laws, who create themselves. To that end we must become the best learners and discoverers of everything that is lawful and necessary in the world: we must become *physicists* in order to be able to be *creators* in this sense—while hitherto all valuations and ideals have been based on *ignorance* of physics or were constructed so as to *contradict* it. Therefore: long live physics! And even more so that which *compels* us to turn to physics—our honesty![67]

---

[66] Cf. section 270 and 270n, above.

[67] We might question the claim that in order to become autonomous "we must become physicists" and discover "everything that is lawful and necessary in the world." We might well wonder whether Nietzsche is using the term "physics" in some extended sense, comparable to the use of *"chemistry"* in the first section of *Human, All-Too-Human*, which is entitled "Chemistry of Concepts and Sensations." There the problem is: "How can anything develop out of its opposite; for example ... logic out of unlogic ... living for others out of egoism, truth out of errors?" And the point is that "this chemistry" might lead to the result "that in this area, too, the most magnificent colors have been derived from lowly, even despised materials. Now we might suppose that in "Long live physics!" Nietzsche is thinking of a *"physics* of moral feelings and judgments." But he is not.

What he argues in the penultimate paragraph above is that (a) no two actions can ever be the same actions; that (b) even those moral regulations which concern themselves with the inside of actions (with motives and feelings) really stay on the surface; that (c) human actions are "impenetrable" and "unknowable"; that (d) our moral judgments are among the most important and "powerful" causes of our actions; but that (e) "in any particular case the law of their mechanism is indemonstrable."

Although this list does not cover all of his points, it is clearly possible to accept some of these claims while questioning or denying others. One may grant (a) not only in the weak, tautologous sense but also in the

336

Nature's stinginess.— Why has nature been so stingy with human beings that it did not allow them to shine—one more, one less, each according to the plenitude of his own light? Why are great human beings not as beautifully visible in their rise and setting as the sun? How much more unambiguous that would make all life among men!

337

The "humaneness" of the future.— When I contemplate the present age with the eyes of some remote age, I can find nothing

---

strong and interesting sense that poses a problem for the kind of ethic that Jean-Paul Sartre proposed in "Existentialism is a Humanism" (reprinted in Kaufmann, *Existentialism from Dostoevsky to Sartre*); here Nietzsche is much more radical than Sartre; (b) is also plausible in a strong and interesting sense; (c) is less clear but means presumably that we can never be sure that any account of the causes and motivations of an action is true; something important may have been left out; and we cannot judge the relative importance or "power" of different causes and motives; (d) is remarkable because there are passages in which Nietzsche plays down the role of consciousness and treats it more like an epiphenomenon (see Kaufmann, 262–69); (e) does not presuppose any of the four preceding claims but is entirely compatible with all of them; and it is (e) that explains the introduction of physics in the final paragraph. Instead of passing moral judgments, we should "discover everything that is lawful and necessary in the world." Why? Even as one has to know physics to build airplanes and to make flying possible—*apparently* defying the laws of gravity—one also has to know physics to become autonomous: that is Nietzsche's point. Does the analogy hold? It would surely be much more plausible if Nietzsche had spoken of psychology instead of physics. Even "physiology" would have been more plausible, and "physics" seems farfetched unless we assume that what is meant is the study of nature (*physis* in Greek). Since Nietzsche himself did *not* turn to physics, it seems clear that he intended a sharp and inclusive contrast with *metaphysics*. Cf. section 293 and "we godless anti-metaphysicians" in section 344; also *Human, All-Too-Human*, sections 6, 9, and 18. His many contemptuous references to metaphysics invite comparison with the writings of positivists, but Nietzsche also questions the science, and specifically the *physics*, of his time—see *Beyond Good and Evil*, sections 14 and 22 (BWN, 211f. and 220f.) and *The Will to Power*, notes 623, 636, *et passim*.

more remarkable in present-day humanity than its distinctive virtue and disease which goes by the name of "the historical sense." This is the beginning of something altogether new and strange in history: If this seed should be given a few centuries and more, it might ultimately become a marvelous growth with an equally marvelous scent that might make our old earth more agreeable to live on. We of the present day are only just beginning to form the chain of a very powerful future feeling, link for link—we hardly know what we are doing. It almost seems to us as if it were not a matter of a new feeling but rather a decrease in all old feelings; the historical sense is still so poor and cold, and many people are attacked by it as by a frost and made still poorer and colder. To others it appears as a sign of stealthily approaching old age, and they see our planet as a melancholy invalid who wants to forget his present condition and therefore writes the history of his youth. This is actually one color of this new feeling: Anyone who manages to experience the history of humanity as a whole as *his own history* will feel in an enormously generalized way all the grief of an invalid who thinks of health, of an old man who thinks of the dreams of his youth, of a lover deprived of his beloved, of the martyr whose ideal is perishing, of the hero on the evening after a battle that has decided nothing but brought him wounds and the loss of his friend. But if one endured, if one *could* endure this immense sum of grief of all kinds while yet being the hero who, as the second day of battle breaks, welcomes the dawn and his fortune, being a person whose horizon encompasses thousands of years past and future, being the heir of all the nobility of all past spirit—an heir with a sense of obligation, the most aristocratic of old nobles and at the same time the first of a new nobility—the like of which no age has yet seen or dreamed of; if one could burden one's soul with all of this— the oldest, the newest, losses, hopes, conquests, and the victories of humanity; if one could finally contain all this in one soul and crowd it into a single feeling—this would surely have to result in a happiness that humanity has not known so far: the happiness of a god full of power and love, full of tears and laughter, a happiness that, like the sun in the evening, continually bestows its inexhaustible riches, pouring them into the sea, feeling richest, as the sun does, only when even the poorest fisherman is still rowing with golden oars! This godlike feeling would then be called—humaneness.

338

The will to suffer and those who feel pity.— Is it good for you yourselves to be above all full of pity? And is it good for those who suffer? But let us leave the first question unanswered for a moment.

Our personal and profoundest suffering is incomprehensible and inaccessible to almost everyone; here we remain hidden from our neighbor, even if we eat from one pot. But whenever people *notice* that we suffer, they interpret our suffering superficially. It is the very essence of the emotion of pity that it strips away from the suffering of others whatever is distinctively personal. Our "benefactors" are, more than our enemies, people who make our worth and will smaller. When people try to benefit someone in distress, the intellectual frivolity with which those moved by pity assume the role of fate is for the most part outrageous; one simply knows nothing of the whole inner sequence and intricacies that are distress for *me* or for *you*. The whole economy of my soul and the balance effected by "distress," the way new springs and needs break open, the way in which old wounds are healing, the way whole periods of the past are shed—all such things that may be involved in distress are of no concern to our dear pitying friends; they wish to *help* and have no thought of the personal necessity of distress, although terrors, deprivations, impoverishments, midnights, adventures, risks, and blunders are as necessary for me and for you as are their opposites. It never occurs to them that, to put it mystically, the path to one's own heaven always leads through the voluptuousness of one's own hell. No, the "religion of pity" (or "the heart") commands them to help, and they believe that they have helped most when they have helped most quickly.

If you, who adhere to this religion, have the same attitude toward yourselves that you have toward your fellow men; if you refuse to let your own suffering lie upon you even for an hour and if you constantly try to prevent and forestall all possible distress way ahead of time; if you experience suffering and displeasure as evil, hateful, worthy of annihilation, and as a defect of existence, then it is clear that besides your religion of pity you also harbor another religion in your heart that is perhaps the mother of the religion of pity: the *religion of comfortableness*. How little you know of human *happiness*, you comfortable and benevolent people, for happiness and unhappiness are sisters and even twins that either grow up together or, as in your case, *remain small* together. But now back to the first question!

How is it at all possible to keep to one's own way? Constantly, some clamor or other calls us aside; rarely does our eye behold anything that does not require us to drop our own preoccupation instantly to help. I know, there are a hundred decent and praiseworthy ways of losing *my own way*, and they are truly highly "moral"! Indeed, those who now preach the morality of pity even take the view that precisely this and only this is moral—to lose one's *own* way in order to come to the assistance of a neighbor. I know just as certainly that I only need to expose myself to the sight of some genuine distress and I am lost. And if a suffering friend said to me, "Look, I am about to die; please promise me to die with me," I should promise it; and the sight of a small mountain tribe fighting for its liberty would persuade me to offer it my hand and my life— if for good reasons I may choose for once two bad examples. All such arousing of pity and calling for help is secretly seductive, for our "own way" is too hard and demanding and too remote from the love and gratitude of others, and we do not really mind escaping from it—and from our very own conscience—to flee into the conscience of the others and into the lovely temple of the "religion of pity."

As soon as any war breaks out anywhere, there also breaks out precisely among the noblest people a pleasure that, to be sure, is kept secret: Rapturously, they throw themselves into the new danger of *death* because the sacrifice for the fatherland seems to them to offer the long desired permission—*to dodge their goal*; war offers them a detour to suicide, but a detour with a good conscience. And while I shall keep silent about some points, I do not want to remain silent about my morality which says to me: Live in seclusion so that you *can* live for yourself. Live in *ignorance* about what seems most important to your age. Between yourself and today lay the skin of at least three centuries. And the clamor of today, the noise of wars and revolutions should be a mere murmur for you. You will also wish to help—but only those whose distress you *understand* entirely because they share with you one suffering and one hope —your friends—and only in the manner in which you help yourself. I want to make them bolder, more persevering, simpler, gayer. I want to teach them what is understood by so few today, least of all by these preachers of pity: *to share not suffering but joy.*[68]

339

Vita femina.[69]— For seeing the ultimate beauties of a work, no knowledge or good will is sufficient; this requires the rarest of lucky accidents: The clouds that veil these peaks have to lift for once so that we see them glowing in the sun. Not only do we have to stand in precisely the right spot in order to see this, but the unveiling must have been accomplished by our own soul because it needed some external expression and parable, as if it were a matter of having something to hold on to and retain control of itself. But it is so rare for all of this to coincide that I am inclined to believe that the highest peaks of everything good, whether it be a work, a deed, humanity, or nature, have so far remained concealed and veiled from the great majority and even from the best human beings. But what does unveil itself for us, *unveils itself for us once only.*

The Greeks, to be sure, prayed: "Everything beautiful twice and even three times!" They implored the gods with good reason, for ungodly reality gives us the beautiful either not at all or once only. I mean to say that the world is overfull of beautiful things but nevertheless poor, very poor when it comes to

---

[68] This is one of Nietzsche's best statements of his case against pity. Cf. Kaufmann, 363–71.

[69] Life is a woman.

beautiful moments and unveilings of these things. But perhaps this is the most powerful magic of life: it is covered by a veil interwoven with gold, a veil of beautiful possibilities, sparkling with promise, resistance, bashfulness, mockery, pity, and seduction. Yes, life is a woman.

340

The dying Socrates.— I admire the courage and wisdom of Socrates in everything he did, said—and did not say. This mocking and enamored monster and pied piper of Athens, who made the most overweening youths tremble and sob, was not only the wisest chatterer of all time: he was equally great in silence. I wish he had remained taciturn also at the last moment of his life; in that case he might belong to a still higher order of spirits. Whether it was death or the poison or piety or malice—something loosened his tongue at that moment and he said: "O Crito, I owe Asclepius a rooster." This ridiculous and terrible "last word" means for those who have ears: "O Crito, *life is a disease.*" Is it possible that a man like him, who had lived cheerfully and like a soldier in the sight of everyone, should have been a pessimist? He had merely kept a cheerful mien while concealing all his life long his ultimate judgment, his inmost feeling. Socrates, Socrates *suffered life!* And then he still revenged himself—with this veiled, gruesome, pious, and blasphemous saying. Did a Socrates need such revenge? Did his overrich virtue lack an ounce of magnanimity? —Alas, my friends, we must overcome even the Greeks![70]

---

[70] Socrates' last words imply that he has been cured of a disease, for Asclepius was the god of medicine.

For the close connection between this section and the two that follow it, concluding the original version of the book, see the section on "Structure" in the Introduction.

As for Socrates, he is a central figure in Nietzsche's work, and this section is therefore important. Its place directly before Nietzsche's first presentation of his doctrine of the eternal recurrence and the beginning of *Zarathustra* suggests that Nietzsche wished to give it special weight.

At one time it was widely claimed that Nietzsche hated Socrates, and the evidence was simply not examined carefully. In 1948 I published an article, examining *all* the passages in which Nietzsche dealt with Soc-

341

The greatest weight.[71]— What, if some day or night a demon were to steal after you into your loneliest loneliness and say to you: "This life as you now live it and have lived it, you will have to live once more and innumerable times more; and there will be nothing new in it, but every pain and every joy and every thought and sigh and everything unutterably small or great in your life will have to return to you, all in the same succession and sequence—even this spider and this moonlight between the trees, and even this moment and I myself. The eternal hourglass of existence is turned upside down again and again, and you with it, speck of dust!"

Would you not throw yourself down and gnash your teeth and curse the demon who spoke thus? Or have you once experienced a tremendous moment when you would have answered him: "You are a god and never have I heard anything more

---

rates, in his notes as well as his books, pro or con, and called it, "Nietzsche's Admiration for Socrates." This title was retained when a revised version of the article was incorporated in my *Nietzsche* as Chapter 13.

Since then the subject has been taken up by several writers—there are entire books on the subject. Some writers have been misled by the title of my discussion and assume that it deals only with the passages expressing admiration. Actually, it deals, at length, not only with the "negative" references but also places the whole problem in the setting of a full-scale examination of Nietzsche's thought—including his views of reason, passion, and Christianity. In any case, the first sentence of this section (340) is as striking a tribute as Nietzsche, or anyone else, ever paid to anyone.

For a better understanding of Nietzsche's attitude to Socrates it is also illuminating to follow his references to Epicurus through the present book, beginning with section 45 and the long note on it.

[71] *Das grösste Schwergewicht*. Literally, the noun means heavyweight, and this term is actually used to designate the heaviest class in boxing; but it is also used quite commonly for "main emphasis" or "stress." In an earlier version of this aphorism, I rendered the title "The greatest stress." My reasons for concluding that "weight" is better are spelled out in the section on the Eternal Recurrence in the Introduction.

Nietzsche himself considered section 341 the first proclamation of "the basic idea of *Zarathustra*" (*Ecce Homo*, BWN, 752), meaning the eternal recurrence. But see also sections 109, 233, and 285.

divine." If this thought gained possession of you, it would change you as you are or perhaps crush you. The question in each and every thing, "Do you desire this once more and innumerable times more?" would lie upon your actions as the greatest weight. Or how well disposed would you have to become to yourself and to life *to crave nothing more fervently* than this ultimate eternal confirmation and seal?

342

Incipit tragoedia.[72]— When Zarathustra was thirty years old, he left his home and Lake Urmi and went into the mountains. There he enjoyed his spirit and his solitude, and for ten years did not tire of that. But at last his heart changed—and one

---

[72] *The tragedy begins.* Cf. the end of section 1 of Nietzsche's Preface. This aphorism, which concludes Book IV and thus stood at the end of the original edition of *The Gay Science*, is almost identical with section 1 of "Zarathustra's Prologue," which opens Nietzsche's next book. But in *The Gay Science* Nietzsche printed it as a single paragraph, like all of the numbered sections of *The Gay Science*, regardless of their length, while in *Zarathustra* it is broken up into twelve very short paragraphs, in keeping with the style of *Zarathustra*. Thus the text in *Zarathustra* has periods and then begins a new sentence after "serpent" and "receive it." The only *substantive* difference is that in *Zarathustra* "Lake Urmi" is changed to "the lake of his home." (Other differences between the text above and my translation of *Zarathustra* are due to the fact that I have tried to improve on my old version instead of simply copying it.)

Lake Urmi or Urmia is a lake in northwestern Iran, between the massif of Ararat, whose highest peak rises to almost 17,000 feet, and Mt. Savalan, which is also over 15,000 feet. The original readers of *The Gay Science* might well be put in mind of the historical Zarathustra, the founder of the religion of ancient Iran, who is also known as Zoroaster. The ancient Greeks thought he had lived 6,000 years before Xerxes invaded Greece in the fifth century B.C.; some recent scholars have dated him around 1,000 B.C.; but most scholars now consider him a contemporary of the prophet Jeremiah and believe that Zarathustra's religious reforms, around 600 B.C., helped to trigger the Persian conquest of the Babylonian empire which, incidentally, put an end to the Babylonian exile of the Jews.

Nietzsche's reasons for choosing "Zarathustra" as his mouthpiece are discussed by him in *Ecce Homo* (BWN, 783f.); also somewhat differently by Kaufmann, 198f.

morning he rose with the dawn, stepped before the sun, and spoke to it thus:

"You great star, what would your happiness be if you did not have those for whom you shine? For ten years you have climbed up to my cave: You would have become weary of your light and of the journey had it not been for me and my eagle and my serpent; but we waited for you every morning, took your overflow from you, and blessed you for it. Behold, I am sick of my wisdom, like a bee that has gathered too much honey; I need hands outstretched to receive it; I want to give away and distribute until the wise among men enjoy their folly once again and the poor their riches. For that I must descend to the depths, as you do in the evening when you go behind the sea and still bring light to the underworld, you over-rich star. Like you I must *go under*,[73] as men put it to whom I wish to descend. Bless me then, you calm eye that can look without envy even upon an all too great happiness. Bless the cup that wants to overflow in order that the water may flow from it golden and carry the reflection of your rapture everywhere. Behold, this cup wants to become empty again, and Zarathustra wants to become man again." —Thus Zarathustra began to go under.

---

[73] In German, the last word of this section is *Untergang*; and here the German word is *untergehen*, emphasized in the original. These German words recur often in "Zarathustra's Prologue"—along with other "under-" and "over-" words. Even in the present section they are immediately preceded by "underworld" and "over-rich." Among the other "over-" words the most important are "overcome" (*überwinden*) and "overman" (*Übermensch*). There is no English equivalent for *untergehen* (literally, going under). The German verb is used for the setting of the sun, for drowning, and above all for perishing. In German, Spengler's *Decline of the West* was called *Der Untergang des Abendlandes*; and *Untergang* generally suggests decline and destruction.

Nietzsche is not suggesting that it would have been better for Zarathustra to stay in the mountains instead of returning among men. See section 4 of "Zarathustra's Prologue": "I love those who do not know how to live, except by going under, for they are those who cross over [the bridge to the overman]." Cf. also section 283 above on living dangerously.

BOOK FIVE

———◆———

WE FEARLESS ONES

Carcasse, tu trembles?
Tu tremblerais bien davantage, si
tu savais, où je te mène.

TURENNE*

———————————

* "You tremble, carcass? You would tremble a lot more if you knew where I am taking you."

Henri de la Tour d'Auvergne, Vicomte de Turenne (1611–75), was one of the greatest French generals of all time, made Marshal of France in 1643, and buried in the Invalides in Paris by order of Napoleon.

Cf. Paul Robert, *Dictionnaire alphabétique et analogique de la langue française* (Paris, 1951) under *carcasse*:

"Quelquefois, pendant une bataille, il (Turenne) ne pouvait s'empêcher de trembler; . . . alors, il parlait à son corps comme on parle à un serviteur. Il lui disait: 'Tu trembles, carcasse; mais si tu savais où je vais te mener tout à l'heure, tu tremblerais bien davantage.' Lavisse, *Histoire de France* (*Cours moyen, 1ʳᵉ et 2ᵉ années*), Ch. XIV, p. 107."
(Sometimes during a battle he could not help trembling. Then he talked to his body as one talks to a servant. He said to it: "You tremble, carcass; but if you knew where I am taking you right now, you would tremble a lot more.")

The striking motto explains Nietzsche's conception of fearlessness.

The meaning of our cheerfulness.[1]— The greatest recent event—that "God is dead,"[2] that the belief in the Christian god has become unbelievable[3]—is already beginning to cast its first shadows over Europe. For the few at least, whose eyes—the *suspicion* in whose eyes is strong and subtle enough for this spectacle, some sun seems to have set[4] and some ancient and profound trust has been turned into doubt; to them our old world must appear daily more like evening, more mistrustful, stranger, "older." But in the main one may say: The event itself is far too great, too distant, too remote from the multitude's capacity for comprehension even for the tidings of it to be thought of as having *arrived* as yet. Much less may one suppose that many people know as yet *what* this event really means —and how much must collapse now that this faith has been undermined because it was built upon this faith, propped up by it, grown into it; for example, the whole of our European morality. This long plenitude and sequence of breakdown, destruction, ruin, and cataclysm[5] that is now impending—who could guess enough of it today to be compelled to play the teacher and advance proclaimer of this monstrous logic of terror, the prophet of a gloom and an eclipse of the sun whose like has probably never yet occurred on earth?

Even we born guessers of riddles who are, as it were, waiting on the mountains,[6] posted between today and tomorrow, stretched in the contradiction between today and tomorrow, we firstlings and premature births of the coming century, to whom the shadows that must soon envelop Europe really *should* have appeared by now—why is it that even we look forward to the

---

[1] *Heiterkeit:* a reference to the title and tenor of *The Gay Science.*

[2] Cf. sections 108ff. and 125 above, as well as 108n.

[3] This clause is clearly offered as an explanation of "God is dead."

[4] *untergegangen:* cf. the last note on section 342.

[5] *Abbruch, Zerstörung, Untergang, Umsturz.*

[6] Posted in high places so that they will see as soon as possible what is approaching from a distance.

approaching gloom without any real sense of involvement and above all without any worry and fear for *ourselves*?[7] Are we perhaps still too much under the impression of the *initial consequences* of this event—and these initial consequences, the consequences for *ourselves*, are quite the opposite of what one might perhaps expect: They are not at all sad and gloomy but rather like a new and scarcely describable kind of light, happiness, relief, exhilaration, encouragement, dawn.

Indeed, we philosophers and "free spirits" feel, when we hear the news that "the old god is dead," as if a new dawn shone on us; our heart overflows with gratitude, amazement, premonitions, expectation. At long last the horizon appears free to us again, even if it should not be bright; at long last our ships may venture out again, venture out to face any danger; all the daring of the lover of knowledge is permitted again; the sea, *our* sea, lies open again; perhaps there has never yet been such an "open sea."—[8]

344

How we, too, are still pious.— In science convictions have no rights of citizenship, as one says with good reason. Only when they decide to descend to the modesty of hypotheses, of a provisional experimental point of view, of a regulative fiction, they may be granted admission and even a certain value in the realm of knowledge—though always with the restriction that they remain under police supervision, under the police of mistrust. —But does this not mean, if you consider it more precisely, that a conviction may obtain admission to science only when it *ceases* to be a conviction? Would it not be the first step in the discipline of the scientific spirit that one would not permit oneself any more convictions?

Probably this is so; only we still have to ask: *To make it possible for this discipline to begin,* must there not be some prior conviction—even one that is so commanding and uncon-

---

[7] A gloss on the title of Book V.
[8] Note how section 125 above was introduced by 124, and cf. also 283, 289, 291.

ditional that it sacrifices all other convictions to itself? We see that science also rests on a faith; there simply is no science "without presuppositions." The question whether *truth* is needed must not only have been affirmed in advance, but affirmed to such a degree that the principle, the faith, the conviction finds expression: *"Nothing* is needed *more* than truth, and in relation to it everything else has only second-rate value."

This unconditional will to truth—what is it? Is it the will *not to allow oneself to be deceived*? Or is it the will *not to deceive*? For the will to truth could be interpreted in the second way, too—if only the special case "I do not want to deceive myself" is subsumed under the generalization "I do not want to deceive." But why not deceive? But why not allow oneself to be deceived?

Note that the reasons for the former principle belong to an altogether different realm from those for the second. One does not want to allow oneself to be deceived because one assumes that it is harmful, dangerous, calamitous to be deceived. In this sense, science would be a long-range prudence, a caution, a utility; but one could object in all fairness: How is that? Is wanting not to allow oneself to be deceived really less harmful, less dangerous, less calamitous? What do you know in advance of the character of existence to be able to decide whether the greater advantage is on the side of the unconditionally mistrustful or of the unconditionally trusting? But if both should be required, much trust *as well as* much mistrust, from where would science then be permitted to take its unconditional faith or conviction on which it rests, that truth is more important than any other thing, including every other conviction? Precisely this conviction could never have come into being if both truth and untruth constantly proved to be useful, which is the case. Thus—the faith in science, which after all exists undeniably, cannot owe its origin to such a calculus of utility; it must have originated *in spite of* the fact that the disutility and dangerousness of "the will to truth," of "truth at any price" is proved to it constantly. "At any price": how well we understand these words once we have offered and slaughtered one faith after another on this altar!

Consequently, "will to truth" does *not* mean "I will not allow myself to be deceived" but—there is no alternative—"I will not deceive, not even myself"; *and with that we stand on moral ground.* For you only have to ask yourself carefully, "Why do you not want to deceive?" especially if it should seem—and it does seem!—as if life aimed at semblance, meaning error, deception, simulation, delusion, self-delusion, and when the great sweep of life has actually always shown itself to be on the side of the most unscrupulous *polytropoi.*[9] Charitably interpreted, such a resolve might perhaps be a quixotism,[10] a minor slightly mad enthusiasm; but it might also be something more serious, namely, a principle that is hostile to life and destructive. —"Will to truth"—that might be a concealed will to death.[11]

Thus the question "Why science?" leads back to the moral problem: *Why have morality at all* when life, nature, and history are "not moral"? No doubt, those who are truthful in that audacious and ultimate sense that is presupposed by the faith in science *thus affirm another world* than the world of life, nature, and history; and insofar as they affirm this "other

---

[9] This Greek word (Nietzsche uses the Greek characters) is applied to Odysseus in the first line of the *Odyssey*.

There is no English equivalent. The meaning ranges from much turned to much traveled, versatile, wily, and manifold. In German there are two good ways of rendering it: *den vielgewandten* and, better yet, *den vielverschlagenen. Viel* is much; *gewandt*, turned, skilled, dexterous; *verschlagen*, driven off course, shipwrecked or stranded—and crafty.

Nietzsche's point is, of course, that Odysseus owed his survival on many occasions to his virtuosity in deception: At this point we should remember the arguments in sections 110 and 111 above.

If life often depends on deception—on deceiving oneself as well as others—then the unconditional desire for truth, truth at any price, depends on a standard independent of our survival—a standard to which we willingly sacrifice ourselves. To that extent we are still "pious."

Without a doubt, Nietzsche includes himself when he says, a few lines later, "we seekers after knowledge today, we godless anti-metaphysicians." Cf. his impassioned insistence on the intellectual conscience in sections 2, 319, and 335.

[10] It is relevant that Nietzsche loved Don Quixote and tended to identify himself with him. See Kaufmann, 71.

[11] The notion of a will to death was resurrected by Freud in *Beyond the Pleasure Principle*, in 1920.

world"—look, must they not by the same token negate its
counterpart, this world, *our* world?—But you will have gathered what I am driving at, namely, that it is still a *metaphysical
faith* upon which our faith in science rests—that even we seekers after knowledge today, we godless anti-metaphysicians still
take our fire, too, from the flame lit by a faith that is thousands
of years old, that Christian faith which was also the faith of
Plato, that God is the truth, that truth is divine. —But what if
this should become more and more incredible, if nothing should
prove to be divine any more unless it were error, blindness, the
lie—if God himself should prove to be our most enduring
lie?—[12]

345

Morality as a problem.— The lack of personality always takes
its revenge: A weakened, thin, extinguished personality that
denies itself is no longer fit for anything good—least of all for
philosophy. "Selflessness" has no value either in heaven or on
earth. All great problems demand *great love*, and of that only
strong, round, secure spirits who have a firm grip on themselves
are capable. It makes the most telling difference whether a
thinker has a personal relationship to his problems and finds in
them his destiny, his distress, and his greatest happiness, or an
"impersonal" one, meaning that he can do no better than to
touch them and grasp them with the antennae of cold, curious
thought. In the latter case nothing will come of it; that much
one can promise in advance, for even if great problems should
allow themselves to be *grasped* by them they would not permit
frogs and weaklings to *hold on* to them; such has been their
taste from time immemorial—a taste, incidentally, that they
share with all redoubtable females.
    Why is it then that I have never yet encountered anybody,

---

[12] Nietzsche quotes from this section in the third essay of his *Genealogy
of Morals*, section 24 (BWN, 588), and says at the end of section 24:
"Whoever feels that this has been stated too briefly should read the
section of *The Gay Science* entitled 'How we, too, are still pious' (section 344), or preferably the entire fifth book . . ."

not even in books, who approached morality in this personal way and who knew morality as a problem, and this problem as his own personal distress, torment, voluptuousness, and passion? It is evident that up to now morality was no problem at all but, on the contrary, precisely that on which after all mistrust, discord, and contradiction one could agree—the hallowed place of peace where our thinkers took a rest even from themselves, took a deep breath, and felt revived. I see nobody who ventured a *critique* of moral valuations; I miss even the slightest attempts of scientific curiosity, of the refined, experimental imagination of psychologists and historians that readily anticipates a problem and catches it in flight without quite knowing what it has caught. I have scarcely detected a few meager preliminary efforts to explore the *history of the origins* of these feelings and valuations (which is something quite different from a critique and again different from a history of ethical systems). In one particular case I have done everything to encourage a sympathy and talent for this kind of history—in vain, as it seems to me today.[13]

These historians of morality (mostly Englishmen) do not amount to much. Usually they themselves are still quite unsuspectingly obedient to one particular morality and, without knowing it, serve that as shield-bearers and followers—for example, by sharing that popular superstition of Christian Europe which people keep mouthing so guilelessly to this day, that what is characteristic of moral actions is selflessness, self-sacrifice, or sympathy and pity. Their usual mistaken premise

---

[13] The preface to the *Genealogy of Morals* (BWN, 453f. and 457) shows that Nietzsche is alluding to Paul Rée, the author of *Der Ursprung der moralischen Empfindungen* (1877) and *Die Entstehung des Gewissens* (1885). Cf. Kaufmann, 48–64, taking note of 50n.

Binion, p. 137n, confirms that Rée is meant in the passage above but mistakenly assigns it to the Preface and not to section 345. Binion says that in the *Genealogy* Nietzsche "mentioned only Rée's *Ursprung* but meant rather Rée's *Entstehung*, alone purportedly a derivation of conscience." Actually, Nietzsche describes his reactions to Rée's *Ursprung* without commenting on the derivation of conscience; and Binion also overlooks that the second section of Rée's *Ursprung* is entitled *"Der Ursprung des Gewissens"* (The Origin of Conscience).

is that they affirm some consensus of the nations, at least of tame nations, concerning certain principles of morals, and then they infer from this that these principles must be unconditionally binding also for you and me; or, conversely, they see the truth that among different nations moral valuations are *necessarily* different and then infer from this that *no* morality is at all binding. Both procedures are equally childish.

The mistake made by the more refined among them is that they uncover and criticize the perhaps foolish opinions of a people about their morality, or of humanity about all human morality—opinions about its origin, religious sanction, the superstition of free will,[14] and things of that sort—and then suppose that they have criticized the morality itself. But the value of a command "thou shalt" is still fundamentally different from and independent of such opinions about it and the weeds of error that may have overgrown it—just as certainly as the value of a medication for a sick person is completely independent of whether he thinks about medicine scientifically or the way old women do. Even if a morality has grown out of an error, the realization of this fact would not as much as touch the problem of its value.[15]

Thus nobody up to now has examined the *value* of that most famous of all medicines which is called morality; and the first step would be—for once to *question* it. Well then, precisely this is our task.—[16]

346

Our question mark.— But you do not understand this? Indeed, people will have trouble understanding us. We are looking

---

[14] Cf. the section on "The error of free will" in *Twilight of the Idols* (VPN, 499ff.) and *Beyond Good and Evil,* section 19 (BWN, 215–17).
[15] What is here suggested is that the value of a morality depends on its relation to health, or life, or ultimately power.
[16] The task is to question whether the effects of morality on those who are moral are beneficial. This question, of course, does not commit one to the assumption that there is only one standard of value. One might make a start by comparing what has become of man under different moralities and by asking what might become of him without any morality.

for words; perhaps we are also looking for ears. Who are we anyway? If we simply called ourselves, using an old expression, godless, or unbelievers, or perhaps immoralists, we do not believe that this would even come close to designating us: We are all three in such an advanced stage that one—that *you*, my curious friends—could never comprehend how we feel at this point. Ours is no longer the bitterness and passion of the person who has torn himself away and still feels compelled to turn his unbelief into a new belief, a purpose, a martyrdom. We have become cold, hard, and tough in the realization that the way of this world is anything but divine; even by human standards it is not rational, merciful, or just. We know it well, the world in which we live is ungodly, immoral, "inhuman"; we have interpreted it far too long in a false and mendacious way, in accordance with the wishes of our reverence, which is to say, according to our *needs*. For man is a reverent animal. But he is also mistrustful; and that the world is *not* worth what we thought it was, that is about as certain as anything of which our mistrust has finally got hold. The more mistrust, the more philosophy.

We are far from claiming that the world is worth *less*; indeed it would seem laughable to us today if man were to insist on inventing values that were supposed to *excel* the value of the actual world. This is precisely what we have turned our backs on as an extravagant aberration of human vanity and unreason that for a long time was not recognized as such. It found its final expression in modern pessimism,[17] and a more ancient and stronger expression in the teaching of Buddha; but it is part of Christianity also, if more doubtfully and ambiguously so but not for that reason any less seductive.

The whole pose of "man *against* the world," of man as a "world-negating" principle, of man as the measure of the value of things, as judge of the world who in the end places existence itself upon his scales and finds it wanting—the monstrous insipidity of this pose has finally come home to us and we are sick of it. We laugh as soon as we encounter the juxtaposition of "man *and* world," separated by the sublime presumption of the little word "and." But look, when we laugh like that, have

---

[17] Schopenhauer's philosophy.

we not simply carried the contempt for man one step further? And thus also pessimism, the contempt for that existence which is knowable by *us*? Have we not exposed ourselves to the suspicion of an opposition—an opposition between the world in which we were at home up to now with our reverences that perhaps made it possible for us to *endure* life, and another world *that consists of us*—an inexorable, fundamental, and deepest suspicion about ourselves that is more and more gaining worse and worse control of us Europeans and that could easily confront coming generations with the terrifying Either/Or: "Either abolish your reverences or—*yourselves*!" The latter would be nihilism; but would not the former also be—nihilism?[18]—This is *our* question mark.

347

Believers and their need to believe.— How much one needs a *faith*[19] in order to flourish, how much that is "firm" and that one does not wish to be shaken because one *clings* to it, that is a measure of the degree of one's strength (or, to put the point more clearly, of one's weakness).[20] Christianity, it seems to me, is still needed by most people in old Europe even today;[21] therefore it still finds believers. For this is how man is: An article of faith could be refuted before him a thousand times—if he needed it, he would consider it "true" again and again, in accordance with that famous "proof of strength" of which the Bible speaks.[22]

---

[18] A few interpreters of Nietzsche have claimed that he was, by his own lights, a nihilist; but they have generally failed to specify the meaning of this term. Here two forms of nihilism are mentioned, and it is clear that Nietzsche is not a nihilist in either sense.

[19] In German there is only one word for belief and faith, *Glaube*; and to believe is *glauben*.

[20] This crucial point, which recurs elsewhere in Nietzsche's writings, makes clear, we might say, "how he is *not* pious," and thus needs to be considered in interpreting section 344 above.

[21] This was written in 1886.

[22] Nietzsche also refers to the "proof of strength" in section 50 of *The Antichrist* and in notes 171 and 452 of *The Will to Power*. But it is

Metaphysics is still needed by some; but so is that impetuous *demand for certainty*[23] that today discharges itself among large numbers of people in a scientific-positivistic form. The demand that one *wants* by all means that something should be firm (while on account of the ardor of this demand one is easier and more negligent about the demonstration of this certainty)—this, too, is still the demand for a support, a prop, in short, that *instinct of weakness* which, to be sure, does not create religious, metaphysical systems, and convictions of all kinds but—conserves them.

Actually, what is steaming around all of these positivistic systems is the vapor of a certain pessimistic gloom, something that smells of weariness, fatalism, disappointment, and fear of new disappointments—or else ostentatious wrath, a bad mood, the anarchism of indignation, and whatever other symptoms and masquerades of the feeling of weakness there may be. Even the vehemence with which our most intelligent contemporaries lose themselves in wretched nooks and crannies, for example, into patriotism[24] (I mean what the French call *chauvinisme* and the

---

only in the passage above that Nietzsche claims that "the Bible speaks" of it. The reference is to I Corinthians 2.4, where the King James Bible has "in demonstration of the Spirit and of power" and Luther *"in Beweisung des Geistes und der Kraft."*

In theological and homiletical quotations the old-fashioned *Beweisung* gave way to *Beweis* (proof—the word Nietzsche uses) during the nineteenth century. Since Schleiermacher this passage became very popular, and the parallelism of *Geist* and *Kraft* was replaced by either *Geist* or, as in Nietzsche's case, *Kraft.* I am indebted to Professor Otto A. Piper for this information.

[23] At first glance, this critique of the "demand for certainty" may seem to be at odds with section 2 above where *"the desire for certainty"* is what "separates the higher human beings from the lower." But when both passages are read in context, the contradiction disappears. Section 2 deals with *"The intellectual conscience"* and the importance of giving ourselves an account of what speaks for *and against* our beliefs. What is attacked is the easy certainty of those who fail to consider objections. Actually, "the desire for certainty" is not the best phrase for what is clearly meant; "the desire for intellectual cleanliness" would be better: what counts is the desire to determine whether one is entitled to feel certain.

[24] *Vaterländerei.*

Germans "German") or into petty aesthetic creeds after the manner of French *naturalisme* (which drags up and bares only that part of nature which inspires nausea and simultaneous amazement—today people like to call this part *la vérité vraie*[25]) or into nihilism à la Petersburg (meaning the *belief in unbelief* even to the point of martyrdom[26]) always manifests above all the *need* for a faith, a support, backbone, something to fall back on.

Faith is always coveted most and needed most urgently where will is lacking; for will, as the affect of command, is the decisive sign of sovereignty and strength. In other words, the less one knows how to command, the more urgently one covets someone who commands, who commands severely—a god, prince, class, physician, father confessor, dogma, or party conscience. From this one might perhaps gather that the two world religions, Buddhism and Christianity, may have owed their origin and above all their sudden spread to a tremendous collapse and *disease of the will.* And that is what actually happened: both religions encountered a situation in which the will had become diseased, giving rise to a demand that had become utterly desperate for some "thou shalt." Both religions taught fanaticism in ages in which the will had become exhausted, and thus they offered innumerable people some support, a new possibility of willing, some delight in willing. For fanaticism is the only "strength of the will" that even the weak and insecure can be brought to attain, being a sort of hypnotism of the whole system of the senses and the intellect for the benefit of an excessive nourishment (hypertrophy) of a single point of view and feeling that henceforth becomes dominant—which the Christian calls his *faith.* Once a human being reaches the fundamental conviction that he *must* be commanded, he becomes "a believer." Conversely, one could conceive of such a pleasure and power of self-determination, such a *freedom* of the will[27] that

---

[25] the true truth.

[26] Again it is clear that Nietzsche dissociates himself from nihilism.

[27] *This* conception of "freedom of the will" (*alias,* autonomy) does not involve any belief in what Nietzsche called "the superstition of free will" in section 345 (*alias,* the exemption of human actions from an otherwise universal determinism).

the spirit would take leave of all faith and every wish for certainty, being practiced in maintaining himself on insubstantial ropes and possibilities and dancing even near abysses. Such a spirit would be the *free spirit* par excellence.[28]

348

On the origin of scholars. — In Europe scholars grow out of all kinds of classes and social conditions, like plants that require no particular soil. Therefore they belong by their very nature and quite involuntarily to the carriers of the democratic idea. But this origin betrays itself. Once one has trained one's eyes to recognize in a scholarly treatise the scholar's intellectual *idiosyncrasy*—every scholar has one—and to catch it in the act, one will almost always behold behind this the scholar's "prehistory," his family, and especially their occupations and crafts.

Where the feeling finds expression "Now this has been proved and I am done with it," it is generally the ancestor in the blood and instinct of the scholar who approves from his point of view "the finished job"; the faith in a proof is merely a symptom of what in a hard-working family has for ages been considered "good workmanship." One example: When the sons of clerks and office workers of every kind, whose main task it has always been to bring order into diverse materials, to distribute it over different files, and in general to schematize things, become scholars, they manifest a tendency to consider a problem almost as solved when they have merely schematized it. There are philosophers who are fundamentally merely schematizers; for them the formal aspect of their fathers' occupation has become content. The talent for classifications, for tables of categories,[29] betrays something; one pays a price for being the child of one's parents.[30]

---

[28] Nietzsche still wants to be a free spirit in the best sense of that word —a liberated, autonomous spirit. Cf. *Twilight*, section 49 (VPN, 554). Cf. also *The Antichrist*, sections 50–55 (VPN, 631–42).

[29] An allusion to Kant.

[30] *Man ist nicht ungestraft das Kind seiner Eltern.* Cf. Ottilie's Diary in Goethe's *Elective Affinities*, 2, 7: *Es wandelt niemand ungestraft unter Palmen* (no one walks under palmtrees without paying for it).

The son of an advocate will have to be an advocate as a scholar, too; he wants above all that his cause should be judged right, and next to that perhaps also that it should be right. The sons of Protestant ministers[31] and school teachers may be recognized by their naive certainty when, as scholars, they consider their cause proved when they have merely stated it with vigor and warmth; they are thoroughly used to being *believed*, as that was part of their fathers' job. A Jew, on the other hand, in keeping with the business circles and the past of his people, is least of all used to being believed. Consider Jewish scholars in this light: All of them have a high regard for logic, that is for *compelling* agreement by force of reasons; they know, with that they are bound to win even where they encounter race and class prejudices and where one does not like to believe them. For nothing is more democratic than logic; it is no respecter of persons and makes no distinction between crooked and straight noses. (Incidentally, Europe owes the Jews no small thanks for making people think more logically and for establishing *cleanlier* intellectual habits—nobody more so than the Germans who are a lamentably *déraisonnable*[32] race who to this day are still in need of having their "heads washed" first. Wherever Jews have won influence they have taught men to make finer distinctions, more rigorous inferences, and to write in a more luminous and cleanly fashion; their task was ever to bring a people "to listen to *raison*."[33])

349

Once more the origin of scholars.— The wish to preserve oneself is the symptom of a condition of distress, of a limitation of the really fundamental instinct of life which aims at *the expansion of power* and, wishing for that, frequently risks and

---

[31] Nietzsche's father and grandfathers had been Protestant ministers. He may not have realized that further back many of his ancestors had been butchers.

[32] unreasonable.

[33] reason. The French words underline Nietzsche's determination to dissociate himself from the Germans—and from German anti-Semitism.

even sacrifices self-preservation.[34] It should be considered symptomatic when some philosophers—for example, Spinoza who was consumptive—considered the instinct of self-preservation decisive and *had* to see it that way; for they were individuals in conditions of distress.

That our modern natural sciences have become so thoroughly entangled in this Spinozistic dogma (most recently and worst of all, Darwinism with its incomprehensibly onesided doctrine of the "struggle for existence") is probably due to the origins of most natural scientists: In this respect they belong to the "common people"; their ancestors were poor and undistinguished people who knew the difficulties of survival only too well at firsthand. The whole of English Darwinism breathes something like the musty air of English overpopulation, like the smell of the distress and overcrowding of small people.[35] But a natural scientist should come out of his human nook; and in nature it is not conditions of distress that are *dominant* but overflow and squandering, even to the point of absurdity. The struggle for existence is only an *exception*, a temporary restriction of the will to life. The great and small struggle always revolves around superiority,[36] around growth and expansion, around power—in accordance with the will to power which is the will of life.

350

In honor of the homines religiosi.[37]— The fight against the church is certainly among other things—for it means many things—also the fight of the more common, merrier, more familiar, ingenuous, and superficial type against the dominion of the graver, deeper, more meditative, that is, more evil and suspi-

---

[34] This whole section provides some reasons for Nietzsche's doctrine of the will to *power* as opposed to the more fashionable notion of a will to *life* or *survival*.

[35] Cf. "Anti-Darwin" in *Twilight* (VPN, 522f.): "One should not mistake Malthus for nature." Thomas Robert Malthus (1766–1834) had published his immensely influential *An Essay on the Principle of Population* in 1798.

[36] *Übergewicht.*

[37] the religious, or the religious type.

cious human beings who brood with an enduring suspicion about the value of existence and also about their own value; the common instinct of the people, their sensuous jollity, their "good heart" rebelled against them. The entire Roman church rests upon a southern suspicion about the nature of man, and this is always misunderstood in the north. The European south has inherited this suspicion from the depths of the Orient, from primeval and mysterious Asia and its contemplation. Protestantism already is a people's rebellion for the benefit of the ingenuous, guileless, and superficial (the north has always been more good-natured and shallower than the south); but it was only the French Revolution that actually and solemnly placed the scepter in the hands of "the good human being" (the sheep, the ass, the goose, and all who are incurably shallow squallers, ripe for the nut house of "modern ideas").

351

In honor of the priestly type.— I rather think that it is precisely from what the common people[38] take for wisdom (and who today is not "common people"?)—this clever, bovine piety, peace of mind, and meekness of country pastors that lies in the meadow and *observes* life seriously while ruminating— that the philosophers have always felt most remote, probably because they were not sufficiently "common people" or country pastors for that. It is likely that they of all people will be the last to learn to believe that the common people could possibly understand anything of what is most remote from them: the great *passion* of the seeker after knowledge who lives and must live continually in the thundercloud of the highest problems and the heaviest responsibilities (by no means as an observer, outside, indifferent, secure, and objective).

The common people revere an altogether different human type when they construct *their* ideal of "the sage," and they are amply entitled to lavish the best words and honors on this type —namely, the mild, serious and simple-minded, chaste priestly

---

[38] Throughout this section *Volk* is rendered as common people. Quotation marks are Nietzsche's.

type and what is related to it. When the common people stand in awe of wisdom, their praise is intended for this type. And to whom would the common people have more reason to show gratitude than these men who belong to them and come from among them but as men who are consecrated, selected, and *sacrificed* for the welfare of the common people—they themselves believe that they are being sacrificed to God. It is to these men that the common people can spill their hearts with impunity, to them one can *get rid of* one's secrets, worries, and worse matters (for as a human being "communicates himself" he gets rid of himself, and when one "has confessed" one forgets).

It is a deep need that commands this; for the filth of the soul also requires sewers with pure and purifying waters in them, it requires rapid streams of love and strong, humble, pure hearts who are willing to perform such a service of non-public hygiene, sacrificing *themselves*—for this does involve a sacrifice, and a priest is and remains a human sacrifice.

The common people attribute *wisdom* to such serious men of "faith" who have become quiet, meaning that they have acquired knowledge and are "certain"[39] compared to one's own uncertainty. Who would want to deny them this word and this reverence?—But it is also fair, conversely, when philosophers consider priests as still "common people" and *not* men of knowledge—above all, because they simply do not believe in any "men of knowledge"; in this belief, or rather superstition, they smell the "common people." It was *modesty* that invented the word "philosopher" in Greece[40] and left the magnificent overweening presumption in calling oneself wise to the actors of the spirit—the modesty of such monsters of pride and sovereignty as Pythagoras, as Plato—.[41]

---

[39] *sicher* means secure as well as certain, and *Unsicherheit* means insecurity as well as uncertainty.

[40] Which means literally, lover of wisdom.

[41] The claim here is that not only Socrates made a point of not knowing matters of which many others falsely claimed to have knowledge but that even such "monsters of pride" as Plato did not believe they had knowledge. This claim is at the very least debatable.

352

How morality is scarcely dispensable.— A naked human being is generally a shameful sight. I am speaking of us Europeans (and not even of female Europeans!). Suppose that, owing to some magician's malice, the most cheerful company at table suddenly saw itself disrobed and undressed; I believe that not only their cheerfulness would vanish and that the strongest appetite would be discouraged—[42] it seems that we Europeans simply cannot dispense with that masquerade which one calls clothes.

Now consider the way "moral man" is dressed up, how he is veiled behind moral formulas and concepts of decency—the way our actions are benevolently concealed by the concepts of duty, virtue, sense of community, honorableness, self-denial—should the reasons for all this not be equally good? I am not suggesting that all this is meant to mask human malice and villainy—the wild animal in us; my idea is, on the contrary, that it is precisely as *tame animals* that we are a shameful sight and in need of the moral disguise, that the "inner man" in Europe is not by a long shot bad enough to show himself without shame (or to be *beautiful*). The European disguises himself *with morality* because he has become a sick, sickly, crippled animal that has good reasons for being "tame"; for he is almost an abortion, scarce half made up,[43] weak, awkward.

It is not the ferocity of the beast of prey that requires a moral disguise but the herd animal with its profound mediocrity, timidity, and boredom with itself. With morality the European

---

[42] Here the dash marks a real break; one is led to expect a continuation that does not materialize. It should be kept in mind that this was written in 1886, during the Victorian era.

[43] *etwas Halbes:* literally, something half. The translation alludes to the opening monologue of *Richard III:* . . .

   I, that am curtail'd of this fair proportion,
   Cheated of feature by dissembling Nature,
   Deform'd, unfinish'd, sent before my time
   Into this breathing world, scarce half made up . . .

dresses up—let us confess it!—to look nobler, more important, more respectable, "divine"—[44]

353

On the origin of religions.— The distinctive invention of the founders of religions is, first: to posit a particular kind of life and everyday customs that have the effect of a *disciplina voluntatis*[45] and at the same time abolish boredom—and then: to bestow on this life style an *interpretation* that makes it appear to be illuminated by the highest value so that this life style becomes something for which one fights and under certain circumstances sacrifices one's life. Actually, the second of these two inventions is more essential. The first, the way of life, was usually there before, but alongside other ways of life and without any sense of its special value. The significance and originality of the founder of a religion usually consists of his *seeing* it, *selecting* it, and *guessing* for the first time to what use it can be put, how it can be interpreted.

Jesus (or Paul), for example, found how small people lived in the Roman province—a modest, virtuous, pinched life. He offered an exegesis, he read the highest meaning and value into it—and with this also the courage to despise every other way of life, the quiet Herrnhut[46] fanaticism, the secret, subterranean self-confidence that grows and grows and finally is ready "to overcome the world" (that is, Rome and the upper classes throughout the Empire). Buddha likewise found a human type, in his case scattered through all classes and social strata of his people, that was good and good-natured from inertia (and

---

[44] There is no period, as if the thought broke off as in a note. The central idea is close to Zarathustra's "I have often laughed at the weaklings who thought themselves good because they had no claws" ("On those who are sublime," VPN, 230): Instead of standing revealed as a creature without claws, one pretends that one is ferocious and that only a high regard for morality keeps one from doing terrible things. Cf. also the section on "Whether we have become more moral" in *Twilight* (VPN, 538f.).

[45] discipline of the will.

[46] The Moravian brotherhood; cf. *Will to Power*, section 911 and 911n.

above all inoffensive); also from inertia, this type lived abstinently, almost without needs. He understood how such a human type must inevitably roll, with its whole *vis inertiae*,[47] into a faith that promises to *prevent* the recurrence of terrestrial troubles (meaning work and action in general). To understand that was his genius. To become the founder of a religion one must be psychologically infallible in one's knowledge of a certain average type of souls who have not yet *recognized* that they belong together. It is he that brings them together. The founding of a religion therefore always becomes a long festival of recognition.—

354

On the "genius of the species."[48]— The problem of consciousness (more precisely, of becoming conscious of something) confronts us only when we begin to comprehend how we could dispense with it; and now physiology and the history of animals place us at the beginning of such comprehension (it took them two centuries to catch up with *Leibniz's* suspicion which soared ahead). For we could think, feel, will, and remember, and we could also "act" in every sense of that word, and yet none of all this would have to "enter our consciousness" (as one says metaphorically). The whole of life would be possible without, as it were, seeing itself in a mirror. Even now, for that matter, by far the greatest portion of our life actually takes place without this mirror effect; and this is true even of our thinking, feeling, and willing life, however offensive this may sound to older philosophers. *For what purpose*, then, any consciousness at all when it is in the main *superfluous*?

Now, if you are willing to listen to my answer and the perhaps extravagant surmise that it involves, it seems to me as if

---

[47] force of inertia.
[48] In the 1950s and 1960s many English-speaking philosophers discussed the possibility of a "private language." The literature on the subject was dominated by the work of Ludwig Wittgenstein (1889–1951) but might have profited from some attention to this section. Whether Wittgenstein knew it is uncertain; but the opening of the following section (355) reminds one of Wittgenstein's *style*.

the subtlety and strength of consciousness always were proportionate[49] to a man's (or animal's) *capacity for communication*,
and as if this capacity in turn were proportionate to the *need
for communication*. But this last point is not to be understood
as if the individual human being who happens to be a master
in communicating and making understandable his needs must
also be most dependent on others in his needs. But it does seem
to me as if it were that way when we consider whole races and
chains of generations: Where need and distress have forced
men for a long time to communicate and to understand each
other quickly and subtly, the ultimate result is an excess of this
strength and art of communication—as it were, a capacity that
has gradually been accumulated and now waits for an heir who
might squander it. (Those who are called artists are these heirs;
so are orators, preachers, writers—all of them people who always come at the end of a long chain, "late born" every one of
them in the best sense of that word and, as I have said, by their
nature squanderers.)

Supposing that this observation is correct, I may now proceed
to the surmise that *consciousness has developed only under the
pressure of the need for communication*; that from the start it
was needed and useful only between human beings (particularly
between those who commanded and those who obeyed); and
that it also developed only in proportion to the degree of this
utility. Consciousness is really only a net of communication between human beings; it is only as such that it had to develop;
a solitary human being who lived like a beast of prey would
not have needed it. That our actions, thoughts, feelings, and
movements enter our own consciousness—at least a part of
them—that is the result of a "must" that for a terribly long
time lorded it over man. As the most endangered animal, he
needed help and protection, he needed his peers, he had to learn
to express his distress and to make himself understood; and for
all of this he needed "consciousness" first of all, he needed to
"know" himself what distressed him, he needed to "know" how
he felt, he needed to "know" what he thought. For, to say it
once more: Man, like every living being, thinks continually

---

[49] *im Verhältnis zur* could also be rendered more weakly "related to."

without knowing it; the thinking that rises to *consciousness* is only the smallest part of all this—the most superficial and worst part—for only this conscious thinking *takes the form of words, which is to say signs of communication*, and this fact uncovers the origin of consciousness.

In brief, the development of language and the development of consciousness (*not* of reason but merely of the way reason enters consciousness) go hand in hand. Add to this that not only language serves as a bridge between human beings but also a mien, a pressure, a gesture. The emergence of our sense impressions into our own consciousness, the ability to fix them and, as it were, exhibit them externally, increased proportionately with the need to communicate them to *others* by means of signs. The human being inventing signs is at the same time the human being who becomes ever more keenly conscious of himself. It was only as a social animal that man acquired self-consciousness—which he is still in the process of doing, more and more.

My idea is, as you see, that consciousness does not really belong to man's individual existence but rather to his social or herd nature; that, as follows from this, it has developed subtlety only insofar as this is required by social or herd utility. Consequently, given the best will in the world to understand ourselves as individually as possible, "to know ourselves," each of us will always succeed in becoming conscious only of what is not individual but "average." Our thoughts themselves are continually governed by the character of consciousness—by the "genius of the species" that commands it—and translated back into the perspective of the herd. Fundamentally, all our actions are altogether incomparably personal, unique, and infinitely individual; there is no doubt of that. But as soon as we translate them into consciousness *they no longer seem to be.*

This is the essence of phenomenalism and perspectivism as *I* understand them: Owing to the nature of *animal consciousness*, the world of which we can become conscious is only a surface- and sign-world, a world that is made common and meaner;[50] whatever becomes conscious *becomes* by the same token shal-

---

[50] *eine verallgemeinerte, eine vergemeinerte Welt.*

low, thin, relatively stupid, general, sign, herd signal; all becoming conscious involves a great and thorough corruption, falsification, reduction to superficialities, and generalization. Ultimately, the growth of consciousness becomes a danger; and anyone who lives among the most conscious Europeans even knows that it is a disease.

You will guess that it is not the opposition of subject and object that concerns me here: This distinction I leave to the epistemologists who have become entangled in the snares of grammar (the metaphysics of the people). It is even less the opposition of "thing-in-itself" and appearance; for we do not "know"[51] nearly enough to be entitled to any such distinction. We simply lack any organ for knowledge,[52] for "truth": we "know"[53] (or believe or imagine) just as much as may be *useful* in the interests of the human herd, the species; and even what is here called "utility" is ultimately also a mere belief, something imaginary, and perhaps precisely that most calamitous stupidity of which we shall perish some day.

355

The origin of our concept of "knowledge."[54]— I take this explanation from the street. I heard one of the common people say, "he knew me right away."[55] Then I asked myself: What is it that the common people take for knowledge? What do they want when they want "knowledge"? Nothing more than this: Something strange is to be reduced to something *familiar*.[56] And we philosophers—have we really meant *more* than this when we have spoken of knowledge? What is familiar means what we are used to so that we no longer marvel at it, our everyday, some rule in which we are stuck, anything at all in which we feel at home. Look, isn't our need for knowledge precisely this

---

[51] *"erkennen."*
[52] *das Erkennen.*
[53] *"wissen."*
[54] *"Erkenntnis."*
[55] *"er hat mich erkannt."*
[56] *etwas Bekanntes.*

need for the familiar, the will to uncover under everything strange, unusual, and questionable something that no longer disturbs us? Is it not the *instinct of fear* that bids us to know? And is the jubilation of those who attain knowledge not the jubilation over the restoration of a sense of security?

Here is a philosopher who fancied that the world was "known" when he had reduced it to the "idea."[57] Was it not because the "idea" was so familiar to him and he was so well used to it—because he hardly was afraid of the "idea" any more?

How easily these men of knowledge are satisfied! Just have a look at their principles and their solutions of the world riddle with this in mind! When they find something in things—under them, or behind them—that is unfortunately quite familiar to us, such as our multiplication tables or our logic, or our willing and desiring—how happy they are right away! For "what is familiar is known"[58]: on this they are agreed. Even the most cautious among them suppose that what is familiar is at least *more easily knowable* than what is strange, and that, for example, sound method demands that we start from the "inner world," from the "facts of consciousness," because this world is *more familiar to us.* Error of errors! What is familiar is what we are used to; and what we are used to is most difficult to "know"—that is, to see as a problem; that is, to see as strange, as distant, as "outside us."

The great certainty of the natural sciences in comparison with psychology and the critique of the elements of consciousness—one might almost say, with the *unnatural* sciences—is due

---

[57] Nietzsche may have been thinking of Hegel, but the passage is surely meant to be applicable to more than one philosopher.   *0*

[58] *"was bekannt ist, ist erkannt."* Nietzsche was no Hegel scholar and may not have realized that Hegel had said in the Preface to his *Phenomenology of the Spirit*: "What is familiar is not known simply because it is familiar" (*Das Bekannte überhaupt ist darum, weil es bekannt ist, nicht erkannt:* see Kaufmann, *Hegel: Reinterpretation, Texts, and Commentary,* p. 406f.) Thus Hegel anticipated not only Nietzsche's play on words but also the point that what is known by acquaintance, and thus familiar, is not for that reason also known in the stronger sense of "known," or comprehended.

precisely to the fact that they choose for their object what is *strange*, while it is almost contradictory and absurd to even *try* to choose for an object what is not-strange.[59]

356

How things will become ever more "artistic" in Europe.— Even today, in our time of transition when so many factors cease to compel men, the care to make a living still compels almost all male Europeans to adopt a particular *role*, their so-called occupation. A few retain the freedom, a merely apparent freedom, to choose this role for themselves; for most men it is chosen. The result is rather strange. As they attain a more advanced age, almost all Europeans confound themselves with their role; they become the victims of their own "good performance"; they themselves have forgotten how much accidents, moods, and caprice disposed of them when the question of their "vocation" was decided—and how many other roles they might perhaps have been *able* to play; for now it is too late. Considered more deeply, the role has actually *become* character; and art, nature.

There have been ages when men believed with rigid confidence, even with piety, in their predestination for precisely this occupation, precisely this way of earning a living, and simply refused to acknowledge the element of accident, role, and caprice. With the help of this faith, classes, guilds, and hereditary trade privileges managed to erect those monsters of social pyramids that distinguish the Middle Ages and to whose credit one can adduce at least one thing: durability (and duration is a first-rate value on earth). But there are opposite ages, really democratic, where people give up this faith, and a certain cocky faith and opposite point of view advance more and more into the foreground—the Athenian faith that first becomes noticeable

[59] While Nietzsche agrees with Hegel that familiarity does not imply knowledge in the strong sense which we might call "comprehension," Hegel thought that such comprehension was possible and constituted the task of philosophy: "To comprehend *what is*, is the task of philosophy" (in the preface to his *Philosophy of Right*). Nietzsche argues above that such "comprehension" involves self-deception.

in the Periclean age, the faith of the Americans today that is more and more becoming the European faith as well: The individual becomes convinced that he can do just about everything and *can manage almost any role*, and everybody experiments with himself, improvises, makes new experiments, enjoys his experiments; and all nature ceases and becomes art.

After accepting this *role faith*—an artist's faith, if you will—the Greeks, as is well known, went step for step through a rather odd metamorphosis that does not merit imitation in all respects: *They really became actors.* As such they enchanted and overcame all the world and finally even "the power that had overcome the world" (for the *Graeculus histrio*[60] vanquished Rome, and *not*, as innocents usually say, Greek culture). But what I fear, what is so palpable that today one could grasp it with one's hands, if one felt like grasping it, is that we modern men are even now pretty far along on the same road; and whenever a human being begins to discover how he is playing a role and how he *can* be an actor, he *becomes* an actor.

With this a new human flora and fauna emerge that could never have grown in more solid and limited ages; or at least they would be left there "below" under the ban and suspicion of lacking honor. It is thus that the maddest and most interesting ages of history always emerge, when the "actors," *all* kinds of actors, become the real masters. As this happens, another human type is disadvantaged more and more and finally made impossible; above all, the great "architects": The strength to build becomes paralyzed; the courage to make plans that encompass the distant future is discouraged; those with a genius for organization become scarce: who would still dare to undertake projects that would require thousands of years for their completion? For what is dying out is the fundamental faith that would enable us to calculate, to promise, to anticipate the future in plans of such scope, and to sacrifice the future to them—namely, the faith that man has value and meaning only insofar as he is *a stone in a great edifice*; and to that end he must be *solid* first of all, a "stone"—and above all not an actor!

---

[60] the little Greek actor. *Graeculus* was a term used ironically by the Romans.

To say it briefly (for a long time people will still keep silent about it): What will not be built any more henceforth, and *cannot* be built any more, is—a society[61] in the old sense of that word; to build that, everything is lacking, above all the material. *All of us are no longer material for a society;* this is a truth for which the time has come. It is a matter of indifference to me that at present the most myopic, perhaps most honest, but at any rate noisiest human type that we have today, our good socialists, believe, hope, dream, and above all shout and write almost the opposite. Even now one reads their slogan for the future "free society" on all tables and walls.[62] Free society? Yes, yes! But surely you know, gentlemen, what is required for building that? Wooden iron! The well-known wooden iron.[63] And it must not even be wooden.

357

On the old problem: "What is German?"[64]— Recapitulate in your mind the real achievements of philosophical thinking that one owes to Germans. Is there any legitimate sense in which one might give the credit for these achievements to the whole race? May we say that they are at the same time the product of "the German soul," or at least symptoms of that in the sense in which, say, Plato's ideomania, his almost religious madness about Forms, is usually taken also for an event and testimony of "the Greek soul"? Or should the opposite be the truth? Might they be just as individual, just as much *exceptions* from the spirit of the race as was, for example, Goethe's pagan-

---

[61] *Gesellschaft.* The distinction between *Gemeinschaft und Gesellschaft* (community and society), popular to this day, was first popularized by Ferdinand Tönnies in a book with that title, published in 1887, and is not presupposed above.

[62] Cf. the note on Nietzsche's poem "Fool in Despair," pp. 363–364.

[63] In German, a proverbial *contradictio in adiecto.*

[64] A question then much discussed in Germany. Nietzsche's many discussions of it include notably a whole chapter in *Twilight* (VPN, 505–13) and the section on *The Case of Wagner* in *Ecce Homo* (BWN, 773–81).

ism with a good conscience?[65] Or as is Bismarck's Machiavellism with a good conscience, his so-called "*Realpolitik*," among Germans?[66] Might our philosophers actually contradict the *need* of "the German soul"? In short, were the German philosophers really—philosophical *Germans*?

I recall three cases. First, *Leibniz's* incomparable insight that has been vindicated not only against Descartes but against everybody who had philosophized before him—that consciousness is merely an *accidens*[67] of experience[68] and *not* its necessary and essential attribute; that, in other words, what we call consciousness constitutes only one state of our spiritual and psychic world (perhaps a pathological state) and *not by any means the whole of it*. The profundity of this idea has not been exhausted to this day.[69] Is there anything German in this idea? Is there any reason for surmising that no Latin could easily have thought of this reversal of appearances? For it is a reversal.

Let us recall, secondly, *Kant's* tremendous question mark that he placed after the concept of "causality"—without, like Hume, doubting its legitimacy altogether. Rather, Kant began cautiously to delimit the realm within which this concept makes sense (and to this day we are not done with this fixing of limits).

Let us take, thirdly, the astonishing stroke of *Hegel*, who struck right through all our logical habits and bad habits when he dared to teach that species concepts[70] develop *out of each other*. With this proposition the minds of Europe were preformed for the last great scientific movement, Darwinism—for without Hegel there could have been no Darwin. Is there any-

---

[65] Goethe had called himself a pagan, and Heine had called himself the great pagan, number two.

[66] Nietzsche's reaction to Bismarck was overwhelmingly negative. Cf. *Beyond*, sections 241n and 254n; *Ecce Homo*, the first section on the *Untimely Meditations* as well as the Appendix (i.e., BWN, 365, 384, 733, 797, and 799); and the last letter to Burckhardt (VPN, 687). There are many, many other passages about the new German Empire; above all, the two cited in note 64.

[67] accidental property.

[68] *Vorstellung*.

[69] Freud, of course, explored this insight further.

[70] *die Artbegriffe*.

thing German in this Hegelian innovation which first introduced the decisive concept of "development" into science?

Yes, without any doubt. In all three cases we feel that something in ourselves has been "uncovered" and guessed, and we are grateful for it and at the same time surprised. Each of these three propositions is a thoughtful piece of German self-knowledge, self-experience, self-understanding. "Our inner world is much richer, more comprehensive, more concealed," we feel with Leibniz. As Germans, we doubt with Kant the ultimate validity of the knowledge attained by the natural sciences and altogether everything that *can* be known *causaliter*;[71] whatever is know*able* immediately seems to us less valuable on that account. We Germans are Hegelians even if there never had been any Hegel, insofar as we (unlike all Latins) instinctively attribute a deeper meaning and greater value to becoming and development than to what "is"; we hardly believe in the justification of the concept of "being"[72]—and also insofar as we are not inclined to concede that our human logic is logic as such or the only kind of logic (we would rather persuade ourselves that it is merely a special case and perhaps one of the oddest and most stupid cases).

It would be a fourth question whether *Schopenhauer*, too, with his pessimism—that is, the problem of the *value of existence*—had to be precisely a German. I believe not. The event after which this problem was to be expected for certain—an astronomer of the soul could have calculated the very day and hour for it—the decline of the faith in the Christian god, the triumph of scientific atheism, is a generally European event in which all races had their share and for which all deserve credit and honor. Conversely, one might charge precisely the Germans —those Germans who were Schopenhauer's contemporaries— that they *delayed* this triumph of atheism most dangerously for the longest time. Hegel in particular was its delayer par excel-

---

[71] causally.

[72] *"Sein."* Nietzsche's appreciation of Hegel is remarkable in view of Schopenhauer's extensive and vitriolic polemics against Hegel; and Nietzsche's consistent depreciation of "being" provides an interesting contrast to Heidegger's philosophy.

lence, with his grandiose attempt to persuade us of the divinity of existence, appealing as a last resort to our sixth sense, "the historical sense." As a philosopher, Schopenhauer was the *first* admitted and inexorable atheist among us Germans: This was the background of his enmity against Hegel.[73] The ungodliness of existence was for him something given, palpable, indisputable; he always lost his philosopher's composure and became indignant when he saw anyone hesitate or mince matters at this point. This is the locus of his whole integrity; unconditional and honest atheism is simply the *presupposition* of the way he poses his problem, being a triumph achieved finally and with great difficulty by the European conscience, being the most fateful act of two thousand years of discipline for truth that in the end forbids itself the *lie* in faith in God.

You see what it was that really triumphed over the Christian god: Christian morality itself, the concept of truthfulness that was understood ever more rigorously, the father confessor's refinement of the Christian conscience, translated and sublimated[74] into a scientific conscience, into intellectual cleanliness at any price. Looking at nature as if it were proof of the goodness and governance of a god; interpreting history in honor of some divine reason, as a continual testimony of a moral world order and ultimate moral purposes; interpreting one's own experiences as pious people have long enough interpreted theirs, as if everything were providential, a hint, designed and ordained for the sake of the salvation of the soul—that is *all over* now, that has man's conscience *against* it, that is considered indecent and dishonest by every more refined conscience—mendaciousness, feminism, weakness, and cowardice. In this severity, if anywhere, we are *good* Europeans[75] and heirs of Europe's longest and most courageous self-overcoming.

---

[73] This explanation seems rather implausible.

[74] *sublimiert.*

[75] Nietzsche had first introduced the concept of the "good European" in *Human, All-Too-Human,* section 475, with the title "The European human being and the abolition of nations"; and the term recurs often in his works and is usually associated with his opposition to nationalism and anti-Semitism. Cf. section 377 below and the indices to Kaufmann and to *Beyond Good and Evil* and *Ecce Homo* in BWN.

As we thus reject the Christian interpretation and condemn its "meaning" like counterfeit,[76] *Schopenhauer's* question immediately comes to us in a terrifying way: *Has existence any meaning at all?* It will require a few centuries before this question can even be heard completely and in its full depth. What Schopenhauer himself said in answer to this question was— forgive me—hasty, youthful, only a compromise, a way of remaining—remaining stuck—in precisely those Christian-ascetic moral perspectives in which one had *renounced faith* along with the faith in God. But he *posed* the question—as a good European, as I have said, and *not* as a German.

Or is it possible that at least the manner in which the Germans appropriated Schopenhauer's question proves that the Germans did have an inner affinity, preparation, and *need* for his problem? That after Schopenhauer one thought and printed things in Germany, too—by the way, late enough—about the problem he had posed, is certainly not sufficient to decide in favor of such an inner affinity. One might rather adduce the peculiar *ineptitude* of this post-Schopenhauerian pessimism *against* this thesis. Obviously, the Germans did not behave in this affair as if they had been in their own element. This is not by any means an allusion to Eduard von Hartmann.[77] On the contrary, to this day I have not shaken off my old suspicion that he is too *apt* for us. I mean that he may have been a wicked rogue from the start who perhaps made fun not only of German pessimism—but in the end he might even "bequeath" to the Germans in his will how far it was possible even in the age of foundations[78] to make fools of them. But let me ask you: Should

---

[76] *Falschmünzerei.* Nietzsche's frequent use of this term in connection with self-deception influenced André Gide, who entitled what he himself considered his only novel *The Counterfeiters.*

[77] A very popular philosopher (1842–1906) who tried to synthesize the philosophies of Hegel and Schopenhauer. His *Philosophy of the Unconscious* (1869) is still cited occasionally. Nietzsche's contempt for Eduard von Hartmann is evident in all his references to him; cf. *Beyond Good and Evil,* section 204.

[78] *Zeitalter der Gründungen:*
Nietzsche is referring to the so-called *Gründerjahre* when the foundation of the new German Empire (1871) was followed by very rapid industrial growth. This "period of promoterism" and "bubble companies" was soon followed by an economic crisis (1873–74).

we perhaps consider that old humming-top Bahnsen[79] as a credit to the Germans, seing how voluptuously he revolved his life long around his real-dialectical misery and his "personal tough luck"? Perhaps precisely this is German? (I herewith recommend his writings for the purpose for which I have used them myself, as an anti-pessimistic diet, especially on account of their *elegantiae psychologicae*;[80] they should, I think, be effective even for the most constipated bowels and mind.) Or could one count such dilettantes and old spinsters as that mawkish apostle of virginity, Mainländer,[81] as a genuine German? In the last analysis he probably was a Jew (all Jews become mawkish when they moralize). Neither Bahnsen nor Mainländer, not to speak of Eduard von Hartmann, gives us any clear evidence regarding the question whether Schopenhauer's pessimism, his horrified look into a de-deified world that had become stupid, blind, mad, and questionable, his *honest* horror, was not merely an exceptional case among Germans but a *German* event. Everything else that one sees in the foreground—our bold politics and our cheerful fatherlandishness which resolutely enough consider all matters with a view to a not very philosophical principle (*"Deutschland, Deutschland über alles"*[82]), which means *sub specie speciei*,[83] namely the German species, bears emphatic

---

[79] Julius Bahnsen (1830–81) had published books on characterology, philosophy of history, and the tragic as the law of the world. He opposed his own *Realdialektik* to Hegel's dialectic and was one of the very few German philosophers influenced by Schopenhauer.

[80] psychological elegance.

[81] Philipp Mainländer was the pseudonym of Philipp Batz. Born in 1841, he committed suicide in 1876. His *Philosophie der Erlösung* (1876: The Philosophy of Redemption) makes much of the will to death, of virginity, and of suicide. This is the only reference to Mainländer in Nietzsche's works, and a large part of Nietzsche's point is, of course, that Schopenhauer's pessimism had had virtually no influence on German philosophy; the few writers who had been influenced by him were of no consequence.

[82] The German national anthem to which Nietzsche occasionally refers with a sneer: "Germany, Germany above everything . . ."

[83] from the point of view of the species—an allusion to Spinoza's *sub specie aeternitatis* (*Ethics*, V.29: from the point of view of eternity). The parenthetical generalization about "all Jews" in the text above clearly does not apply to Spinoza, and one is left to wonder to whom precisely it is thought to apply.

witness of the opposite. No, the Germans of today are *no* pessimists. And Schopenhauer was a pessimist, to say it once more, as a good European and *not* as a German.—[84]

358

The peasant rebellion of the spirit.— We Europeans confront a world of tremendous ruins. A few things are still towering, much looks decayed and uncanny, while most things already lie on the ground. It is all very picturesque—where has one ever seen more beautiful ruins?—and overgrown by large and small weeds. The church is this city of destruction: We see the religious community of Christianity shaken to its lowest foundations; the faith in God has collapsed; the faith in the Christian-ascetic ideal is still fighting its final battle. An edifice like Christianity that had been built so carefully over such a long period—it was the last construction of the Romans!—naturally could not be destroyed all at once. All kinds of earthquakes had to shake it, all kinds of spirits that bore, dig, gnaw, and moisten have had to help. But what is strangest is this: Those who exerted themselves the most to preserve and conserve Christianity have become precisely its most efficient destroyers—the Germans.

It seems that the Germans do not understand the nature of a church. Are they not spiritual enough for that? or not mistrustful enough? The edifice of the church at any rate rests on a *southern* freedom and enlightenment of the spirit as well as a southern suspicion of nature, man, and spirit; it rests on an altogether different knowledge of man and experience of man than is to be found in the north. The Lutheran Reformation was, in its whole breadth, the indignation of simplicity against

---

[84] When one considers this section as a whole, it differs from the other passages in which Nietzsche deals at length with the Germans (see the first footnote to this section) by not being stridently and centrally anti-German. The achievements of Leibniz, Kant, and Hegel, which are credited to the Germans, are genuine. This suggests that an event after the above section was written, but before *Twilight* was written, changed Nietzsche's mind about the Germans. If so, it was surely the accession to the throne of the last Kaiser (see the first section of the discussion of *Zarathustra* in *Ecce Homo*, including the material cited in note 6: BWN, 753f.). But sections 134, 149, and 377 of *The Gay Science* point toward Nietzsche's final views. See also p. 23f. above.

"multiplicity" or, to speak cautiously, a crude, ingenuous misunderstanding in which there is much that calls for forgiveness.
One failed to understand the expression of a *triumphant* church
and saw nothing but corruption; one misunderstood the noble
skepticism, that *luxury* of skepticism and tolerance which every
triumphant, self-assured power permits itself.

Today it is easy enough to see how in all cardinal questions
of power Luther's disposition was calamitously myopic, superficial, and incautious. He was a man of the common people who
lacked everything that one might inherit from a ruling caste;
he had no instinct for power. Thus his work, his will to restore
that Roman work became, without his knowing or willing it,
nothing but the beginning of a work of destruction. He un-
raveled, he tore up with honest wrath what the old spider had
woven so carefully for such a long time. He surrendered the
holy books to everybody—until they finally got into the hands
of the philologists,[85] who are the destroyers of every faith that
rests on books. He destroyed the concept of the "church" by
throwing away the faith in the inspiration of the church coun-
cils; for the concept of the "church" retains its power only on
condition that the inspiring spirit that founded the church still
lives in it, builds in it, and continues to build its house. He
gave back to the priest sexual intercourse with woman; but
three quarters of the reverence of which the common people,
especially the women among the common people, are capable,

---

[85] This is more amusing than correct. Luther's magnificent translation
of the Bible was made possible by the work of some great philologists.
Johann Reuchlin (1455–1522) made a great reputation as a Greek and
Hebrew scholar, was the first Christian to publish a Hebrew grammar
(1506), and urged the Emperor Maximilian to establish two chairs of
Hebrew learning at every German university. Desiderius Erasmus (1466–
1536) published the Greek text of the New Testament with his own
Latin translation and notes in 1516, and it was reprinted with some
corrections in 1519, 1522, 1527, 1535. The philological value of his edition has been denied outright by modern scholars, but "it revealed that
the Vulgate, the Bible of the church, was not only a second-hand document, but in places an erroneous document. A shock was thus given to
the credit of the clergy ... equal to that which was given in the province
of science by the astronomical discoveries of the 17th century" (*Encyclopaedia Britannica,* 11th ed., vol. 9, p. 732).

rests on the faith that a person who is an exception at this point will be an exception in other respects as well; it is here that the popular faith in something superhuman in man, in the miracle, in the redeeming god in man, finds its subtlest and most insidious advocate. Luther, having given the priest woman, had to *take* away from him auricular confession; that was right psychologically. With that development the Christian priest was, at bottom, abolished, for his most profound utility had always been that he was a holy ear, a silent well, a grave for secrets. "Everyone his own priest"—behind such formulas and their peasant cunning there was hidden in Luther the abysmal hatred against "the higher human being" and the dominion of "the higher human beings" as conceived by the church. He smashed an ideal that he could not attain, while he seemed to abhor and to be fighting only against the degeneration of this ideal. Actually, he, the man who had found it impossible to be a monk, pushed away the *dominion* of the *homines religiosi*, and thus he himself made within the *ecclesiastical* social order what in relation to the *civic* social order he attacked so intolerantly—namely, a "peasant rebellion."

What afterward grew out of his Reformation, good as well as bad, might be calculated approximately today; but who would be naive enough to praise or blame Luther on account of these consequences? He is innocent of everything; he did not know what he was doing. The European spirit became shallower, particularly in the north—*more good-natured*, if you prefer a moral term—and there is no doubt that this development advanced a large step with the Lutheran Reformation. The mobility and restlessness of the spirit, its thirst for independence, its faith in a right to liberty, its "naturalness"—all this also grew owing to the Reformation. If in connection with this last point one wanted to concede it the value of having prepared and favored what we today revere as "modern science," one would surely have to add that it also shares the responsibility for the degeneration of the modern scholar, for his lack of reverence, shame, and depth, for the whole naive guilelessness and ostentatious ingenuousness in matters of knowledge—in short, for that *plebeianism of the spirit* which is a peculiarity of the last two centuries and from which even pessimism has not yet liberated us.

"Modern ideas" also belong to this peasant rebellion of the north against the colder, more ambiguous and mistrustful spirit of the south that built its greatest monument in the Christian church. Let us not forget in the end what a church is, as opposed to any "state." A church is above all a structure for ruling[86] that secures the highest rank for the *more spiritual* human beings and that *believes* in the power of spirituality to the extent of forbidding itself the use of all the cruder instruments of force; and on this score alone the church is under all circumstances a *nobler* institution than the state.[87]

---

[86] *Herrschafts-Gebilde.*
[87] Cf. the last note on the preceding section: Again there is a significant change in 1888. Some of the motifs sounded here and in some of Nietzsche's earlier works are retained, but the image of Luther in *The Antichrist* is nevertheless importantly different: "like Luther, like Leibniz, Kant was one more clog for German honesty, which was none too steady in the first place" (section 10, VPN, 577); " 'Faith' was at all times, for example, in Luther, only a cloak, a pretext, a *screen* behind which the instincts played their game—a shrewd *blindness* about the dominance of *certain* instincts" (section 39, VPN, 613); "Luther . . . the opposition-type of the strong spirit who has *become* free" (section 54, VPN, 639); and above all, "Luther *restored the church*: he attacked it. . . . Oh, these Germans what they have cost us already! In vain—that has always been the doing of the Germans. The Reformation, Leibniz, Kant and so-called German philosophy, the Wars of 'Liberation' [against Napoleon], the *Reich*—each time and in vain for something that had already been attained, for something irrevocable" (section 61, VPN, 654; cf. *Ecce Homo,* the second section of the discussion of *The Case of Wagner,* BWN, 776).

That Nietzsche felt a certain ambivalence about Luther is hardly remarkable; anyone who knows enough about Luther is likely to admire some aspects of his character and his accomplishments while being appalled by others. And there is some consistency in Nietzsche's image of Luther; even some of the same epithets keep recurring. But in *The Gay Science* he is said to have destroyed the church, while in 1888 Nietzsche blames him for having restored the church by attacking it. As it happens, he did destroy the church in an obvious and very important sense—but he also revitalized Christianity for some time. And in *The Antichrist* and in *Ecce Homo* Nietzsche has in mind Christianity rather than the edifice of the church.

What has changed emphatically in the works written in 1888 is the tenor of Nietzsche's remarks about the Germans; he sees them as an utter disaster.

359

The revenge against the spirit and other ulterior motives[88] *of morality.*— Morality—where do you suppose that it finds its most dangerous and insidious advocates?

There is a human being who has turned out badly,[89] who does not have enough spirit to be able to enjoy it but just enough education to realize this; he is bored, disgusted, and despises himself; having inherited some money, he is deprived even of the last comfort, "the blessings of work," self-forgetfulness in "daily labor." Such a person who is fundamentally ashamed of his existence—perhaps he also harbors a few little vices—and on the other hand cannot keep himself from becoming more and more spoiled and irritable by reading books to which he is not entitled or by associating with more spiritual company than he can digest; such a human being who has become poisoned through and through—for spirit becomes poison, education becomes poison, possessions become poison, solitude becomes poison for those who have turned out badly in this way—eventually ends up in a state of habitual revenge, will to revenge.

What do you suppose he finds necessary, absolutely necessary, to give himself in his own eyes the appearance of superiority over more spiritual people and to attain the pleasure of an *accomplished revenge* at least in his imagination? Always *morality*; you can bet on that. Always big moral words. Always the rub-a-dub of justice, wisdom, holiness, virtue. Always the Stoicism of gesture (how well Stoicism conceals what one lacks!). Always the cloak of prudent silence, of affability, of mildness, and whatever may be the names of all the other idealistic cloaks in which incurable self-despisers, as well as the incurably vain, strut about.

Do not misunderstand me: Among such born *enemies of the spirit* there comes into being occasionally the rare piece of humanity that the common people revere, using such names as saint and sage. It is from among men of this sort that those monsters of morality come who make noise, who make history

---

[88] literally: backgrounds (*Hintergründe*).
[89] *ein missratener Mensch.*

—St. Augustine is one of them. Fear of the spirit, revenge against the spirit—how often these propelling vices have become the roots of virtues! Even nothing less than virtues.

And a confidential question: Even the claim that they possessed *wisdom*, which has been made here and there on earth by philosophers, the maddest and most immodest of all claims—has it not always been to date, in India as well as in Greece, *a screen above all*? At times perhaps a screen chosen with pedagogical intent, which hallows so many lies; one has a tender regard for those still in the process of becoming, of growing—for disciples, who must often be defended against themselves by means of faith in a person (by means of an error).

Much more often, however, it is a screen behind which the philosopher saves himself because he has become weary, old, cold, hard—as a premonition that the end is near, like the prudence animals have before they die: they go off by themselves, become still, choose solitude, hide in caves, and become *wise*.

What? Wisdom as a screen behind which the philosopher hides from—spirit?—

360

Two kinds of causes that are often confounded.— This seems to me to be one of my most essential steps and advances: I have learned to distinguish the cause of acting from the cause of acting in a particular way, in a particular direction, with a particular goal. The first kind of cause is a quantum of dammed-up energy that is waiting to be used up somehow, for something, while the second kind is, compared to this energy, something quite insignificant, for the most part a little accident in accordance with which this quantum "discharges" itself in one particular way—a match versus a ton of powder. Among these little accidents and "matches" I include so-called "purposes" as well as the even much more so-called "vocations": They are relatively random,[90] arbitrary, almost indifferent in relation to the tremendous quantum of energy that presses, as

---

[90] *beliebig.*

I have said, to be used up somehow. The usual view is different: People are accustomed to consider the goal (purposes, vocations, etc.) as the *driving force,* in keeping with a very ancient error; but it is merely the *directing* force—one has mistaken the helmsman for the steam. And not even always the helmsman, the directing force.

Is the "goal," the "purpose" not often enough a beautifying pretext, a self-deception of vanity after the event that does not want to acknowledge that the ship is *following* the current into which it has entered accidentally? that it "wills" to go that way *because it—must?* that is has a direction, to be sure, but—no helmsman at all?

We still need a critique of the concept of "purpose."

361

On the problem of the actor.— The problem of the actor has troubled me for the longest time. I felt unsure (and sometimes still do) whether it is not only from this angle that one can get at the dangerous concept of the "artist"—a concept that has so far been treated with unpardonable generosity. Falseness with a good conscience; the delight in simulation exploding as a power that pushes aside one's so-called "character," flooding it and at times extinguishing it; the inner craving for a role and mask, for *appearance*; an excess of the capacity for all kinds of adaptations that can no longer be satisfied in the service of the most immediate and narrowest utility—all of this is perhaps not *only* peculiar to the actor?

Such an instinct will have developed most easily in families of the lower classes who had to survive under changing pressures and coercions, in deep dependency, who had to cut their coat according to the cloth, always adapting themselves again to new circumstances, who always had to change their mien and posture, until they learned gradually to turn their coat with *every* wind and thus virtually to *become* a coat—and masters of the incorporated and inveterate art of eternally playing hide-and-seek, which in the case of animals is called mimicry—until eventually this capacity, accumulated from generation to generation, becomes domineering, unreasonable, and intractable, an instinct that learns to lord it over other instincts, and generates the actor, the "artist" (the zany, the teller of lies, the buffoon, fool, clown at first, as well as the classical servant, Gil Blas;[91] for it is in such types that we find the pre-history of the artist and often enough even of the "genius").

In superior social conditions, too, a similar human type develops under similar pressures; only in such cases the histrionic instinct is usually barely kept under control by another instinct; for example, in the case of "diplomats." Incidentally, I am inclined to believe that a good diplomat would always be free to become a good stage actor if he wished—if only he were "free."

As for the *Jews*, the people who possess the art of adaptability par excellence, this train of thought suggests immediately that one might see them virtually as a world-historical arrangement for the production of actors, a veritable breeding ground for actors. And it really is high time to ask: What good actor today is *not*—a Jew? The Jew as a born "man of letters,"[92] as the true master of the European press, also exercises his power by virtue of his histrionic gifts; for the man of letters is essentially an actor: He plays the "expert," the "specialist."

Finally, *women*. Reflect on the whole history of women: do they not *have* to be first of all and above all else actresses? Listen to physicians who have hypnotized women;[93] finally, love them—let yourself be "hypnotized by them"! What is always the end result? That they "put on something" even when they take off everything.[94]

Woman is so artistic.

---

91 See the note on section 77 above.

92 *Literat,* though translated in the best dictionaries as "man of letters, writer," often has derogatory overtones. See section 366.

93 *Frauenzimmer* usually has derogatory overtones. This whole sentence, like many of Nietzsche's generalizations about women, descends to a lower level—stylistically as well as in content. It seems to be intended merely to lead up to the pun that follows.

94 *Dass sie "sich geben," selbst noch, wenn sie—sich geben.* Literally: that they "give themselves" (that is, act or play a part) even when they —give themselves.

362

Our faith that Europe will become more virile.— We owe it
to Napoleon (and not by any means to the French Revolution,
which aimed at the "brotherhood" of nations and a blooming
universal exchange of hearts[95]) that we now confront a succession of a few warlike centuries that have no parallel in history;
in short, that we have entered *the classical age of war*, of scientific and at the same time popular war on the largest scale (in
weapons, talents, and discipline). All coming centuries will look
back on it with envy and awe for its perfection. For the national
movement out of which this war glory is growing is only the
counter-shock against Napoleon and would not exist except for
Napoleon. He should receive credit some day for the fact that
in Europe the *man* has again become master over the business-
man and the philistine—and perhaps even over "woman" who
has been pampered by Christianity and the enthusiastic spirit
of the eighteenth century, and even more by "modern ideas."
Napoleon, who considered modern ideas and civilization itself
almost as a personal enemy,[96] proved himself through this enmity as one of the greatest continuators of the Renaissance; he
brought back again a whole slab of antiquity, perhaps even the
decisive piece, the piece of granite. And who knows whether
this slab of antiquity might not finally become master again
over the national movement, and whether it must not become
the heir and continuator of Napoleon in an *affirmative* sense;
for what he wanted was one unified Europe, as is known—as
mistress of the earth.—[97]

363

How each sex has its own prejudice about love.— Despite
all the concessions that I am willing to make to the prejudice
in favor of monogamy, I will never admit the claim that man

---

[95] *allgemeinen blumichten Herzens-Austausch* is very colloquial and
ironical.
[96] *Feindin:* a female enemy; in German, civilization is feminine.
[97] Nietzsche's consistent opposition to nationalism is clear enough, his
image of a unified Europe is not. He never discusses the quest for
colonies in Africa.

and woman have *equal* rights in love; these do not exist. For man and woman have different conceptions of love; and it is one of the conditions of love in both sexes that neither sex presupposes the same feeling and the same concept of "love" in the other. What woman means by love is clear enough: total devotion (not mere surrender[98]) with soul and body, without any consideration or reserve, rather with shame and horror at the thought of a devotion that might be subject to special clauses or conditions. In this absence of conditions her love is a *faith*; woman has no other faith.

Man, when he loves a woman, wants precisely this love from her and is thus himself as far as can be from the presupposition of feminine love. Supposing, however, that there should also be men to whom the desire for total devotion is not alien; well, then they simply are—not men. A man who loves like a woman becomes a slave; while a woman who loves like a woman becomes *a more perfect woman*.

A woman's passion in its unconditional renunciation of rights of her own presupposes precisely that on the other side there is no equal pathos, no equal will to renunciation; for if both partners felt impelled by love to renounce themselves, we should then get—I do not know what; perhaps an empty space?

Woman wants to be taken and accepted as a possession, wants to be absorbed into the concept of possession, possessed. Consequently, she wants someone who *takes*, who does not give himself or give himself away; on the contrary, he is supposed to become richer in "himself"—through the accretion of strength, happiness, and faith given him by the woman who gives herself. Woman gives herself away, man acquires more— I do not see how one can get around this natural opposition by means of social contracts or with the best will in the world to be just, desirable as it may be not to remind oneself constantly how harsh, terrible, enigmatic, and immoral this antagonism is. For love, thought of in its entirety as great and full, is nature, and being nature it is in all eternity something "immoral."

---

[98] *vollkommene Hingabe (nicht nur Hingebung)*. To capture the play on words, one might use "devotedness" instead of "surrender," for the German here is ambiguous; but *Hingebung* recurs in the last sentence of this section where it clearly means "surrender."

Faithfulness is accordingly included in woman's love; it follows from the definition. In man, it *can* easily develop in the wake of his love, perhaps as gratitude or as an idiosyncratic taste and so-called elective affinity; but it is not an *essential* element of his love—so definitely not that one might almost speak with some justification of a natural counterplay of love and faithfulness in man. For his love consists of wanting to *have* and not of renunciation and giving away; but *wanting* to have always comes to an end with *having.*

It is actually man's more refined and suspicious lust for possession that rarely admits his "having," and then only late, and thus permits his love to persist. It is even possible for his love to increase after the surrender; he will not readily concede that a woman should have nothing more to give him.—

364

The hermit speaks.— The art of associating with people depends essentially on an aptitude (requiring long practice) for accepting and eating a meal in whose cuisine one has no confidence. If you come to the table ravenously hungry, it is all very easy ("the worst company can be *felt*," as Mephistopheles says[99]); but one does not have this ravenous hunger when one needs it. How hard it is to digest one's fellow men!

First principle: to summon one's courage as in misfortune, to fall to boldly, to admire oneself in the process, to grit one's teeth on one's repugnance, and to swallow one's nausea.

Second principle: to "improve" one's fellow man, by praise, for example, so that he begins to sweat out his delight in himself, or to grab a corner of his good or "interesting" qualities and to pull at it until the whole virtue comes out and one can hide one's fellow man in its folds.

Third principle: autosuggestion. To fix one's eyes upon the object of association as if it were a glass button, until one ceases to feel any pleasure or displeasure and goes to sleep unnoticed, grows rigid, and acquires poise—a home remedy amply tested

---

[99] *lässt sich fühlen.* What Mephistopheles says in Goethe's *Faust,* line 1637, is: "[Even] the worst company allows you to feel [*lässt dich fühlen*] that you are a human being among human beings." In the Musarion edition, *sich* has been changed to *dich.*

in marriage and friendship and praised as indispensable, but not yet formulated scientifically. Its popular name is—patience.—

365

The hermit speaks once more.— We, too, associate with "people"; we, too, modestly don the dress in which (*as which*) others know us, respect us, look for us—and then we appear in company, meaning among people who are disguised without wanting to admit it. We, too, do what all prudent masks do, and in response to every curiosity that does not concern our "dress" we politely place a chair against the door. But there are also other ways and tricks when it comes to associating with or passing among men[100]—for example, as a ghost, which is altogether advisable if one wants to get rid of them quickly and make them afraid. Example: One reaches out for us but gets no hold of us. That is frightening. Or we enter through a closed door. Or after all lights have been extinguished. Or after we have died.

The last is the trick of *posthumous* people par excellence. ("What did you think?" one of them once asked impatiently; "would we feel like enduring the estrangement,[101] the cold and quiet of the grave around us—this whole subterranean, concealed, mute, undiscovered solitude that among us is called life but might just as well be called death—if we did not know what will *become* of us, and that it is only after death that we shall enter *our* life and become alive, oh, very much alive, we posthumous people!") [102]

---

[100] *um unter Menschen, mit Menschen "umzugehn"*: taken with the two immediately preceding words, the verb means "associate"; taken with the first three words it brings to mind a ghost.

[101] *Fremde.*

[102] Cf. section 262 above; also "Some are born posthumously" (both in the Preface to *The Antichrist*, VPN, 568, and in the first section of the third chapter of *Ecce Homo*, BWN, 715); also "One pays dearly for immortality; one has to die several times while still alive" (in section 5 of the discussion of *Zarathustra* in *Ecce Homo*, BWN, 759).

One occasionally sees the following graffiti: " 'God is dead.' Nietzsche. 'Nietzsche is dead.' God."

Rarely, someone adds a third line; e.g., " 'Neitsche is spelled wrong.' Kaufmann." The best third line I have seen is: " 'Some are born posthumously.' Nietzsche."

366

Faced with a scholarly book.— We do not belong to those who have ideas only among books, when stimulated by books. It is our habit to think outdoors—walking, leaping, climbing, dancing, preferably on lonely mountains or near the sea where even the trails become thoughtful. Our first questions about the value of a book, of a human being, or a musical composition are: Can they walk? Even more, can they dance?

We read rarely, but not worse on that account. How quickly we guess how someone has come by his ideas; whether it was while sitting in front of his inkwell, with a pinched belly, his head bowed low over the paper—in which case we are quickly finished with his book, too! Cramped intestines betray themselves—you can bet on that—no less than closet air, closet ceilings, closet narrowness.—This was what I felt just now as I closed a very decent scholarly book—gratefully, very gratefully, but also with a sense of relief.

Almost always the books of scholars are somehow oppressive, oppressed; the "specialist" emerges somewhere—his zeal, his seriousness, his fury, his overestimation of the nook in which he sits and spins, his hunched back; every specialist has his hunched back. Every scholarly book also mirrors a soul that has become crooked; every craft makes crooked.[103]

You see the friends of your youth again after they have taken possession of their specialty—and always the opposite has happened, too! Always they themselves are now possessed by it and obsessed with it. Grown into their nook, crumpled beyond recognition, unfree, deprived of their balance, emaciated and angular all over except for one place where they are downright rotund—one feels moved and falls silent when one sees them again this way. Every craft, even if it should have a golden floor, has a leaden ceiling over it that presses and presses down upon the soul until that becomes queer and crooked. Nothing can be done about that. Let nobody suppose that one could possibly avoid such crippling by some artifice of education. On this

---

[103] Here the translation is more suggestive than the original: *jedes Handwerk zieht krumm.* The German noun does not have the overtones of craftiness.

earth one pays dearly for every kind of *mastery*, and perhaps one pays too dearly for everything. For having a specialty one pays by also being the victim of this specialty. But you would have it otherwise—cheaper and fairer and above all more comfortable—isn't that right, my dear contemporaries? Well then, but in that case you also immediately get something else: instead of the craftsman and master, the "man of letters,"[104] the dexterous, "polydexterous"[105] man of letters who, to be sure, lacks the hunched back—not counting the posture he assumes before you, being the salesman of the spirit and the "carrier" of culture—the man of letters who really *is* nothing but "represents" almost everything, playing and "substituting" for the expert, and taking it upon himself in all modesty to get himself paid, honored, and celebrated in place of the expert.

No, my scholarly friends, I bless you even for your hunched backs. And for despising, as I do, the "men of letters" and culture parasites. And for not knowing how to make a business of the spirit. And for having opinions that cannot be translated into financial values. And for not representing anything that you are not. And because your sole aim is to become masters of your craft, with reverence for every kind of mastery and competence, and with uncompromising opposition to everything that is semblance, half-genuine, dressed up, virtuosolike, demagogical, or histrionic in *litteris et artibus*[106]—to everything that cannot prove to you its unconditional *probity* in discipline and prior training.

(Even genius does not compensate for such a deficiency, however much it may deceive people about it. This becomes clear to anyone who has ever watched our most gifted painters and musicians from nearby. All of them, with scarcely any exception, know how to use cunning inventions of manners, of makeshift devices, and even of principles to give themselves after the event an artificial *semblance* of such probity, of such solidity of training and culture—without, of course, managing to deceive

---

[104] See section 361n, above.
[105] *den gewandten "vielgewendeten"*: see section 344n above on *polytropoi*.
[106] arts and letters.

themselves, without silencing for good their own bad conscience. For you surely know that all great modern artists suffer
from a guilty conscience.)

367

The first distinction to be made regarding works of art.[107]—
All thought, poetry, painting, compositions, even buildings and
sculptures, belong either to monological art or to art before
witnesses. In the second class we must include even the apparently monological art that involves faith in God, the whole
lyricism of prayer. For the pious there is as yet no solitude; this
invention was made only by us, the godless. I do not know of
any more profound difference in the whole orientation of an
artist than this, whether he looks at his work in progress (at
"himself") from the point of view of the witness, or whether
he "has forgotten the world," which is the essential feature of
all monological art; it is based *on forgetting*, it is the music of
forgetting.

368

The cynic speaks.[108]— My objections to the music of Wagner
are physiological objections; why should I trouble to dress them
up in aesthetic formulas? My "fact" is that I no longer breathe
easily once this music begins to affect me; that my foot soon
resents it and rebels; my foot feels the need for rhythm, dance,
march; it demands of music first of all those delights which are
found in *good* walking, striding, leaping, and dancing. But does
not my stomach protest, too? my heart? my circulation? my
intestines? Do I not become hoarse as I listen?

And so I ask myself: What is it that my whole body really
expects of music? I believe, its own *ease*[109]: as if all animal

---

[107] Cf. the last three paragraphs of section 370 below.
[108] A revised version of this section was included by Nietzsche in his
Nietzsche contra Wagner, under the title *"Where I offer objections"*
(VPN, 664–66). A few of the changes Nietzsche made are noted below.
[109] *Erleichterung:* being made easier, having a weight taken off.

functions should be quickened by easy, bold, exuberant, self-assured rhythms; as if iron, leaden life should be gilded by good golden and tender harmonies. My melancholy[110] wants to rest in the hiding places and abysses of *perfection*: that is why I need music. What is the drama to me? What, the convulsions of its moral ecstasies which give the common people satisfaction? What, the whole gesture hocus-pocus of the actor?

You will guess that I am essentially anti-theatrical[111]—but Wagner was, conversely, essentially a man of the theater and an actor, the most enthusiastic mimomaniac of all time, also as a musician. And, incidentally, if it was Wagner's theory that "the drama is the end, the music is always a mere means," his *practice* was always, from beginning to end, "the pose is the end; the drama, also the music, is always merely a means to *that*." Music as a means to clarify, strengthen, and lend inward dimension to the dramatic gesture and the actor's appeal to the senses—and the Wagnerian drama, a mere occasion for many dramatic poses! Besides all other instincts, he had the commanding instincts of a great actor in absolutely everything—and, as already mentioned, also as a musician.

I once made this clear to an upright Wagnerian, not without trouble;[112] and I had reasons for adding: "Do be a little more honest with yourself! After all, we are not in the theater.[113] In the theater one is honest only in the mass; as an individual one lies, one lies to oneself. One leaves oneself at home when one goes to the theater, one renounces the right to one's own tongue and choice, to one's taste, even to one's courage as one has it and exercises it between one's own four walls against both God

---

110 *Schwermut:* literally, heavy mood, this is the ordinary word for melancholy.
111 In NCW Nietzsche added: "Confronted with the theater, this mass art par excellence, I feel that profound scorn at the bottom of my soul which every artist today feels. *Success* in the theater—with that one drops in my respect forever; *failure*—I prick up my ears and begin to respect."
112 The additions in NCW include, at this point: "Clarity and Wagnerian! Not another word is needed."
113 Here and in the following lines, NCW has "Bayreuth" instead of theater.

and man. No one brings along the finest senses of his art to the
theater, nor does the artist who works for the theater.[114] There
one is common people, audience, herd, female, pharisee, voting
cattle, democrat, neighbor, fellow man;[115] there even the most
personal conscience is vanquished by the leveling magic of the
great number; there stupidity has the effect of lasciviousness
and contagion; the neighbor reigns, one becomes a mere
neighbor "[116]

(I forgot to mention how my enlightened Wagnerian replied
to these physiological objections: "Then you really are merely
not healthy enough for our music?")

369

Our side by side.— Don't we have to admit to ourselves, we
artists, that there is an uncanny difference within us between
our taste and our creative power? They stand oddly side by
side, separately, and each grows in its own way. I mean, they
have altogether different degrees and *tempi* of old, young,
mature, mellow, and rotten. A musician, for example, might
create his life long what is utterly at odds with what his
refined listener's ear and listener's heart esteem, enjoy, and
prefer—and he need not even be aware of this contradiction. As
our almost painfully frequent experience shows, one's taste can
easily grow far beyond the reach of the taste of one's powers,
and this need not at all paralyze these powers and keep them from
continued productivity. But the opposite can happen, too—and
this is what I should like to call to the attention of artists. Consider a continually creative person, a "mother" type in the
grand sense, one who knows and hears nothing any more
except about the pregnancies and deliveries of his spirit, one
who simply lacks the time to reflect on himself and his work
and to make comparisons, one who no longer has any desire to

---

[114] In NCW Nietzsche inserted: "Solitude is lacking; whatever is perfect
suffers no witnesses."
[115] The additions in NCW include "idiot," a word that suddenly
assumed importance in Nietzsche's last works. Cf. Kaufmann, p. 340f.
[116] In NCW the section ends at this point.

assert his taste and who simply forgets it, without caring in the least whether it still stands, or lies, or falls—such a person might perhaps eventually produce works *that far excel his own judgment,* so that he utters stupidities about them and himself --utters them and believes them. This seems to me to be almost the norm among fertile artists—nobody knows a child less well than its parents do—and it is true even in the case, to take a tremendous example, of the whole world of Greek art and poetry: it never "knew" what it did.[117]

370

What is romanticism?[118]— It may perhaps be recalled, at least among my friends, that initially I approached the modern world with a few crude errors and overestimations and, in any case, hopefully. Who knows on the basis of what personal experiences, I understood the philosophical pessimism of the nineteenth century as if it were a symptom of a superior force of thought, of more audacious courage, and of more triumphant *fullness* of life than had characterized the eighteenth century, the age of Hume, Kant, Condillac, and the sensualists. Thus tragic insight appeared to me as the distinctive *luxury* of our culture, as its most precious, noblest, and most dangerous squandering, but, in view of its over-richness, as a *permissible* luxury. In the same way, I reinterpreted German music for myself as if it signified a Dionysian power of the German soul: I believed that I heard in it the earthquake through which some primeval force that had been dammed up for ages finally liber-

---

[117] This fruitful suggestion has been largely ignored. My reinterpretation of Hegel differs from most other readings of Hegel by in effect applying this insight to him: What Hegel actually did in his works was quite different from what he thought—and said again and again—needed to be done. The contrast is particularly striking when one compares his preface to the *Phenomenology* with what follows; but the same contrast recurs throughout his work. Another example: Max Weber's practice was far superior to his influential preachment in *Science as a Vocation;* cf. Kaufmann, *Without Guilt and Justice,* 1973, section 76.

[118] A revised version of this section appears in *Nietzsche contra Wagner* under the title "We Antipodes" (VPN, 669–71). A few of the changes are noted below.

ated itself—indifferent whether everything else that one calls culture might begin to tremble. You see, what I failed to recognize at that time both in philosophical pessimism and in German music was what is really their distinctive character—their *romanticism*.

What is romanticism?— Every art, every philosophy may be viewed as a remedy and an aid in the service of growing and struggling life; they always presuppose suffering and sufferers. But there are two kinds of sufferers: first, those who suffer from the *over-fullness of life*—they want a Dionysian art and likewise a tragic view of life, a tragic insight—and then those who suffer from the *impoverishment of life* and seek rest, stillness, calm seas, redemptiom from themselves through art and knowledge, or intoxication, convulsions, anaesthesia, and madness.[119] All romanticism in art and insight corresponds to the dual needs of the latter type, and that included (and includes) Schopenhauer as well as Richard Wagner, to name the two most famous and pronounced romantics whom I *misunderstood* at that time—*not*, incidentally, to their disadvantage, as one need not hesitate in all fairness to admit. He that is richest in the fullness of life, the Dionysian god and man, cannot only afford the sight of the terrible and questionable but even the terrible deed and any luxury of destruction, decomposition, and negation. In his case, what is evil, absurd, and ugly seems, as it were, permissible, owing to an excess of procreating, fertilizing energies that can still turn any desert into lush farmland. Conversely, those who suffer most and are poorest in life would need above all mildness, peacefulness, and goodness in thought as well as deed—if possible, also a god who would be truly a god for the sick, a healer and savior; also logic, the conceptual understandability of existence[120]—for logic calms and gives confidence—in short, a certain warm narrowness that keeps away fear and encloses one in optimistic horizons.

---

[119] The changes in NCW at this point include the insertion: "Revenge against life itself—the most voluptuous kind of frenzy for those so impoverished!"

[120] At this point NCW has: "even for idiots—the typical 'free spirits,' like the 'idealists' and 'beautiful souls,' are all decadents—in short, ..."

Thus I gradually learned to understand Epicurus, the opposite of a Dionysian pessimist; also the "Christian" who is actually only a kind of Epicurean—both are essentially romantics[121]—and my eye grew ever sharper for that most difficult and captious form of *backward inference* in which the most mistakes are made: the backward inference from the work to the maker, from the deed to the doer, from the ideal to those who *need it*, from every way of thinking and valuing to the commanding need behind it.

Regarding all aesthetic values I now avail myself of this main distinction: I ask in every instance, "is it hunger or super-abundance that has here become creative?"[122] At first glance, another distinction may seem preferable—it is far more obvious —namely the question whether the desire to fix, to immortalize, the desire for *being* prompted creation, or the desire for destruction, for change, for future, for *becoming*. But both of these kinds of desire are seen to be ambiguous when one considers them more closely; they can be interpreted in accordance with the first scheme that is, as it seems to me, preferable. The desire for *destruction*, change, and becoming can be an expression of an overflowing energy that is pregnant with future (my term for this is, as is known, "Dionysian"); but it can also be the hatred of the ill-constituted, disinherited, and underprivileged, who destroy, *must* destroy, because what exists, indeed all existence, all being, outrages and provokes them. To understand this feeling, consider our anarchists closely.

The will to *immortalize*[123] also requires a dual interpretation. It can be prompted, first, by gratitude and love; art with this origin will always be an art of apotheoses, perhaps dithyrambic

---

[121] A more sympathetic view of Epicurus still finds expression in sections 45, 277, and 306 above. In NCW the text continues after "Epicurean": "and, with his 'faith makes blessed,' follows the principle of hedonism as far as possible—far beyond any intellectual integrity." See also section 375.

[122] Here NCW continues: "In Goethe, for example, superabundance became creative; in Flaubert, hatred." In NCW the section ends after a few more lines about Flaubert.

Cf. also section 367 above.

[123] Literally: eternalize.

like Rubens, or blissfully mocking like Hafiz, or bright and gracious like Goethe, spreading a Homeric light and glory over all things.[124] But it can also be the tyrannic will of one who suffers deeply, who struggles, is tormented, and would like to turn what is most personal, singular, and narrow, the real idiosyncrasy of his suffering, into a binding law and compulsion—one who, as it were, revenges himself on all things by forcing his own image, the image of his torture, on them, branding them with it. This last version is *romantic pessimism* in its most expressive form, whether it be Schopenhauer's philosophy of will or Wagner's music—romantic pessimism, the last *great* event in the fate of our culture.

(That there still *could* be an altogether different kind of pessimism, a classical type—this premonition and vision belongs to me as inseparable from me, as my *proprium* and *ipsissimum*;[125] only the word "classical" offends my ears, it is

---

[124] It should be noted how different this conception of the Dionysian is from that introduced in *The Birth of Tragedy*, Nietzsche's first book. Nietzsche's celebration of the Dionysian in the later sense, exemplified in the text above, has often been read illicitly into *The Birth of Tragedy*. See Kaufmann, 155f. and 375n.

The last-mentioned note also discusses the insertion of a parenthesis at this point, "(in this case I speak of *Apollinian* art)," pointing out (a) that "this parenthesis is missing in the otherwise almost identical draft for this passage in WM 846" (*The Will to Power*, section 846), and (b) that "Nietzsche, as a matter of fact, does not speak of 'Apollinian' art in such cases: in his other late works he consistently refers to it as 'Dionysian.' This insertion of this parenthesis was plainly an afterthought ... inconsistent even with its immediate context: *vide* the dithyrambic Rubens and Hafiz."

It must be added now (c) that the parenthesis is not to be found in the edition of 1887, the only one published by Nietzsche himself, but only in the later collected editions! This illicit insertion helped to obscure Nietzsche's crucial redefinition of the "Dionysian." See the last note on this section.

(d) The parenthesis *is* found in Nietzsche's own copy of the book, as a marginal notation. This information I owe to Professor Mazzino Montinari. His edition of the text follows the edition of 1887, and he will print the parenthesis only in the philological apparatus, which is surely sound. Such marginal afterthoughts do not necessarily represent Nietzsche's final views.

[125] my own and my quintessence.

far too trite and has become round and indistinct. I call this
pessimism of the future—for it comes! I see it coming!—
Dionysian pessimism.) [126]

371

We incomprehensible ones.— Have we ever complained
because we are misunderstood, misjudged, misidentified, slandered, misheard, and not heard? Precisely this is our fate—oh,
for a long time yet! let us say, to be modest, until 1901—it is
also our distinction; we should not honor ourselves sufficiently
if we wished that it were otherwise. We are misidentified—
because we ourselves keep growing, keep changing, [127] we shed
our old bark, we shed our skins every spring, we keep becoming younger, fuller of future, [128] taller, stronger, we push our

---

[126] These final lines of one of the most important sections of the whole
book are profoundly revealing both for Nietzsche's style and temperament and for the meaning of the Dionysian in his later work. Now the
Dionysian is no longer contrasted with the Apollinian; it is contrasted
instead with the romantic and the Christian. In all of the books after
Zarathustra, the "Apollinian" is hardly ever mentioned (section 10 of
the penultimate chapter of *Twilight* and the first section of the discussion of *The Birth of Tragedy* in *Ecce Homo* seem to be the only exceptions), while Dionysus and the Dionysian assume momentous importance for Nietzsche. The Dionysus whom Nietzsche celebrates in his late
works is not the counterpart of Apollo; and in *The Birth of Tragedy*,
where Dionysus *is* the counterpart of Apollo, he is not celebrated.

Anyone who wonders what Dionysus represents in the late works
where he is apotheosized by Nietzsche could hardly do better than to
begin with section 370 of *The Gay Science*. Here the Dionysian is associated with superabundance (the *über*-words Nietzsche uses include
Überreichtum, Überfülle, Überschuss, Überfluss, übervoll) and contrasted
with a desire for revenge that is born of the sense of being underprivileged—what Nietzsche elsewhere calls *ressentiment*. Apollo had
never been associated with resentment in Nietzsche's work; but now
Christianity is associated with it more and more.

For the conception of Dionysus and the Dionysian see also *The Will
to Power*, note 1052, *Ecce Homo* (the Index lists the relevant passages),
and *Twilight*, section 49 (VPN, 554).

[127] In German *wachsen* (grow) and *wechseln* (change) have the same
root, which repays reflection. The point Nietzsche makes here is directly
relevant to the preceding note.

[128] *zukünftiger*.

roots ever more powerfully into the depths—into evil—while at the same time we embrace the heavens ever more lovingly, more broadly, imbibing their light ever more thirstly with all our twigs and leaves. Like trees we grow—this is hard to understand, as is all of life—not in one place only but everywhere, not in one direction but equally upward and outward and inward and downward; our energy is at work simultaneously in the trunk, branches, and roots; we are no longer free to do only one particular thing, to *be* only one particular thing.

This is our fate, as I have said; we grow in *height*; and even if this should be our fatality—for we dwell ever closer to the lightning—well, we do not on that account honor it less; it remains that which we do not wish to share, to make public[129]— the fatality of the heights, *our* fatality.

372

Why we are no idealists.— Formerly philosophers were afraid of the senses. Have we perhaps unlearned this fear too much? Today all of us are believers in the senses,[130] we philosophers of the present and the future, *not* in theory but in praxis, in practice.

They, however, thought that the senses might lure them away from their own world, from the cold realm of "ideas," to some dangerous southern island where they feared that their philosopher's virtues might melt away like snow in the sun. Having "wax in one's ears" was then almost a condition of philosophizing; a real philosopher no longer listened to life insofar as life is music; he *denied* the music of life—it is an ancient philosopher's superstition that all music is sirens' music.[131]

---

[129] *nicht teilen, nicht mitteilen.*

[130] *Sensualisten:* cf. the reference to Condillac and the sensualists near the beginning of section 370. Both "sensualist" and "sensationalist" have irrelevant connotations; the relevant "ism," for which both terms have been used, claims that all knowledge is derived from sensations. But what matters to Nietzsche is our attitude toward the senses.

[131] In the twelfth canto of the *Odyssey*, Odysseus stops the ears of his companions with wax to keep them from hearing the sirens' song as their ship approaches the sirens' island, and he has himself bound to the mast.

We today are inclined to make the opposite judgment (which actually could be equally wrong), namely that *ideas* are worse seductresses than our senses, for all their cold and anemic appearance, and not even in spite of this appearance: they have always lived on the "blood" of the philosopher, they always consumed his senses and even, if you will believe us, his "heart." These old philosophers were heartless; philosophizing was always a kind of vampirism. Looking at these figures, even Spinoza, don't you have a sense of something profoundly enigmatic and uncanny? Don't you notice the spectacle that unrolls before you, how they *become ever paler*—how desensualization is interpreted more and more ideally? Don't you sense a long concealed vampire in the background who begins with the senses and in the end is left with, and leaves, mere bones, mere clatter? I mean categories, formulas, *words* (for, forgive me, what was left of Spinoza, *amor intellectualis dei*,[132] is mere clatter and no more than that: What is *amor*, what *deus*, if there is not a drop of blood in them?).

In sum: All philosophical idealism to date was something like a disease, unless it was, as it was in Plato's case, the caution of an over-rich and dangerous health, the fear of *overpowerful* senses, the prudence of a prudent Socratic.—Perhaps we moderns are merely not healthy enough *to be in need of* Plato's idealism? And we are not afraid of the senses because—[133]

---

[132] intellectual love of God (*Ethics* V.33ff. The work ends with V.42).

[133] The unwritten thought that completes this sentence is clearly: our senses are not as over-powerful as his were. The startling implication is that Plato was healthier than "we" are. In the last chapter of *Twilight* (section 2; cf. also the second chapter) Nietzsche adopts a very different tone in speaking of Plato. And right here, too, one might expect Nietzsche to be put off by Plato's otherworldliness. From the passage that ends with "sirens' music" Nietzsche might have moved on to a contrast with himself as an "artistic Socrates," a Socrates who makes music—two images he had introduced in *The Birth of Tragedy*. In the text above, "the *backward inference* . . . from the ideal to those who *need it*" (section 370, above) comes to a premature end, and it is not only syntactically that the section suddenly breaks off. It is clear that Nietzsche later changed his mind; also that his tone above is more attractive than in the later passages. But having put a point nicely, he did not stop thinking about the problem; and as he thought more about it he came to see more.

373

"Science" as a prejudice.— It follows from the laws of the order of rank[134] that scholars, insofar as they belong to the spiritual middle class, can never catch sight of the really great problems and question marks; moreover, their courage and their eyes simply do not reach that far—and above all, their needs which led them to become scholars in the first place, their inmost assumptions and desires that things might be such and such, their fears and hopes all come to rest and are satisfied too soon. Take, for example, that pedantic Englishman, Herbert Spencer. What makes him "enthuse" in his way and then leads him to draw a line of hope, a horizon of desirability—that eventual reconciliation of "egoism and altruism" about which he raves—almost nauseates the likes of us; a human race that adopted such Spencerian perspectives as its ultimate perspectives would seem to us worthy of contempt, of annihilation![135]

---

[134] For this concept see especially *Beyond Good and Evil* and *The Will to Power*: the many relevant passages are listed in the Indices.

[135] Cf. William James: "The white-robed harp-playing heaven of our sabbath schools, and the ladylike tea-table elysium represented in Mr. Spencer's Data of Ethics, as the final consummation of progress, are exactly on a par in this respect,—lubberlands ... *tedium vitae* is the only sentiment they awaken in our breasts.... If the generations of mankind suffered and laid down their lives; if prophets confessed and martyrs sang in the fire ... for no other end than that a race of creatures of such unexampled insipidity should succeed, and protract *in saecula saeculorum* their contented and inoffensive lives,—why, at such a rate ... better ring down the curtain before the last act of the play, so that a business that began so importantly may be saved from so singularly flat a winding up" ("The Dilemma of Determinism," first published in 1884 and reprinted in many collections of William James's essays).

Nietzsche's works contain no references to James, and James's treatment of Nietzsche in *The Varieties of Religious Experience* (1902) is rather disappointing. In his discussion of "The Value of Saintliness" James claims, erroneously, that "For Nietzsche the saint represents little but sneakingness and slavishness"; he then quotes a long passage from the *Genealogy of Morals*, III, section 14, in which there is no mention whatever of saints; and in a footnote James admits, "I have abridged, and in one place transposed, a sentence." Then he proceeds, with rather misplaced condescension: "Poor Nietzsche's antipathy is itself sickly enough ..." (four pages from the end of Lecture XV).

But the mere fact that he had to experience as his highest hope something that to others appears and may appear only as a disgusting possibility poses a question mark that Spencer would have been incapable of foreseeing.

It is no different with the faith with which so many materialistic natural scientists rest content nowadays, the faith in a world that is supposed to have its equivalent and its measure in human thought and human valuations—a "world of truth" that can be mastered completely and forever with the aid of our square little reason. What? Do we really want to permit existence to be degraded for us like this—reduced to a mere exercise for a calculator and an indoor diversion for mathematicians? Above all, one should not wish to divest existence of its *rich ambiguity*[136]: that is a dictate of good taste, gentlemen, the taste of reverence for everything that lies beyond your horizon. That the only justifiable interpretation of the world should be one in which *you* are justified because one can continue to work and do research scientifically in *your* sense (you really mean, mechanistically?)—an interpretation that permits counting, calculating, weighing, seeing, and touching, and nothing more—that is a crudity and naiveté, assuming that it is not a mental illness, an idiocy.[137]

Would it not be rather probable that, conversely, precisely the most superficial and external aspect of existence—what is most apparent, its skin and sensualization—would be grasped first—and might even be the only thing that allowed itself to be grasped? A "scientific" interpretation of the world, as you understand it, might therefore still be one of the *most stupid* of all possible interpretations of the world, meaning that it would be one of the poorest in meaning. This thought is intended for the ears and consciences of our mechanists who nowadays like to pass as philosophers and insist that mechanics is the doctrine of the first and last laws on which all existence must be based as on a ground floor. But an essentially mechanical world would be an essentially *meaningless* world. Assum-

---

[136] *seines vieldeutigen Charakters:* this critique of positivism left its mark on German existentialism.

[137] Cf. the penultimate note on section 368 above.

ing that one estimated the *value* of a piece of music according
to how much of it could be counted, calculated, and expressed
in formulas: how absurd would such a "scientific" estimation
of music be! What would one have comprehended, understood,
grasped of it? Nothing, really nothing of what is "music" in it!

374

Our new "infinite."— How far the perspective character of
existence extends or indeed whether existence has any other
character than this; whether existence without interpretation,
without "sense," does not become "nonsense"; whether, on the
other hand, all existence is not essentially actively engaged in
interpretation[138]—that cannot be decided even by the most
industrious and most scrupulously conscientious analysis and
self-examination of the intellect; for in the course of this analysis the human intellect cannot avoid seeing itself in its own
perspectives, and *only* in these. We cannot look around our
own corner: it is a hopeless curiosity that wants to know what
other kinds of intellects and perspectives there *might* be; for
example, whether some beings might be able to experience time
backward, or alternately forward and backward (which would
involve another direction of life and another concept of cause
and effect). But I should think that today we are at least far
from the ridiculous immodesty that would be involved in de-
creeing from our corner that perspectives are permitted only
from this corner. Rather has the world become "infinite" for us
all over again, inasmuch as we cannot reject the possibility that
it may include infinite interpretations. Once more we are seized
by a great shudder; but who would feel inclined immediately to
deify again after the old manner this monster of an unknown
world? And to worship the unknown henceforth as "the
Unknown One"? Alas, too many *ungodly* possibilities of interpretation are included in the unknown, too much devilry,

---

[138] *ob . . . nicht alles Dasein essentiell ein auslegendes Dasein ist.* It is
only in Heidegger that *Dasein* refers only to human existence. In
Nietzsche and in ordinary German it refers to existence in general.

stupidity, and foolishness of interpretation—even our own human, all too human folly, which we know.

375

Why we look like Epicureans.[139]— We are cautious, we modern men, about ultimate convictions. Our mistrust lies in wait for the enchantments and deceptions of the conscience that are involved in every strong faith, every unconditional Yes and No.[140] How is this to be explained? Perhaps what is to be found here is largely the care of the "burned child," of the disappointed idealist; but there is also another, superior component: the jubilant curiosity of one who formerly stood in his corner and was driven to despair by his corner, and now delights and luxuriates in the opposite of a corner, in the boundless, in what is "free as such." Thus an almost Epicurean bent for knowledge develops that will not easily let go of the questionable character of things; also an aversion to big moral words and gestures; a taste that rejects all crude, four-square opposites and is proudly conscious of its practice in having reservations. For this constitutes our pride, this slight tightening of the reins as our urge for certainty races ahead, this self-control of the rider during his wildest rides; for we still ride mad and fiery horses, and when we hesitate it is least of all danger that makes us hesitate.

376

Our slow periods.— This is how all artists and people of "works" feel, the motherly human type: at every division of their lives, which are always divided by a work, they believe that they have reached their goal; they would always patiently accept death with the feeling, "now we are ripe for it." This is not the expression of weariness—rather of a certain autumnal sunniness and mildness that the work itself, the fact that the work has become ripe, always leaves behind in the author. Then the

---

[139] Cf. sections 45, 277, 306, and 370 above, including the notes.
[140] Cf. *The Antichrist*, sections 50–55, as well as section 344 above.

tempo of life slows down and becomes thick like honey—even to the point of long *fermata,* of the faith in long *fermata.*[141]

377

We who are homeless.— Among Europeans today there is no lack of those who are entitled to call themselves homeless in a distinctive and honorable sense: it is to them that I especially commend my secret wisdom and *gaya scienza.* For their fate is hard, their hopes are uncertain; it is quite a feat to devise some comfort for them—but what avail? We children of the future, how *could* we be at home in this today? We feel disfavor for all ideals that might lead one to feel at home even in this fragile, broken time of transition; as for its "realities," we do not believe that they will *last.* The ice that still supports people today has become very thin; the wind that brings the thaw is blowing; we ourselves who are homeless constitute a force that breaks open ice and other all too thin "realities."

We "conserve" nothing; neither do we want to return to any past periods;[142] we are not by any means "liberal"; we do not work for "progress"; we do not need to plug up our ears against the sirens who in the market place sing of the future: their song about "equal rights," "a free society," "no more masters and no servants" has no allure for us. We simply do not consider it desirable that a realm of justice and concord should be established on earth (because it would certainly be the realm of the deepest leveling and *chinoiserie*[143]); we are delighted with all who love, as we do, danger, war, and adventures, who refuse to compromise, to be captured, reconciled, and castrated; we count ourselves among conquerors; we think about the necessity for new orders, also for a new slavery—for every strengthening and enhancement of the human type also involves a new kind of enslavement. Is it not clear that with all this we are bound to feel ill at ease in an age that likes to claim

---

[141] A prolongation at the performer's discretion of a musical note, chord, or rest beyond its given time value.

[142] Occasional interpretations have assumed that Nietzsche did.

[143] *Chineserei:* cf. section 24 above.

the distinction of being the most humane, the mildest, and the most righteous age that the sun has ever seen? It is bad enough that precisely when we hear these beautiful words we have the ugliest suspicions. What we find in them is merely an expression—and a masquerade—of a profound weakening, of weariness, of old age, of declining energies. What can it matter to us what tinsel the sick may use to cover up their weakness? Let them parade it as their *virtue*; after all, there is no doubt that weakness makes one mild, oh so mild, so righteous, so inoffensive, so "humane"!

The "religion of pity" to which one would like to convert us—oh, we know the hysterical little males and females well enough who today need precisely this religion as a veil and make-up. We are no humanitarians; we should never dare to permit ourselves to speak of our "love of humanity"; our kind is not actor enough for that. Or not Saint-Simonist[144] enough, not French enough. One really has to be afflicted with a *Gallic* excess of erotic irritability and enamored impatience to approach in all honesty the whole of humanity with one's lust!

Humanity! Has there ever been a more hideous old woman among all old women—(unless it were "truth"[145]: a question for philosophers)? No, we do not love humanity;[146] but on the other hand we are not nearly "German" enough, in the sense in which the word "German" is constantly being used nowadays, to advocate nationalism and race hatred and to be able to take pleasure in the national scabies of the heart and blood poisoning that now leads the nations of Europe to delimit and barricade themselves against each other as if it were a matter of quarantine. For that we are too openminded, too malicious, too spoiled, also too well informed, too "traveled": we far prefer to live on mountains, apart, "untimely," in past or future centuries, merely in order to keep ourselves from experiencing the silent rage to which we know we should be condemned as

---

[144] Claude-Henri Saint-Simon (1760–1825) was a leading representative of French utopian socialism.

[145] Cf. the third poem in the Appendix, below: "In the South."

[146] Cf. "Zarathustra's Prologue": "Man is something that shall be overcome" (VPN, 124ff.).

eyewitnesses of politics that are desolating the German spirit by making it vain and that is, moreover, *petty* politics: to keep its own creation from immediately falling apart again, is it not finding it necessary to plant it between two deadly hatreds? *must* it not desire the eternalization of the European system of a lot of petty states?[147]

We who are homeless are too manifold and mixed racially and in our descent, being "modern men," and consequently do not feel tempted to participate in the mendacious racial self-admiration and racial indecency that parades in Germany today as a sign of a German way of thinking and that is doubly false and obscene among the people of the "historical sense."[148] We are, in one word—and let this be our word of honor—*good Europeans*, the heirs of Europe, the rich, oversupplied, but also overly obligated heirs of thousands of years of European spirit. As such, we have also outgrown Christianity and are averse to it—precisely because we have grown out of it, because our ancestors were Christians who in their Christianity were uncompromisingly upright: for their faith they willingly sacrificed possessions and position, blood and fatherland. We—do the same. For what? For our unbelief? For every kind of unbelief? No, you know better than that, friends! The hidden Yes in you is stronger than all Nos and Maybes that afflict you and your age like a disease; and when you have to embark on the sea, you emigrants, you, too, are compelled to this by—a *faith*![149]

378

"And become bright again."— We, openhanded and rich in spirit, standing by the road like open wells with no intention

---

[147] *Kleinstaaterei* harks back to *kleine Politik*. It would be easy to quote parts of this section *out of context* so as to give the impression that Nietzsche was a forerunner of fascism. But his remarks about nationalism and race hatred and his use of such expressions as "scabies of the heart and blood poisoning" are clearly intended to dissociate him from those tendencies which finally reached their fruition in National Socialism.

[148] Again, Nietzsche leaves no doubt about his distaste for the proto-Nazis in Germany.

[149] Cf. section 344 above.

to fend off anyone who feels like drawing from us—we unfortunately do not know how to defend ourselves where we want to: we have no way of preventing people from *darkening* us: the time in which we live throws into us what is most timebound; its dirty birds drop their filth into us; boys their gewgaws; and exhausted wanderers who come to us to rest, their little and large miseries. But we shall do what we have always done: whatever one casts into us, we take down into our depth —for we are deep, we do not forget—*and become bright again.*[150]

379

The fool interrupts.— The writer of this book is no misanthrope; today one pays too dearly for hatred of man. If one would hate the way man was hated formerly, Timonically,[151] wholly, without exception, with a full heart, with the whole *love* of hatred, then one would have to renounce contempt. And how much fine joy, how much patience, how much graciousness even do we owe precisely to our contempt! Moreover, it makes us the "elect of God": refined contempt is our taste and privilege, our art, our virtue perhaps, as we are the most modern of moderns.

---

[150] A prose poem like this should not be reduced to a single interpretation; but that is no reason for not offering even one reading.

Nietzsche's writings attract all kinds of readers and interpreters who force timely concerns on him: some read their personal problems into his books; others, whatever happens to be fashionable in the world of intellect; boys, their adolescent confusions; and many others, simply filth. Neither a writer himself while he is alive, nor a well-meaning interpreter later on can prevent all this. Endless misunderstandings are the price of immortality. But while one cannot keep people from darkening Nietzsche, no one has prevented him from becoming bright again.

Another reading, perhaps less interesting but surely also intended by the author: A writer is saddened and made gloomy again and again by his encounters with others; but if he is deep enough, and above all creative enough, he will become bright again.

[151] The story of Timon's misanthropy is related by Plutarch in his life of Antony. Lucian wrote a dialogue on him. And Shakespeare, in his *Timon of Athens,* has given superlative expression to Timon's hatred of man.

Hatred, on the other hand, places people on a par, vis-à-vis; in hatred there is honor; finally, in hatred there is *fear*, a good and ample element of fear. We fearless ones, however, we more spiritual human beings of this age, we know our own advantage well enough to live without fear of this age precisely because we are more spiritual. We shall hardly be decapitated, imprisoned, or exiled; not even our books will be banned or burned. The age loves the spirit; it loves and needs us, even if we should have to make clear to it that we are virtuosos of contempt; that every association with human beings makes us shudder slightly; that for all our mildness, patience, geniality,[152] and politeness, we cannot persuade our nose to give up its prejudice against the proximity of a human being; that we love nature the less humanly it behaves, and art when it is the artist's escape from man, or the artist's mockery of man, or the artist's mockery of himself.

380

"The wanderer" speaks.— If one would like to see our European morality for once as it looks from a distance, and if one would like to measure it against other moralities, past and future, then one has to proceed like a wanderer who wants to know how high the towers in a town are: he *leaves* the town. "Thoughts about moral prejudices,"[153] if they are not meant to be prejudices about prejudices, presuppose a position *outside* morality, some point beyond good and evil[154] to which one has to rise, climb, or fly—and in the present case at least a point beyond *our* good and evil, a freedom from everything "European," by which I mean the sum of the imperious value judgments that have become part of our flesh and blood. That one *wants* to go precisely out there, up there, may be a minor madness, a peculiar and unreasonable "you must"—for we seekers

---

[152] *Menschenfreundlichkeit.*

[153] This had been the subtitle of Nietzsche's *The Dawn* (1881), reissued with a new preface in 1886.

[154] This, of course, was the title of a book Nietzsche had published in 1886.

for knowledge also have our idiosyncrasies of "unfree will"—
the question is whether one really *can* get up there.

This may depend on manifold conditions. In the main the
question is how light or heavy we are—the problem of our
"specific gravity." One has to be *very light* to drive one's will
to knowledge into such a distance and, as it were, beyond one's
time, to create for oneself eyes to survey millennia and, moreover, clear skies in these eyes. One must have liberated oneself
from many things that oppress, inhibit, hold down, and make
heavy precisely us Europeans today. The human being of such
a beyond who wants to behold the supreme measures of value
of his time must first of all "overcome" this time in himself—
this is the test of his strength—and consequently not only his
time but also his prior aversion and contradiction *against* this
time, his suffering from this time, his un-timeliness, his *romanticism.*

381

On the question of being understandable.— One does not
only wish to be understood when one writes; one wishes just
as surely *not* to be understood. It is not by any means necessarily an objection to a book when anyone finds it impossible
to understand: perhaps that was part of the author's intention—
he did not want to be understood by just "anybody." All the
nobler spirits and tastes select their audience when they wish to
communicate; and choosing that, one at the same time erects
barriers against "the others." All the more subtle laws of any
style have their origin at this point: they at the same time keep
away, create a distance, forbid "entrance," understanding, as
said above—while they open the ears of those whose ears are
related to ours.

And let me say this among ourselves and about my own case:
I don't want either my ignorance or the liveliness of my temperament to keep me from being understandable for *you*, my
friends—not the liveliness, however much it compels me to
tackle a matter swiftly to tackle it at all. For I approach deep
problems like cold baths: quickly into them and quickly out
again. That one does not get to the depths that way, not deep

enough down, is the superstition of those afraid of the water, the enemies of cold water; they speak without experience. The freezing cold makes one swift.

And to ask this incidentally: does a matter necessarily remain ununderstood and unfathomed merely because it has been touched only in flight, glanced at, in a flash? Is it absolutely imperative that one settles down on it? that one has brooded over it as over an egg? *Diu noctuque incubando,*[155] as Newton

---

[155] By incubating it day and night.

The Newton scholars I have consulted neither recall this phrase nor believe that this poetic use of *"diu noctuque"* in the sense of "continually" rather than more literally "by day and by night" is in keeping with Newton's Latin style. Now it happens that in his lecture notes of 1875–76 Nietzsche relates how Newton was asked "How ever did you arrive at your discoveries?" and replied, "By *always thinking unto them*" (Musarion ed., V, 324) *This* quotation is found in the Newton literature (e.g., E.N. daC. Andrade, *Sir Isaac Newton,* 1954, at the beginning of chapter III). In a later note Nietzsche distinguished three types of philosophers, "not counting those few who ... alone deserve to be called 'thinkers.' These think day and night and do not even notice this any longer, as those who live in a blacksmith's shop no longer hear the noise ... like Newton who was once asked how he had arrived at his discoveries and replied simply: 'by always thinking unto them'" (IX, 360). Possibly, Nietzsche then came to associate Newton with "night and day" and eventually, knowing that Newton had written in Latin, assumed that what Newton had answered was *diu noctuque incubando.* This is only a surmise; but seeing that Nietzsche had been a professor of classical philology, and had published articles in Latin, it stands to reason that he sometimes was not sure whether he had read something in Latin or in German; and he might even have read about Newton in French.

In the summer of 1886, approximately three months before he wrote Book V, Nietzsche wrote Overbeck from Sils Maria: "All in all, R. W. [Wagner] has so far been the only one, at least the first, who had some feeling for what I am like. (Of which [Erwin] Rohde, for example, to my regret, does not seem to have even the remotest idea . . .) In this university atmosphere the best people degenerate: I continually feel that the background and ultimate power even in such types as R. is a damned general indifference [*Wurschtigkeit*] and a total lack of faith in their own stuff. That someone like I has been living among problems *diu noctuque incubando* and has his distress and happiness there alone— who would have any empathy for that? R. Wagner, as I've mentioned, did; and that is why Tribschen [where Nietzsche visited the Wagners

said of himself? At least there are truths that are singularly shy and ticklish and cannot be caught except suddenly—that must be *surprised* or left alone.

Finally, my brevity has yet another value: given such questions as concern me, I must say many things briefly in order that they may be heard still more briefly. For, being an immoralist, one has to take steps against corrupting innocents—I mean, asses and old maids of both sexes whom life offers nothing but their innocence. Even more, my writings should inspire, elevate, and encourage them to be virtuous. I cannot imagine anything on earth that would be a merrier sight than inspired old asses and maids who feel excited by the sweet sentiments of virtue; and "this I have seen"—thus spoke Zarathustra.

So much regarding brevity. Matters stand worse with my ignorance which I do not try to conceal from myself. There are hours when I feel ashamed of it—to be sure, also hours when I feel ashamed of feeling ashamed. Perhaps all of us philosophers are in a bad position nowadays regarding knowledge: science keeps growing, and the most scholarly among us are close to discovering that they know too little. But it would be still worse if it were different—and we knew *too much*; our task is and remains above all not to mistake ourselves for others. We *are* something different from scholars, although it is unavoidable for us to be also, among other things, scholarly. We have different needs, grow differently, and also have a different digestion: we need more, we also need less. How much a spirit needs for its nourishment, for this there is no formula; but if its taste is for independence, for quick coming and going, for roaming, perhaps for adventures for which only the swiftest

---

when he was a young professor at Basel] was such a recreation for me, while now I no longer have any place or people that are any recreation for me."

The swiftness of Nietzsche's tempo and his distaste for academic heaviness, which he associated with a *lack* of seriousness, are easily misunderstood. He did live day and night with the problems that he discussed in his inimitable way. My commentary aims to show how he dived into them again and again, often from different vantage points, to explore them more and more fully. Cf. Kaufmann, Chapter 2, "Nietzsche's Method."

are a match, it is better for such a spirit to live in freedom with little to eat than unfree and stuffed. It is not fat but the greatest possible suppleness and strength that a good dancer desires from his nourishment—and I would not know what the spirit of a philosopher might wish more to be than a good dancer. For the dance is his ideal, also his art, and finally also his only piety, his "service of God."

382

The great health.— Being new, nameless, hard to understand, we premature births of an as yet unproven future need for a new goal also a new means—namely, a new health, stronger, more seasoned, tougher, more audacious, and gayer than any previous health. Whoever has a soul that craves to have experienced the whole range of values and desiderata to date, and to have sailed around all the coasts of this ideal "mediterranean"; whoever wants to know from the adventures of his own most authentic experience how a discoverer and conqueror of the ideal feels, and also an artist, a saint, a legislator, a sage, a scholar, a pious man, a soothsayer,[156] and one who stands divinely apart in the old style—needs one thing above everything else: the *great health*—that one does not merely have but also acquires continually, and must acquire because one gives it up again and again, and must give it up.

And now, after we have long been on our way in this manner, we argonauts of the ideal, with more daring perhaps than is prudent, and have suffered shipwreck and damage often enough, but are, to repeat it, healthier than one likes to permit us, dangerously healthy, ever again healthy—it will seem to us as if, as a reward, we now confronted an as yet undiscovered country whose boundaries nobody has surveyed yet, something beyond all the lands and nooks of the ideal so far, a world so overrich in what is beautiful, strange, questionable, terrible, and divine that our curiosity as well as our craving to possess it has got beside itself—alas, now nothing will sate us any more!

---

[156] "A soothsayer" is omitted in *Ecce Homo,* where this entire section is quoted in section 2 of the discussion of *Zarathustra* (BWN, 754f.).

After such vistas and with such a burning hunger in our conscience and science,[157] how could we still be satisfied with *present-day man*? It may be too bad but it is inevitable that we find it difficult to remain serious when we look at his worthiest goals and hopes, and perhaps we do not even bother to look any more.

Another ideal runs ahead of us, a strange, tempting, dangerous ideal to which we should not wish to persuade anybody because we do not readily concede *the right to it* to anyone: the ideal of a spirit who plays naively—that is, not deliberately but from overflowing power and abundance—with all that was hitherto called holy, good, untouchable, divine; for whom those supreme things that the people naturally accept as their value standards, signify danger, decay, debasement, or at least recreation, blindness, and temporary self-oblivion; the ideal of a human, superhuman well-being and benevolence[158] that will often appear *inhuman*—for example, when it confronts all earthly seriousness so far, all solemnity in gesture, word, tone, eye, morality, and task so far, as if it were their most incarnate and involuntary parody—and in spite of all of this, it is perhaps only with him that *great seriousness* really begins, that the real question mark is posed for the first time, that the destiny of the soul changes, the hand moves forward, the tragedy *begins*.[159]

383

Epilogue.— But as I slowly, slowly paint this gloomy question mark at the end[160] and am still willing to remind my readers of the virtues of the right reader—what forgotten and unknown virtues they are!—it happens that I hear all around me the most malicious, cheerful, and koboldish laughter: the spirits of my own book are attacking me, pull my ears, and call me back to order. "We can no longer stand it," they shout at me; "away, away with this raven-black music! Are we not

---

[157] *In Wissen und Gewissen.*
[158] *Wohlseins und Wohlwollens.*
[159] Cf. the title of section 342, which marked the conclusion of the original edition of *The Gay Science.*
[160] The reference is to the last sentence of the preceding section.

surrounded by bright morning? And by soft green grass and grounds, the kingdom of the dance? Has there ever been a better hour for gaiety? Who will sing a song for us, a morning song, so sunny, so light, so fledged that it will *not* chase away the blues[161] but invite them instead to join in the singing and dancing? And even simple, rustic bagpipes would be better than such mysterious sounds, such swampy croaking, voices from the grave and marmot whistles as you have employed so far to regale us in your wilderness, Mr. Hermit and Musician of the Future![162] No! Not such tones! Let us strike up more agreeable, more joyous tones!"[163]

Is that your pleasure, my impatient friends? Well then, who would not like to please you? My bagpipes are waiting, and so is my throat—which may sound a bit rough; but put up with it, after all we are in the mountains. At least what you are about to hear is new; and if you do not understand it, if you mis-understand the *singer*, what does it matter? That happens to be "the singer's curse."[164] His music and manner you will be able to hear that much better, and to his pipes—dance that much better. Is that your *will*?

---

[161] Instead of "blues" the German has *Grillen*, twice: first in the sense of "the blues," moping, sadness; then in the literal sense of the word, "crickets."

[162] *Zukunftsmusikant:* Wagner's music had been known as *Zukunfts-musik*; Nietzsche's first book had been derided by a hostile philologist as "philology of the future"; and Nietzsche had come to refer occasionally to the philosophers of the future. Above all, cf. some of the preceding sections, such as 377 and 382.

[163] In Beethoven's Ninth Symphony, the "Ode to Joy" (*Freude*) is intro-duced by a baritone, singing: "O friends, not these tones. Let us strike up more agreeable, more joyous tones!"

[164] The title of a famous ballad by Ludwig Uhland (1787–1862). In the poem, the singer pronounces the curse, calling down ruin upon a castle and telling a king that his very name shall be forgotten. Nietzsche is suggesting that it is the singer's curse not to be understood—even to be misunderstood. In context, he is referring particularly to the Appendix of Songs that follows immediately upon this section: even readers who fail to fathom these "songs" may enjoy them.

APPENDIX

———◆———

SONGS OF
PRINCE VOGELFREI*

---

* *Vogelfrei,* literally "bird-free" or free as a bird, usually signifies an outlaw whom anybody may shoot at sight. The ambiguity is, of course, intentional. The author of *Beyond Good and Evil,* which had appeared during the previous year, sees himself as outside the law; but several of the poems concern birds and establish the connection, especially "In the South," which originally bore the title *Prinz Vogelfrei.* The name has been left untranslated above not only to preserve the ambiguity but also because in German it sounds like a real name, the more so because one of the very greatest early German poets was Walther von der Vogelweide.

An Goethe[1]

Das Unvergängliche
Ist nur dein Gleichnis!
Gott der Verfängliche
Ist Dichter-Erschleichnis . . .

Welt-rad, das rollende,
Streift Ziel auf Ziel:
Not—nennt's der Grollende,
Der Narr nennt's—Spiel . . .

Welt-spiel, das herrische,
Mischt Sein und Schein:—
Das Ewig-Närrische
Mischt *uns*—hinein! . . .

Dichters Berufung

Als ich jüngst, mich zu erquicken,
Unter dunklen Bäumen sass,
Hört ich ticken, leise ticken,
Zierlich, wie nach Takt und Mass.
Böse wurd' ich, zog Gesichter,—
Endlich aber gab ich nach,
Bis ich gar, gleich einem Dichter,
Selber mit im Tiktak sprach.

---

[1] Cf. the last lines of the Second Part of *Faust*:
CHORUS MYSTICUS:
    Alles Vergängliche
    Ist nur ein Gleichnis;
    Das Unzulängliche,
    Hier wird's Ereignis;
    Das Unbeschreibliche,
    Hier ist's getan;
    Das Ewig-Weibliche
    Zieht uns hinan.

To Goethe[2]

The indestructible
is but your invention.
God, the ineluctable,
poetic pretension.

World wheel, while rolling on,
skims aim on aim:
Fate, says the sullen one,
fools call it a game.

World game, the ruling force,
blends false and true:
the eternally fooling force
blends us in too.

The Poet's Call

In the woods upon the ground,
I was sitting at my leisure
When a distant ticking sound
Seemed to beat an endless measure.
I got mad, began to show it,
There was nothing I could do,
Until I, just like a poet,
Spoke in that strange ticktock, too.

---

[2] Cf. *Goethe's Faust,* tr. Walter Kaufmann, Doubleday & Co., 1961,
p. 503:
CHORUS MYSTICUS:
      What is destructible
      Is but a parable;
      What fails ineluctably,
      The undeclarable,
      Here it was seen,
      Here it was action;
      The Eternal-Feminine
      Lures to perfection.

Wie mir so im Versemachen
Silb' um Silb' ihr Hopsa sprang,
Musst' ich plötzlich lachen, lachen
Eine Viertelstunde lang.
Du ein Dichter? Du ein Dichter?
Steht's mit deinem Kopf so schlecht?
—„Ja, mein Herr, Sie sind ein Dichter"
Achselzuckt der Vogel Specht.

Wessen harr' ich hier im Busche?
Wem doch laur' ich Räuber auf?
Ist's ein Spruch? Ein Bild? Im Husche
Sitzt mein Reim ihm hintendrauf.
Was nur schlüpft und hüpft, gleich sticht der
Dichter sich's zum Vers zurecht.
—„Ja, mein Herr, Sie sind ein Dichter"
Achselzuckt der Vogel Specht.

Reime, mein' ich, sind wie Pfeile?
Wie das zappelt, zittert, springt,
Wenn der Pfeil in edle Teile
Des Lazertenleibchens dringt!
Ach, ihr sterbt dran, arme Wichter,
Oder taumelt wie bezecht!
—„Ja, mein Herr, Sie sind ein Dichter"
Achselzuckt der Vogel Specht.

Schiefe Sprüchlein voller Eile,
Trunkne Wörtlein, wie sich's drängt!
Bis ihr alle, Zeil' an Zeile,
An der Tiktakkette hängt.
Und es gibt grausam Gelichter,
Das dies—freut? Sind Dichter—schlecht?
—„Ja, mein Herr, Sie sind ein Dichter"
Achselzuckt der Vogel Specht.

Höhnst du, Vogel? Willst du scherzen?
Steht's mit meinem Kopf schon schlimm,
Schlimmer stünd's mit meinem Herzen?

I kept making verses. After
Lots of them did their ding-dong,
I was overcome by laughter
And laughed fifteen minutes long.
You a poet? You a poet?
Has your head become that sick?
—"Yes, my friend, you are a poet,"
Mocks the pecker with a flick.

I'm a robber, what's the quarry
I await here, wasting time?
Maxim? Image? I am sorry,
I have pinned you with a rhyme.
All that runs or leaps—I slow it
Down to rhyme, nothing's too quick.
—"Yes, my friend, you are a poet,"
Mocks the pecker with a flick.

Rhymes are deadly little arrows.
See the tremor, see the quiver
When they pierce the vital marrows
Of the lizard, or his liver!
You are dying, and you know it,
Or reel like a lunatic.
—"Yes, my friend, you are a poet,"
Mocks the pecker with a flick.

Silly maxims, made in haste,
Drunken phrases, crowd in pain,
Wriggling, lined up to my taste,
On the silly ticktock chain.
Scalawags that dared you, rue it.
This—you like? Are poets sick?
—"Yes, my friend, you are a poet,"
Mocks the pecker with a flick.

Is this meant to be a joke?
First you said my head was ill,
Now my heart, you pecking bloke,

Fürchte, fürchte meinen Grimm!—
Doch der Dichter—Reime flicht er
Selbst im Grimm noch schlecht und recht.
—„Ja, mein Herr, Sie sind ein Dichter"
Achselzuckt der Vogel Specht.

Im Süden

So häng' ich denn auf krummem Aste
Und schaukle meine Müdigkeit.
Ein Vogel lud mich her zu Gaste,
Ein Vogelnest ist's, drin ich raste.
Wo bin ich doch? Ach, weit! Ach, weit!

Das weisse Meer liegt eingeschlafen,
Und purpurn steht ein Segel drauf.
Fels, Feigenbäume, Turm und Hafen,
Idylle rings, Geblök von Schafen,—
Unschuld des Südens, nimm mich auf!

Nur Schritt für Schritt—das ist kein Leben,
Stets Bein vor Bein macht deutsch und schwer.
Ich hiess den Wind mich aufwärts heben,
Ich lernte mit den Vögeln schweben,—
Nach Süden flog ich übers Meer.

Vernunft! Verdriessliches Geschäfte!
Das bringt uns allzubald ans Ziel!
Im Fliegen lernt' ich, was mich äffte,—
Schon fühl' ich Mut und Blut und Säfte
Zu neuem Leben, neuem Spiel . . .

Einsam zu denken nenn' ich weise,
Doch einsam singen—wäre dumm!
So hört ein Lied zu eurem Preise
Und setzt euch still um mich im Kreise,
Ihr schlimmen Vögelchen, herum!

So jung, so falsch, so umgetrieben
Scheint ganz ihr mir gemacht zum Lieben

Fear, oh fear my evil will!—
But the poet rhymes, although it
Angers him: he has a tic.
—"Yes, my friend, you are a poet,"
Mocks the pecker with a flick.

In the South

On a crooked branch I sway
And rock my weariness to rest.
A bird invited me to stay,
And I sit in a bird-built nest.
But where am I? Far, far away.

The white sea stretches, fast asleep,
A crimson sail, bucolic scents,
A rock, fig trees, the harbor's sweep,
Idyls around me, bleating sheep:
Accept me, southern innocence!

Step upon step—this heavy stride
Is German, not life—a disease:
To lift me up, I asked the breeze,
And with the birds I learned to glide;
Southward I flew, across the seas.

Reason is businesslike—a flood
That brings us too soon to our aim.
In flight I rose above the mud;
Now I have courage, sap, and blood
For a new life, for a new game.

To think in solitude is wise;
Singing in solitude is silly.
Hence I shall sing, dear birds, your praise,
And you shall listen, willy-nilly,
You wicked, dear birds, to my lays.

So young, so false, so full of schemes,
You seem to live in loving dreams,

Und jedem schönen Zeitvertreib?
Im Norden—ich gesteh's mit Zaudern—
Liebt' ich ein Weibchen, alt zum Schaudern:
„Die Wahrheit" hiess dies alte Weib . . .

Die fromme Beppa

Solang noch hübsch mein Leibchen,
Lohnt sich's schon, fromm zu sein.
Man weiss, Gott liebt die Weibchen,
Die hübschen obendrein.
Er wird's dem armen Mönchlein
Gewisslich gern verzeihn,
Dass er, gleich manchem Mönchlein,
So gern will bei mir sein.

Kein grauer Kirchenvater!
Nein, jung noch und oft rot,
Oft trotz dem grausten Kater
Voll Eifersucht und Not.
Ich liebe nicht die Greise,
Er liebt die Alten nicht:
Wie wunderlich und weise
Hat Gott dies eingericht'!

Die Kirche weiss zu leben,
Sie prüft Herz und Gesicht.
Stets will sie mir vergeben,—
Ja, wer vergibt mir nicht!
Man lispelt mit dem Mündchen,
Man knixt und geht hinaus,
Und mit dem neuen Sündchen
Löscht man das alte aus.

Gelobt sei Gott auf Erden,
Der hübsche Mädchen liebt
Und derlei Herzbeschwerden
Sich selber gern vergibt.
Solang noch hübsch mein Leibchen,

Attuned to all the games of youth.
Up north—embarrassing to tell—
I loved a creepy ancient belle:
The name of this old hag was Truth.

Pious Beppa

As long as I look classy,
Piety is no pity.
We know, God loves a lassy,
At least if she is pretty.
And my poor little monk
He'll pardon cheerfully
That like many a monk
He loves to be with me.

No church father who's sallow!
But blushing youthful greed:
Hung over, they still wallow
In jealousy and need.
He does not love old age,
The old are not my line:
How marvelous and sage
Is our Lord's design!

The church knows how to live,
It tries the heart and face,
Sees me, and will forgive:
Who does not show me grace?
One lisps of deep chagrin,
A curtsey, and good-bye—
And with another sin
One wipes old sins away.

Praise be to God who lives
And loves the pretty maids,
And who gladly forgives
Himself his escapades.
As long as I look classy,

Lohnt sich's schon fromm zu sein:
Als altes Wackelweibchen
Mag mich der Teufel frein!

Der geheimnisvolle Nachen

Gestern nachts, als alles schlief,
Kaum der Wind mit ungewissen
Seufzern durch die Gassen lief,
Gab mir Ruhe nicht das Kissen,
Noch der Mohn, noch, was sonst tief
Schlafen macht,—ein gut Gewissen.

Endlich schlug ich mir den Schlaf
Aus dem Sinn und lief zum Strande.
Mondhell war's und mild, ich traf
Mann und Kahn auf warmem Sande,
Schläfrig beide, Hirt und Schaf:—
Schläfrig stiess der Kahn vom Lande.

Eine Stunde, leicht auch zwei,
Oder war's ein Jahr?—da sanken
Plötzlich mir Sinn und Gedanken
In ein ew'ges Einerlei,
Und ein Abgrund ohne Schranken
Tat sich auf:—da war's vorbei!

—Morgen kam: auf schwarzen Tiefen
Steht ein Kahn und ruht und ruht ...
Was geschah? so rief's, so riefen
Hundert bald: was gab es? Blut?—
Nichts geschah! Wir schliefen, schliefen
Alle—ach, so gut! so gut!

Liebeserklärung
(bei der aber der Dichter in eine Grube fiel—)

O Wunder! Fliegt er noch?
Er steigt empor, und seine Flügel ruhn?
Was hebt und trägt ihn doch?
Was ist ihm Ziel und Zug und Zügel nun?

Piety is no pity:
When I am old and gassy,
The Devil take my kitty!

The Mysterious Bark

Last night all appeared to doze,
Unsteady the wind that wailed
Softly lest it break repose;
Only I on my bed flailed,
Poppy and good conscience, those
Trusted soporifics, failed.

Finally, I foreswore sleep,
Got up, and ran to the strand.
There was moonlight where it's steep,
Man and bark on the warm sand,
Sleepy both shepherd and sheep—
Sleepily we left the land.

One hour passed, or two, or three—
Or a year—when suddenly
All my thoughts and mind were drowned
In timeless monotony:
An abyss without a ground
Opened up—not one more sound.

Morning came, on the black deep
Rests a bark, rests on the swell.
What has happened? Hundreds keep
Asking that. Who died? Who fell?
Nothing happened! We found sleep,
All of us—we slept so well.

Declaration of Love
(In the course of which the poet fell into a pit)

Wonder! Does he still fly?
He soars, and yet his wings are still?
What buoys him up so high?
What are his goal, his way, his will?

Gleich Stern und Ewigkeit
Lebt er in Höh'n jetzt, die das Leben flieht,
  Mitleidig selbst dem Neid—:
Und hoch flog, wer ihn auch nur schweben sieht!

  O Vogel Albatross!
Zur Höhe treibt's mit ew'gem Triebe mich.
  Ich dachte dein: da floss
Mir Trän' um Träne,—ja, ich liebe dich!

Lied
eines theokritischen Ziegenhirten

Da lieg' ich, krank im Gedärm,—
Mich fressen die Wanzen.
Und drüben noch Licht und Lärm!
Ich hör's, sie tanzen ...

Sie wollte um diese Stund'
Zu mir sich schleichen.
Ich warte wie ein Hund,—
Es kommt kein Zeichen.

Das Kreuz, als sie's versprach?
Wie konnte sie lügen?
—Oder läuft sie jedem nach,
Wie meine Ziegen?

Woher ihr seidner Rock?—
Ah, meine Stolze?
Es wohnt noch mancher Bock
An diesem Holze?

—Wie kraus und giftig macht
Verliebtes Warten!

Timeless now and starry,
He lives at heights that life seeks to avoid;
   For envy he feels sorry—
And high soar all who merely see him buoyed.

   O albatross, I'm swept
Up high, by an eternal impulse spurred:
   I thought of you and wept
Tear upon tear—I love you, noble bird!

Song of a Theocritical Goatherd[3]

Here I lie with intestinal blight,
Bedbugs advancing;
Over there, still noise and light;
I hear them dancing.

She promised—she is late—
She would be mine;
But like a dog I wait,
And there's no sign.

She swore again and again:
Was it by rote?
Does she run after all men,
Just like a goat?

You give yourself such airs:
Who gave you silk?
How do I know who shares
Your goatlike ilk?

We're poisoned by love when we wait,
It makes us barbaric:

---

[3] Theocritus, a Greek poet of the early third century B.C., has been called the father of pastoral poetry. The pun on the poet's name is less pronounced in the original German. The fly agaric (*amanita muscaria*) is probably the best known poisonous fungus of Europe. The German original has *Giftpilz*: poisonous fungus.

So wächst bei schwüler Nacht
Giftpilz im Garten.

Die Liebe zehrt an mir
Gleich sieben Übeln,—
Nichts mag ich essen schier.
Lebt wohl, ihr Zwiebeln!

Der Mond ging schon ins Meer,
Müd' sind alle Sterne,
Grau kommt der Tag daher,—
Ich stürbe gerne.

„Diesen ungewissen Seelen"

Diesen ungewissen Seelen
Bin ich grimmig gram.
All ihr Ehren ist ein Quälen,
All ihr Lob ist Selbstverdruss und Scham.

Dass ich nicht an ihrem Stricke
Ziehe durch die Zeit,
Dafür grüsst mich ihrer Blicke
Giftig-süsser, hoffnungsloser Neid.

Möchten sie mir herzhaft fluchen
Und die Nase drehn!
Dieser Augen hilflos Suchen
Soll bei mir auf ewig irregehn.

Narr in Verzweiflung

Ach! Was ich schrieb auf Tisch und Wand
Mit Narrenherz und Narrenhand,
Das sollte Tisch und Wand mir zieren? . . .

Thus damp nights generate
The fly agaric.

Love eats me like a blight,
It is the seventh hell.
I've lost my appetite:
Onions, farewell!

The moon set in the sea,
The stars fade in the sky,
The day is dawning gray:
I'd like to die.

"Souls that are unsure"

Souls that are unsure and cloying
I loathe like their acclaim.
All their honors are annoying,
All their praise is self-hatred and shame.

Since I do not join their dances,
Tied to *their* old rope,
I am followed by their glances'
Sweetly poisoned envy without hope.

Let them curse me and despise
My way, let them hiss!
When the seeking of these eyes
Aims at me, it shall forever miss!

Fool in Despair[4]

All that I wrote on table and wall
With a foolish heart and foolish scrawl
Was meant to add a little grace.

---

[4] *Narrenhände / beschmieren Tisch und Wände* (fools' hands deface
table and walls) is a German proverb. *Wassermann*, rendered above
as waterman, could also mean Aquarius, but Nietzsche was not an
Aquarius.

Doch ihr sagt: „Narrenhände schmieren,—
Und Tisch und Wand soll man purgieren,
Bis auch die letzte Spur verschwand!"

Erlaubt! Ich lege Hand mit an—,
Ich lernte Schwamm und Besen führen,
Als Kritiker, als Wassermann.

Doch, wenn die Arbeit abgetan,
Säh' gern ich euch, ihr Überweisen,
Mit Weisheit Tisch und Wand besch . . . . . .

Rimus remedium[5]
Oder: Wie kranke Dichter sich trösten

Aus deinem Munde,
Du speichelflüssige Hexe Zeit,

---

[5] "Rhyme as remedy." In "The Mysterious Bark" the poet speaks of poppy as failing to give him sleep; here poppy is meant to provide relief from pain. In December 1882, in the winter after the first edition of *The Gay Science* had appeared—but these poems were added only in the second edition of 1887—Nietzsche had written Lou Salomé and Paul Rée that he had just taken "an immense dose of opium—from despair. But instead of thus losing my reason, I seem to have *found* it at long last" (See Kaufmann, 58).

In the same stanza, Nietzsche imagines that his fever asks him what reward he expects for living on and continuing with his work in such agony. But of whom is he thinking when he speaks of "the whore and her disdain"? That image is developed in the following stanza: He imagines her leaving him but warns her how cold and rainy the night is outside, and instead of being gentler with her, he gives her a piece of gold.

This fantasy brings to mind Thomas Mann's fictional treatment of Nietzsche's life in his *Doktor Faustus* (1947), where the artist's disease, which heightens his creativity, is contracted from a whore, and it is suggested that the artist owed the brilliance of his work to his illness. Nietzsche seems to be responding to this interpretation, many decades before it was first offered: "You, fever, I should bless?" This poem *could* contain an actual recollection of an encounter with a whore, coupled with the thought that his agonies and his creative work were indissolubly linked and that he *might* therefore be expected to consider his painful existence "happiness," and "bless" his fever. But this reading is surely wrong, and seems never to have occurred to anyone. For

You say: "The hands of fools deface
Table and wall—one must erase
All he has written, all!"

I'd like to help as best I can:
I wield a sponge, as you recall,
As critic and as waterman.

But when the cleaning up is done,
Let's see the super-sage emit
Upon the walls sagacious shit!

Rimus remedium[5]
Or: How sick poets console themselves

From your old lips
O Time, you drooling ghoul,

Nietzsche seems to have had no notion at all that he might have syphilis; and even if this possibility had occurred to him, it is exceedingly improbable that he would have chosen to air it in a poem of this sort.

Who, then, is the "whore"? It could be the world that has no heart and mocks his pain, or Time. If so, "Come back!" would signify the poet's resolve to go on living, after first thinking of using enough opium to kill himself. I take it that this is what Nietzsche had in mind; but it is fascinating to see how his unconscious mind developed an image along the very same lines that Thomas Mann pursued much later at epic lengths. (About Mann's conception, see Kaufmann, 24 and 69.)

The third line from the end *"Wer jetzt nicht hundert Reime hätte"* reminds one of Nietzsche's earlier poems, *"Mitleid hin und her"* (Pity back and forth), which contains the lines *"wohl dem, der jetzt noch— Heimat hat!"* and *"weh dem, der keine Heimat hat!"* (Lucky is he who now still has a home! and: Woe's him that has no home!). In "our" poem there is no longer any question of having a home; but I take it that Nietzsche emphasizes the word "rhymes" at least in part to contrast it with home: The artist is saved by his work, and when Nietzsche is not in the mood for writing philosophy, he falls back on rhymes and writes, for the most part, in a lighter vein. But not always as light as it might look at first glance.

"A glowing bull": Phalaris, a tyrant of Agrigentum in Sicily, tortured his subjects on the slightest suspicion, by roasting them in a brazen bull. Perillus, who had designed the bull, was the first victim. In 552 B.C. the people revolted and put Phalaris himself to death in the same way.

Tropft langsam Stund' auf Stunde.
Umsonst, dass all mein Ekel schreit:
  ,,Fluch, Fluch dem Schlunde
Der Ewigkeit!"

    Welt—ist von Erz:
Ein glühender Stier,—der hört kein Schrein.
Mit fliegenden Dolchen schreibt der Schmerz
Mir ins Gebein:
  ,,Welt hat kein Herz,
Und Dummheit wär's, ihr gram drum sein!"

    Giess alle Mohne,
Giess, Fieber! Gift mir ins Gehirn!
Zu lang schon prüfst du mir Hand und Stirn.
Was frägst du? Was? ,,Zu welchem—Lohne?"
   —Ha! Fluch der Dirn'
Und ihrem Hohne!

    Nein! Komm zurück!
Draussen ist's kalt, ich höre regnen—
Ich sollte dir zärtlicher begegnen?
—Nimm! Hier ist Gold: wie glänzt das Stück!—
  Dich heissen ,,Glück"?
Dich, Fieber, segnen?—

    Die Tür springt auf!
Der Regen sprüht nach meinem Bette:
Wind löscht das Licht,—Unheil in Hauf'!
—Wer jetzt nicht hundert Reime hätte,
  Ich wette, wette,
Der ginge drauf!

Hour upon hour drips.
My nausea cries to no avail:
"Damn, damn the grip
Of your eternal rule!"

World—hard as stones:
A glowing bull—he hears no crying.
Pain writes with daggers that are flying
Into my bones:
"World has no heart;
The fool bears her a grudge and groans."

Pour poppies, pour,
O fever! poison in my brain!
You test my brow too long with pain.
Why do you ask, "For what—reward?"
—Hah! Damn the whore
And her disdain!

No! Come back! Hold!
I hear the rain, outside it's cold—
I should be gentler? You want a caress?
—Take this! It glistens; it is gold.—
You—"happiness"?
You, fever, I should bless?—

A gust—the door
Flies open—rain—my bed gets wet—
The light's blown out—mishaps galore.
—Without a hundred *rhymes*, a wight—
I bet, I bet—
Would be done for!

,,Mein Glück!"[6]

Die Tauben von San Marco seh' ich wieder:
Still ist der Platz, Vormittag ruht darauf.
In sanfter Kühle schick' ich müssig Lieder
Gleich Taubenschwärmen in das Blau hinauf—
    Und locke sie zurück,
Noch einen Reim zu hängen ins Gefieder
—mein Glück! Mein Glück!

Du stilles Himmelsdach, blau-licht, von Seide,
Wie schwebst du schirmend ob des bunten Baus,
Den ich—was sag' ich?'—liebe, fürchte, neide . . .
Die Seele wahrlich tränk' ich gern ihm aus!
    Gäb' ich sie je zurück?—
Nein, still davon, du Augen-Wunderweide!
—mein Glück! Mein Glück!

Du strenger Turm, mit welchem Löwendrange
Stiegst du empor hier, siegreich, sonder Müh'!
Du überklingst den Platz mit tiefem Klange—:
Französisch, wärst du sein accent aigu?
    Blieb' ich gleich dir zurück,
Ich wüsste, aus welch seidenweichem Zwange . . .
—mein Glück! Mein Glück!

Fort, fort Musik! Lass erst die Schatten dunkeln
Und wachsen bis zur braunen lauen Nacht!
Zum Tone ist's zu früh am Tag, noch funkeln
Die Goldzieraten nicht in Rosenpracht,
    Noch blieb viel Tag zurück,
Viel Tag für Dichten, Schleichen, Einsam-Munkeln
—mein Glück! Mein Glück!

---

[6] The title of this poem and its refrain pose a problem. The primary meaning of *Glück* is luck, but it can also mean happiness. Nietzsche's reason for placing the title in quotes is presumably that he is describing *his* conception of happiness of which he assumes that it must strike most readers as almost involving a misuse of the term. "My Luck!" would suggest falsely that the intended meaning is that of the English

"My Happiness!"[6]

The pigeons of San Marco I descry
Again: Calm is the square, still signs of dew.
It's mild and cool. Like swarms of pigeons, I
Send up my songs into the blue,
    And idly lure them back
To add another rhyme before they fly.
    My happiness! My luck!

You light-blue roof of heaven, silky, sheer,
You float above the colored edifice
That I—what am I saying?—*envy*, love, and fear.
I'd like to drain its soul as in a kiss!
    And would I give it back?
No more of that, you sight of endless cheer!
    My happiness! My luck!

You severe tower, with what lion's flair
Did you rise without effort, gloriously!
Sonorous sound you send across the square:
In French you would be its *accent aigu*?
    If I, like you, stayed back,
I would be caught in a soft, silken snare.
    My happiness! My luck!

Begone, O music! Give the shadows time
To grow into a brown, mild night and doze!
It is too early in the day to chime:
The golden ornaments have not turned rose,
    The day is holding back:
Still time to prowl, talk to oneself, and rhyme—
    My happiness! My luck!

---

idiom, which brings to mind such words as "wouldn't you know it?"
But letting every stanza end, "My happiness! My happiness!" would be
rather clumsy and sound very heavy. Moreover, Nietzsche follows a
very regular rhyme scheme in this poem (a, b, a, b, c, a, c), and the
third line from the end always ends with the word *zurück* (back).
Something would be lost if that were changed. Thus several reasons
come together to suggest the above solution.
    Cf. the second poem in the Prelude.

Nach neuen Meeren[7]

Dorthin—will ich: und ich traue
Mir fortan und meinem Griff.
Offen liegt das Meer, ins Blaue
Treibt mein Genueser Schiff.

Alles glänzt mir neu und neuer,
Mittag schläft auf Raum und Zeit—:
Nur dein Auge—ungeheuer
Blickt mich's an, Unendlichkeit!

Sils-Maria[8]

Hier sass ich, wartend, wartend,—doch auf nichts,
Jenseits von Gut und Böse, bald des Lichts

Geniessend, bald des Schattens, ganz nur Spiel,
Ganz See, ganz Mittag, ganz Zeit ohne Ziel.
Da, plötzlich, Freundin! wurde eins zu zwei—
—Und Zarathustra ging an mir vorbei . . .

---

[7] Line 4: In the original, the ship is Genoese (or Genovese)—because Columbus was born in Genoa. Nietzsche spent most of 1881 in Genoa (except for the summer, in Sils Maria); then again the winter and early spring of 1882 and 1883 (some of it in nearby Rapallo, where he wrote Part One of *Zarathustra*).

A draft for this poem bears the title "To L." (i.e., Lou Salomé) and has two more lines of which the first rhymes on *neuer* (newer) and *ungeheuer* (monstrously): *"Mut! Stehst du doch selbst am Steuer, / Lieblichste Victoria!"* Courage! After all, you yourself stand at the helm, / Loveliest Victoria! (Cf. Binion, 1968, p. 94n. and 130–31n.)

For the Columbus theme, cf. sections 124, 283, 289, 291, 343, and 377 above

Toward New Seas[7]

That way is my *will*; I trust
In my mind and in my grip.
Without plan, into the vast
Open sea I head my ship.

All is shining, new and newer,
upon space and time sleeps noon;
Only *your* eye—monstrously,
Stares at me, infinity!

Sils Maria[8]

Here I sat, waiting—not for anything—
Beyond Good and Evil, fancying

Now light, now shadows, all a game,
All lake, all noon, all time without all aim.
Then, suddenly, friend, one turned into two—
And Zarathustra walked into my view.

---

[8] Sils Maria is the village in the Upper Engadine in Switzerland where Nietzsche spent his summers from 1881 until 1888, excepting only 1882. He wrote Part One of *Zarathustra* in Rapallo, on the Riviera, early in 1883, and completed Part Two in Sils Maria that summer. The poem suggests that the idea of Zarathustra himself "came to him" in the summer of 1881 and eased his lonesomeness, turning it into a twosomeness. The "friend" to whom he is telling this (*Freundin* is feminine) is Lou Salomé, in 1882 (See Binion, 1968, p. 130f.). Cf. Nietzsche's account of the origin of *Zarathustra* in his *Ecce Homo* (BWN, p. 751f.). Zarathustra makes his first appearance in section 342 above, originally published in 1882. Cf. also the end of the "Aftersong" that concludes *Beyond Good and Evil*.

An den Mistral
Ein Tanzlied

Mistralwind, du Wolkenjäger,
Trübsalmörder, Himmelsfeger,
Brausender, wie lieb' ich dich!
Sind wir zwei nicht eines Schosses
Erstlingsgabe, eines Loses
Vorbestimmte ewiglich?

Hier auf glatten Felsenwegen
Lauf' ich tanzend dir entgegen,
Tanzend, wie du pfeifst und singst:
Der du ohne Schiff und Ruder
Als der Freiheit freister Bruder
Über wilde Meere springst.

Kaum erwacht, hört' ich dein Rufen,
Stürmte zu den Felsenstufen,
Hin zur gelben Wand am Meer.
Heil! Da kamst du schon gleich hellen
Diamantnen Stromesschnellen
Sieghaft von den Bergen her.

Auf den ebnen Himmelstennen
Sah ich deine Rosse rennen,
Sah den Wagen, der dich trägt,
Sah die Hand dir selber zücken,
Wenn sie auf der Rosse Rücken
Blitzesgleich die Geissel schlägt,—

Sah dich aus dem Wagen springen,
Schneller dich hinabzuschwingen,
Sah dich wie zum Pfeil verkürzt
Senkrecht in die Tiefe stossen,—
Wie ein Goldstrahl durch die Rosen
Erster Morgenröten stürzt.

To the Mistral
A DANCING SONG

Mistral wind, you rain cloud leaper,
sadness killer, heaven sweeper,
how I love you when you roar!
Were we two not generated
in one womb, predestinated
for one lot for evermore?

Here on slippery rocky traces
I dance into your embraces,
dancing as you sing and whistle:
you that, shipless, do not halt,
freedom's freest brother, vault
over raging seas, a missile.

Barely waked, I heard your calling,
stormed to where the rocks are sprawling,
to the gold wall by the sea—
when you came like swiftly dashing
river rapids, diamond-splashing,
from the peaks triumphantly.

Through the heavens' threshing basin
I could see your horses hasten,
saw the carriage you commanded,
saw your hand yourself attack
when upon the horses' back
lightning-like your scourge descended.

From your carriage of disaster
leaping to bear down yet faster,
I saw you in arrow form
vertically downward plunging,
like a golden sunbeam lunging
through the roses of the dawn.

Tanze nun auf tausend Rücken,
Wellenrücken, Wellentücken—
Heil, wer neue Tänze schafft!
Tanzen wir in tausend Weisen,
Frei—sei unsre Kunst geheissen,
Fröhlich—unsre Wissenschaft!

Raffen wir von jeder Blume
Eine Blüte uns zum Ruhme
Und zwei Blätter noch zum Kranz!
Tanzen wir gleich Troubadouren
Zwischen Heiligen und Huren,
Zwischen Gott und Welt den Tanz!

Wer nicht tanzen kann mit Winden,
Wir sich wickeln muss mit Binden,
Angebunden, Krüppelgreis,
Wer da gleicht den Heuchelhänsen,
Ehrentölpeln, Tugendgänsen,
Fort aus unsrem Paradeis!

Wirbeln wir den Staub der Strassen
Allen Kranken in die Nasen,
Scheuchen wir die Krankenbrut!
Lösen wir die ganze Küste
Von dem Odem dürrer Brüste,
Von den Augen ohne Mut!

Jagen wir die Himmelstrüber,
Weltenschwärzer, Wolkenschieber.
Hellen wir das Himmelreich!
Brausen wir . . . o aller freien
Geister Geist, mit dir zu zweien
Braust mein Glück dem Sturme gleich.—

—Und dass ewig das Gedächtnis
Solchen Glücks, nimm sein Vermächtnis,
Nimm den Kranz hier mit hinauf!
Wirf ihn höher, ferner, weiter,
Stürm' empor die Himmelsleiter,
Häng' ihn—an den Sternen auf!

Dance on myriad backs a season,
billows' backs and billows' treason—
we need dances that are new!
Let us dance in myriad manners,
freedom write on *our* art's banners,
our science shall be gay!

Let us break from every flower
one fine blossom for our power
and two leaves to wind a wreath!
Let us dance like troubadours
between holy men and whores,
between god and world beneath!

Who thinks tempests dance too quickly,
all the bandaged and the sickly,
crippled, old, and overnice,
if you fear the wind might hurt you,
honor-fools and geese of virtue—
out of our paradise!

Let us whirl the dusty hazes
right into the sick men's noses,
flush the sick brood everywhere!
Let us free the coast together
from the wilted bosoms' blether,
from the eyes that never dare!

Let us chase the shadow lovers,
world defamers, rain-cloud shovers—
let us brighten up the sky!
All free spirits' spirit, let you
and me thunder; since I met you,
like a tempest roars my joy.

And forever to attest
such great joy, take its bequest,
take this wreath with you up there!
Toss it higher, further, gladder,
storm up on the heavens' ladder,
hang it up—upon a star.

ACKNOWLEDGMENTS

Kevin Ashley read most of the manuscript, checking it against the original German text, and raised scores of questions. His help has been invaluable. He also did most of the work on the Index.

Ira Wade spent a good deal of time helping me to find the source of the epigraph for Book V which, oddly, is not listed in the treasuries of quotations and the biographies of Turenne that we checked, nor in previous editions of Nietzsche or discussions of Nietzsche and the French.

Siegwart Lindenberg is the most helpful critic I know. His detailed comments on the manuscript of my translation of Buber's *I and Thou* were a delight; his critique of what I had thought might be the final version of my own *Without Guilt and Justice* gave me a very hard time because it was so perceptive; and now, coming to my help the third time, he has explained to me a couple of passages that had puzzled me, besides suggesting many minor improvements. I only wish Nietzsche had had such a friend!

As always, it has been a delight to work with Jean Pohoryles at Random House.

Finally, I am grateful that it was given to me to read the proofs of Books IV and V in Sils Maria where some of the central ideas of *The Gay Science* and of his later thought first occurred to Nietzsche; for example, his doctrine of the eternal recurrence, the figure of Zarathustra, and "beyond good and evil." See the penultimate poem in this book. Using the little collection of books in the house where Nietzsche had spent seven summers, I also made some final additions to the commentary.

INDEX

Arabic numbers refer to sections, not to pages. A refers to the Appendix, and the first poem in the Appendix is cited as A1, the last as A14. J refers to "Joke, Cunning, and Revenge: Prelude in German Rhymes." NP means Nietzsche's Preface; TI the Translator's Introduction; n a note; t a title page. Vtn refers to the note on the title page of Book V.

A

Abbruch, *Zerstörung, Untergang, Umsturz,* 343n
accidens, 357, 357n
accidents, 109, 360
actions, 335, 335n, 341, 345, 352, 353, 354, 360; effect of, 233
actors, TI6, 36, 99, 236, 301, 356, 361, 366, 368, 377
adaptability, 361
Aeschylus, 1, 300n
aesthetics, 347, 368, 370
affirmation and renunciation, TI5, 27, 301, 377
age, the, 156, 159, 161, 180, 283, 331, 337, 338, 356, 361, 370, 377, 378, 378n, 379, 382; of foundations, 357, 357n
agreement, law of, 76
air, virile, 293
Ajax, 135
albatross, A6
Albigensian Crusade, TI2
Alcaeus, 83, 83n
alcohol, 42, 134, 134n, 145, 147
Alfieri, Count Vittorio, 91, 91n
Allah, 128
alpha and omega, J36

altruism, 21, 119, 373
Americans, 329, 356
amor fati, 276, 276n
amor intellectualis dei, 372, 372n
amour-plaisir, 123, 123n
amour-vanité, 123, 123n
anaesthetics, 326, 371
anarchists, 370
Andrade, E. N. daC., 381n
animals, mercy for, 99; animals and men, 286, 301, 314, 316, 352, 354, 359, 361
anthem, German national, 357, 357n
anthropomorphisms, 109
anti-idealism, 134n
anti-Semitism, TI6, 32n, 99n, 135n, 348n, 357n
Antony, Mark, 379n
An-und Für-sich's, 23n
aphorisms, TI4, 125n, 126n, 143n
Apollinian art, 370n
Apollo, 84, 370n
appearance, NP4, 54, 58, 88, 309, 344, 354, 361; good will to, 107
applause, 201, 330
appropriation, 118, 192, 249
Arabia, 43, 306
Ararat, 342n

Q

quando etiam sapientibus gloriae

FRIEDRICH NIETZSCHE was born in 1844 in Röcken (Saxony), Germany. He studied classical philology at the universities of Bonn and Leipzig, and in 1869 was appointed to the chair of classical philology at the University of Basel, Switzerland. Ill health led him to resign his professorship ten years later. His works include *The Birth of Tragedy, Thus Spoke Zarathustra, Beyond Good and Evil, On the Genealogy of Morals, The Case of Wagner, Twilight of the Idols, The Antichrist, Nietzsche contra Wagner,* and *Ecce Homo.* He died in 1900. *The Will to Power,* a selection from his notebooks, was published posthumously.

WALTER KAUFMANN was born in Freiburg, Germany, in 1921, came to the United States in 1939, and studied at Williams College and Harvard University. In 1947 he joined the faculty of Princeton University, where he is now Professor of Philosophy. He has held many visiting professorships, including Fulbright grants at Heidelberg and Jerusalem. His books include *Critique of Religion and Philosophy, From Shakespeare to Existentialism, The Faith of a Heretic, Cain and Other Poems, Hegel, Tragedy and Philosophy,* and *Without Guilt and Justice,* as well as verse translations of Goethe's *Faust* and *Twenty German Poets.* The third edition, revised, of Professor Kaufmann's critical study *Nietzsche: Philosopher, Psychologist, Antichrist* is available in Vintage Books. He has translated all of the books by Nietzsche listed in the biographical note about Nietzsche above. The following appear in Vintage Books: *Beyond Good and Evil; The Will to Power*; and, in one volume, *The Birth of Tragedy* and *The Case of Wagner; On the Genealogy of Morals* and *Ecce Homo.*